The
Courthouses
of
Maine

To Kayren
With love and
appreciation
Regie

You will always be
our model of a receptionist
active and french
Love!
John

January 8, 1999
A nice luncheon to help us
all stay in touch,
John
at Poppa + Goose

The
Courthouses
of
Maine

ROBERT K. SLOANE

SENIOR EDITOR
MAINE LAWYERS REVIEW

With an Introduction by
HON. VINCENT L. MCKUSICK
Former Chief Justice, Maine Supreme Judicial Court

MAINE LAWYERS REVIEW
WOOLWICH, MAINE, 1998

Cover photographs: Jacob Sloane

© 1998 Robert Sloane

Published by
Maine Lawyers Review
Woolwich, Maine
1998

Library of Congress Catalog #98-68-161

ISBN 0-9668250-0-4

Design: Edith Allard, Crummet Mountain Design
Layout: Nina Medina, Basil Hill Graphics
Printed and bound by Quebecor Printing
Covers by John P. Pow Company

To Diane Lund
Who brought us together

Acknowledgments

The Courthouses of Maine is based on a series of articles prepared for the *Maine Lawyers Review*. Now, in expanded form, they are the core of the book. Preparation of the articles and this book would not have been possible without the aid and ideas of many people who contributed their assistance willingly and gracefully. I appreciate the help of all those who participated, and sincerely hope they will feel rewarded for their efforts. Those that helped in finding information throughout Maine are listed first, followed by individuals in the 16 counties, and then the family and near-family members who supported the effort.

Hon. Sandra Lynch, and Hon. Conrad Cyr, U. S. Circuit Court of Appeals.

Hon. Brock Hornby and Hon. William Brownell of the U.S. District Court of Maine for material on federal courthouses.

Hon. Vincent L. McKusick, historian of the state courts and contributor of the introduction and three appendices of material.

Hon. Herbert T. Silsby, II of Ellsworth, eminent historian and treasure-trove of history in Maine, particularly Hancock County.

Hon. Thomas E. Delahanty, II, courthouse historian with an outstanding collection of courthouse memorabilia.

Earl Shettleworth, Director of the Maine Historic Preservation Commission

Stephanie Philbrick, David Barry and Don King at the Center for Maine History at the Maine Historical Society

Dr. Harold Osher and Christi Mitchell, Osher Map Library, University of Southern Maine

The staff of the Maine State Library and the Maine State Archives

Katherine Dibble and John Dorsey, Boston Public Library

Frank Sorrentino, Massachusetts Archives

Androscoggin County: Pat Fournier, Androscoggin County Clerk; Mary Pollard; Gridley Barrows, Mike Lord and David Richards, Androscoggin Historic Society

Aroostook County: Joseph Inman; Cary Library in Houlton; John Dunn, Dunn Funeral Home in Houlton

Cumberland County: Jeffrey Henthorn and Lisa Morgan, Regional Court Administrator's Office; Dan Hayes, Cumberland County Executive Office; Jim Wallace, Courthouse Security; Portland Public Library

Franklin County: Richard Mallett, local historian and author; Frank Dingley, Farmington Historical Society

Hancock County: Hon. Herbert T. Silsby, II; Allan Baker, *Ellsworth American*; Sally Foote and Gardiner Gregory, Castine Historical Society

Kennebec County: Nancy Desjardin, Kennebec County Superior Court Clerk; Anthony Douin, Kennebec Historical Society; Lithgow Public Library, Augusta

Knox County: Virginia Lindsey, Knox County Clerk; Rockland Public Library; Mary Jane and Edward Boggs, Jr., Warren; Carl Slocomb, owner of courthouse building in Warren

Lincoln County: Nancy Giles, Lincoln County Clerk; Sharon Simpson, Lincoln County Superior Court; Janet Morgan, Wiscasset Public Library; Ervin Snyder, Jr., Wiscasset lawyer; Jane Tucker, Wiscasset Historical Society

Oxford County: Carol Mahoney, Oxford County Clerk; Ben Conant and Cynthia Immonen, Paris Cape Historical Society; Diane Jones, Fryeburg Historic Society

Penobscot County: Margaret Gardner, Penobscot County Superior Court Clerk; Deborah Thompson, architectural historian of Bangor; Bangor Public Library; Bangor Historical Society; Penobscot County Law Library

Piscataquis County: Lewis Stevens, Piscataquis and Dover-Foxcroft author; Thompson Free Library

Sagadahoc County: Barry Sturgeon, Sagadahoc County Clerk; Richard Snow, Sagadahoc County Court House historian; Patten Free Library

Somerset County, Robin Poland, Somerset County Clerk; Wright Pinkham, former Somerset County Clerk

Waldo County: Marilyn Keene, Waldo County Clerk; Belfast Free Library

Washington County: Hon. Lyman Holmes, Judge of Probate; Val Atwood, Machias Historical Society; Porter Memorial Library, Machias; Calais Free Library

York County: David Adjutant, York County Clerk; Tom Johnson and Virginia Spiller at the Old York Historic Society; Tom Henderson, York Institute Museum/Dyer Library

The staff of *Maine Lawyers Review* — Deborah Firestone, Gail Lowe and Kathy Hooke — who contributed their encouragement, questions and comments as the book progressed. Robert L. Johnston, manager of the production and completion of the book from his special vantage in Gardiner, is due special thanks for bringing the work to a successful conclusion.

I owe a broad spectrum of appreciation to the Lund family. My family joined the Lunds to establish *Maine Lawyers Review* in 1993. Diane Lund organized our team of writers, editors and managers. Erik Lund has been a special partner and friend full of optimism and encouragement. Ted Lund has used his special skills to capture magnificent photographs of the Bangor courthouses.

My family has contributed mightily to the effort. Jacob Sloane, my son, photographed the interiors and exteriors of many of the courthouses. My daughter Sydney helped me along with encouragement and ever-present optimism. From afar, my son Burt enthusiastically supported my every effort. My wife, Regina Healy, was encouraging and urging at appropriate moments, gave discussion and suggestions along the way, and at all times contributed the wit, editing and love essential to completing the work.

Contents

Introduction

This attractive volume reminds us of the prominent place that our county courthouses occupy, both visually and historically, in the public architecture of our State. As soon as each of our sixteen counties achieved its separate existence, its people went to work to construct a building that would be appropriate for the dignity and authority of the courts and that would bring credit to their community. Their efforts, most in the last century, have left us a rich architectural heritage, coupled with a substantial challenge to make the elderly courthouses functionally adequate to meet the heavy demands of our very busy modern courts.

As I followed Bob Sloane's tour of our historic courthouses, my thoughts went beyond the granite and the bricks and mortar to the many thousands of people who have worked there over the many decades. These centers of county government have always housed the county elected officials – commissioners, registers of deeds and probate, sheriffs, etc. – and their staffs and deputies. And they have housed the county probate courts, and also in many cases the municipal courts that preceded the Maine District Court created in the early 1960s.

But when I think of the county courthouses I think first and primarily of the statewide trial courts of general jurisdiction that have "ridden circuit" for jury and nonjury sessions in these county buildings distributed throughout the State. For the first 110 years of Maine history the only statewide trial court was the Supreme Judicial Court; single justices of that Court sat as trial judges in all counties, with their rulings reviewed by the whole Court sitting as the Law Court. Our present statewide Superior Court has in the years since its creation in 1930 progressively taken over almost all of the trial functions of the justices of the Supreme Judicial Court, who themselves are now fully occupied with Law Court and other non-trial work. These state judges of both the Superior Court and the Supreme Judicial Court have always had their chambers in county courthouses convenient to where they lived.[1] Unique among state supreme courts, the Maine Supreme Judicial Court has never had its own building, but rather has always held its Law Court and other sessions in county buildings. With only some ceremonial and other special exceptions, the Law Court in recent years has held all its sessions in the splendid courtroom specifically planned for it when the Cumberland County Courthouse was built in 1908-1910.

It is, and has always been, the judicial activities of these *state* judges that cause the *county* buildings to be universally designated county courthouses. These county buildings are not merely historical landmarks; they are – and have been throughout their history – the everyday workplaces for the judges of our statewide Supreme Judicial and Superior Courts, along with the court clerks, jurors, attorneys, court officers, secretaries, and law clerks necessary for operating those courts. Week-in and week-out and year-in and year-out, these state judges and court personnel have worked in our county courthouses to administer justice.

In honoring the historic courthouses of Maineís sixteen counties, this fine book at the same time honors the judges and their co-workers who over 178 years have made our state judicial system one of the best in the Nation.

September 3, 1998 Vincent L. McKusick
Retired Chief Justice
Supreme Judicial Court

---

[1] To date, 104 justices have sat on the Supreme Judicial Court and 87 on the statewide Superior Court. Their periods of service and the counties of their residence, with a summary, are listed in Appendices A, B and C.

The
Courthouses
of
Maine

The courtroom used by the Supreme Judicial Court in Portland.
Jacob Sloane

ONE

The Courts
Old and New

The courts in Maine evolved from a formal English-based system into a more flexible American system. As settlers moved into the state, new court services were added, based on new jurisdictions formed to meet their geographic needs. Maine was part of Massachusetts until it became a state, and judicial services were provided in the early years under policies set by the government in Boston. But even before statehood in 1820, court services had been expanded deep into the upcountry that would become Maine, and new counties were created to move court services closer to the people. This process continued until 1860 when the last county—Knox—was formed, giving Maine its present total of sixteen counties.

The need for courts developed as Maine began to be settled. British settlers were accustomed to the resolution of disputes and prosecution of criminal activities in the courts of England. In Maine, the first courts were echoes of the formal British system, but with individual forms to adapt to the frontier. Courts were informal and irregularly held. In some instances they were established by towns, and were not initially based on counties, county seats, or even a fixed site. Appeals from judgments were difficult to obtain, and frequently involved hearings in a distant seat of government. [1]

Early courts reflected the discordant and overlapping proprietorships and jurisdictions of the first 100 years of settlement before Maine was united into Yorkshire or York County. The first jurisdictions focused on three geographic areas, defined by the St. Croix River, St. Georges River, the Kennebec River, and the Piscataqua River.[2]

In the territory between the St. Croix and the St. Georges Rivers, the

Court Jurisdictions in Maine

first settlement in the area that would become Maine was established on an island in the St. Croix River in 1604. Although the settlement lasted only a few months, its existence focused the question of ownership by European powers. For half of the years between 1604 and 1713, France held possession of the territory, but only a scattering of transient settlements appeared prior to 1713. With few settlements, no local courts were established until later in the century, when the French and Indian Wars concluded with Britain as the victor.

Between the St. Georges and the Kennebec Rivers, in the area called the Sagadahoc territory, varying conditions affected colonization. Fishing ports were set up at Pemaquid and Monhegan prior to 1618 and, except for these two fairly continuous settlements, Indian warfare limited colonization before 1700. The territory between the Kennebec and the St. Croix Rivers, except for Pemaquid, became part of Nova Scotia in 1621. Forty years later, the Sagadahoc territory, including Pemaquid, was purchased in 1664 by the Duke of York, who called it the County of Cornwall of the Colony of New York. The seat of government, the shire town, was Sheepscot, renamed New Dartmouth and each of the small settlements were assigned a justice of the peace. When New York fell to the Dutch in 1675, Massachusetts claimed jurisdiction of the area east of the Kennebec and established a new county—Devonshire or Devon County. County courts were held by Massachusetts judges in 1674 and 1675. The settlements of Devonshire were destroyed by the Indians in 1676, and resettlement was severely restricted. In 1688 the Duke of York regained his property from Massachusetts and reestablished Cornwall County. When Indians reappeared, further settlement was discouraged for twenty years. The Sagadahoc territory again came under the jurisdiction of Massachusetts in 1691 and became part of York County in 1718. [3]

In southern Maine, between the Piscataqua and the Kennebec Rivers, colonization was characterized by confusing and overlapping jurisdictions. The initial royal grants of land to John Mason and Sir Ferdinando Gorges extended from the Merrimack River to the Kennebec River and 60 miles inland. In 1635, this territory was divided between Mason and Gorges at the Piscataqua River (the present boundary of Maine and New Hampshire). The area between the Piscataqua and the Kennebec in Maine was named New Somersetshire. In 1639 the area was renamed the Province of Maine, under a new patent from Great Britain to Gorges, which extended his holdings to 120 miles inland. This jurisdiction was divided in 1646, during the Civil War in England, and the area north of the Mousam River up to the Kennebec River became the new Province of Lygonia, under the leadership of Alexander Rigby and George Cleeves.

In 1652, taking advantage of postwar confusion in England, Massachusetts claimed the Province of Maine and, with the agreement of settlers, the Province became part of Massachusetts. Claiming all the territory between the headwaters of the Merrimack River and the ocean, the Massachusetts legislature set up a new jurisdiction between the Piscataqua and the Kennebunk Rivers, calling it the County of Yorkshire. The Province of Lygonia joined Massachusetts in 1658 and became part of Yorkshire, extending the county boundaries and jurisdiction to the Kennebec River.

The County of Yorkshire became subject to competing masters for the next forty years. In 1665, following the restoration of the Stuarts to the throne of England, royal commissioners established jurisdiction over not only Yorkshire County, but all of the area as far east as the St. Georges River. The Commissioners reestablished the Province of Maine between the Piscataqua and Kennebec Rivers. Above the Kennebec, the territory became part of Nova Scotia. In 1668 Massachusetts regained control, but was confronted in 1678 by a new claim of ownership by Ferdinando Gorges, grandson of the founder. Massachusetts purchased Gorges' rights to Maine for £1250 and, with new authority, appointed magistrates for Yorkshire County in 1679.

Under the brief Council of New England and the Dominion of New England from 1686 to 1691, New England was one entity from Long Island Sound up to the St. Croix River, ruled by a royal commission under Governor Sir Edmond Andros. With the downfall of the Dominion and a new charter for Massachusetts in 1692, boundaries were reestablished. The territory between the Piscataqua and the St. Georges Rivers became once more the Province of Maine, under Massachusetts jurisdiction. The territory between the St. Georges and the St. Croix Rivers remained a part of Nova Scotia briefly, then became part of the Province of Maine. These boundaries were to remain unchallenged until the American Revolution.

In 1780 the Province of Maine became the District of Maine in the Commonwealth of Massachusetts. The 1783 treaty between Great Britain and the United States after the Revolution established the eastern boundary of Maine at the St. Croix River. The northern boundary, which had been fixed in 1692 as 120 miles north of the mouth of the Piscataqua River in the area west of the Kennebec River, and the St. Lawrence River in the area east of the Kennebec River, was fixed at "the Highlands" (the watershed between the St. Lawrence River and the Maine rivers).

During the War of 1812, the British temporarily occupied Belfast, Bangor, Castine and Machias, and set up a provincial government between the Penobscot and St. Croix Rivers with Castine as a port of entry. After Maine became a state in 1820, the long-standing controversy over the exact boundary between New Brunswick and Maine culminated in the "Aroostook War." Maine's present northeast boundary was determined and formally ratified by the 1842 Treaty of Washington between Great Britain and the United States.

The Evolution of the Courts in Maine

Courts were available to settlers in Maine from the beginning of European settlement. During each stage of the history of Maine, depending on who was in charge, courts were altered to meet the vision of the controlling government. The history of the courts may be divided into three distinct periods:

1. The early colonial times and the era starting when Massachusetts first won control of Maine, 1652-1820;

2. The courts after statehood arrived, 1820-1930; and

3. The present-day court system.

Courts in Early Colonial Times

The colony founded by Sir Ferdinando Gorges operated under a charter obtained from the King of England with the administration of justice through local courts. During this period (roughly 1622 to 1652), courts also informally assisted in the administration of the colony.

About 1640 the first **Executive Council**, a combined legislature and trial court, was held in Saco, representing Maine settlements joined together for purposes of government and advancement of religion. One of its first acts was to grant a bounty of twelve pence for every wolf killed by any settler.

The Council also set up a division of the Gorges colony into two counties with **County Courts** in each to be held two to four times a year. These courts, with both civil and criminal jurisdiction, dealt with misdemeanors, violation of municipal ordinances and all crimes except those involving "life or member," that is, capital crimes or assault and battery. Gorges' manor house in York, the largest building in the settlement, probably served as one site for hearings and adjudication of disputes. Meetinghouses and places of public entertainment—inns and pubs—may also have accommodated informal court proceedings.

In each town a **Town Court** was set up, with commissioners or trial justices appointed to hear trials of small cases. Jurisdiction in civil matters was limited to 40 shillings; these courts had no criminal jurisdiction. Appeals bypassed the County Courts and went directly from local Town Courts to the Council.

After 1652, when Massachusetts assumed responsibility for the Province of Maine, the court system initially followed the Gorges charter specifications, with county and town courts. Provision was made for appeals from decisions, and death penalties were subject to the concurrence of a majority of the **Great and General Court**—the Assembly of

Massachusetts, a combined legislature and trial court sitting in Boston. Although there was no probate court or register of deeds, the recorder of the province, usually the county clerk, recorded wills, administrations of estates and deeds.

In 1691, William and Mary of England gave Massachusetts a new charter with the power to establish courts of justice for the trial of all cases, criminal and civil, arising within the Province. Appointments of judges and justices of the peace were made by the Governor and the Governor's Council. The charter specified a **Superior Court of Judicature**, **Court of Assize and General Gaol Delivery** to travel between the counties to hear criminal and certain civil cases and all appeals from lower courts. Presiding over the court were a chief justice and four other justices, who heard cases involving, for example, property, debt, contract, damages and personal injury. Litigants had a right to trial by jury in cases before the court.

In developing a system that would meet the approval of the English authorities, the General Court in 1699 established for each county a lower tier of courts called the **Inferior Courts** that usually met four times a year, in January, April, July and October.

The **Inferior Court of Common Pleas** heard all civil suits except those in which the crown was a party or a justice of the peace had jurisdiction. Court concerns might include cases between individuals regarding titles to land, ownership of personal property, trespass, contracts, torts involving injury to person or property, maritime commerce, and suits contesting estate settlements. Many civil cases focused on steps in the debt-collection process in commerce. More serious cases would be tried before a jury. Presiding over the courts were magistrates—leading citizens appointed by the General Court and the Governor. In all cases brought before the court, litigants had a right to trial by jury. Appeals would go to the Superior Court of Judicature at one of its subsequent sessions. [4]

The second of the lower courts—the **Court of General Sessions of the Peace**— comprised all the justices of the peace in the county, sitting to hear criminal matters ranging from petty assault, theft, and drunkenness to cursing and fornication, and was called upon for determinations of paternity and assignment of responsibility for financial support as needed. The Court of General Sessions also acted as an administrative body presiding over matters such as county finances, licensing public houses and ferries, and assuring that towns would meet such obligations in road repairs and finding ministers for local churches. Litigants had a right to trial by jury in criminal cases. Appeals went to the next Superior Court session held in the county.

Maine Courts under Massachusetts rule: 1691-1820

A third court—the **Court of Probate**—was established and initially consisted of the Governor and his council. After 1691, a judge was appointed in each county to deal with probating wills and managing and settling estates of deceased persons. In 1784 a Probate Court was formally established for each county, with appointments of the Judge and Register of Probate by the governor and council.

At the base of the judicial hierarchy were **Justices of the Peace**, a one-man court with jurisdiction over civil suits where issues involved no more than 40 shillings and land titles were not in question. Justices of the Peace also had jurisdiction over criminal cases involving profanity, defamation and minor trespasses, for which they could impose fines of up to 20 shillings, and sentence convicted prisoners to the stocks, the whipping post or prison for a maximum of 24 hours. They could also take affidavits and depositions of witnesses. Appeals went to the Court of General Sessions.

These courts were in place up to the Revolutionary War. After the Boston Tea Party, Great Britain passed the Coercive Acts, taking away local and provincial control of the appointment of judges and juries. Citizens of Maine and Massachusetts boycotted the courts under the Act and refused to be sworn as jury members, effectively shutting down the Superior Court for two years. In Cumberland and Lincoln Counties, the

Monumental architectural details of the Cumberland County Courthouse.
Jacob Sloane

inferior courts continued to operate, but without the required juries at every term.

After the Revolution, courts were established that closely resembled those of the former colony. The 1780 Constitution of Massachusetts reconstituted the Superior Court of Judicature as the Supreme Judicial Court. In 1805 the Legislature allowed single justices to travel between county courts, and the full Supreme Judicial Court sat only for capital offenses, issues of law arising on other trials and appeals. The Courts of Common Pleas were also altered in 1805 to take over much of the jurisdiction of the Court of General Sessions of the Peace, which nevertheless retained its responsibilities for granting licenses and for maintaining county buildings and roads.

Maine Courts after Statehood: 1820 to 1930

When Maine became a state in 1820, the courts briefly continued to operate in their prior form. The Act of Separation provided that Massachusetts law and its lower court system would continue until the Maine legislature established new courts. The new Maine constitution, Article VII, Section 1, provided that "The judicial power of this State shall be vested in a Supreme Judicial Court, and such other courts as the legislature shall from time to time establish."

The new **Maine Supreme Judicial Court** continued judicial operations by picking up where its Massachusetts predecessor had left off. In addition to deciding appeals from trial courts as the **Law Court**, the court was also the principal trial court of general jurisdiction. Thus, for the first 35 years of statehood, any murder case or other capital case was tried to a jury before the full Supreme Judicial Court, or at least a majority of the court, making rulings on the admissibility of evidence and instructing the jury. In 1852 the state was divided into three districts, Western, Middle and Eastern, and terms of the Law Court were held only in Portland, Augusta and Bangor.

The **Court of Common Pleas** was reestablished in 1822, but was widely criticized for delays in reaching judgments. In 1831 **County Commissioners** were appointed to take over the tasks of the former Court of General Sessions. The Court of Common Pleas was abolished in 1839 and a new **District Court of Common Pleas** was established with roughly the same jurisdiction. The Supreme Judicial Court's duties continued to include holding sessions in each county.

In 1852 a court reform movement prompted the legislature to abolish the District Court of Common Pleas, combining its functions with the Supreme Judicial Court. Reformers had cited abuses in the appeals process that led to double jury trials—one in District Court and one in the Supreme Judicial Court. The unified court would sit as a Law Court—

primarily for appeals—and individual justices would sit at trials of issues of fact before a jury or without a jury if the parties to the case agreed to waive jury trial. These two divisions of the Supreme Judicial Court were abolished shortly thereafter, and the entire court heard both appellate cases and those formerly assigned to the District Court.

In 1855 another experiment began. **Municipal Courts** were established in Bangor and Portland as intermediate level courts. Initially, municipal courts principally heard cases previously handled by justices of the peace—civil matters where debt or damages did not exceed $100. They were supplemented by **Police Courts** with jurisdiction over minor offenses for which the punishment would be a small fine or a short imprisonment. Trials were not by jury and all cases could be appealed to the Supreme Judicial Court.

The bench in the Supreme Judicial Court in Portland.
Jacob Sloane

The reform period proceeded with the transfer of civil and criminal jurisdiction from the Justices of the Peace to **Trial Justices** in smaller communities in 1860. The great backlog of cases in Cumberland County led to the formation in 1859 of a **County Superior Court** to sit in Portland and hear cases within the county with jurisdiction very similar to that of the Supreme Judicial Court. Additional County Superior Courts were established in Kennebec County in 1878, in Aroostook County in 1885, in Androscoggin County in 1917, and in Penobscot County in 1919. By 1930 a Superior Court had been created for each county of Maine, reestablishing an intermediate level of courts and relieving the Supreme Judicial Court from its dual responsibilities as both an appeals court and a trial court.

A new wave of court reform began in the late 1950s, leading to a dramatic transformation of Maine's court system. Members of the judiciary examined, promoted and implemented changes to the system, and the legislature passed significant revisions in substantive law. During this period federal rights expanded providing equal protection for women and minority groups, court-appointed counsel for indigent defendants, and new procedural safeguards in criminal cases. State and federal environmental legislation and consumer protection statutes and regulations became more complex. All these changes led to an increasing burden on state and federal courts not merely in the amount of litigation, but in its complexity and the amount of judicial time required to deal with it.

The Present Courts of Maine

The Supreme Judicial Court** has a central role as the governing body of the Judicial Department of the State. The Court defines and regulates the practice of law and conduct of attorneys in Maine by the promulgation of the Maine Bar Rules and the Maine Rules of Court. It is the ultimate authority for admitting lawyers to the bar, and for lawyer discipline, including disbarment. The justices of the Supreme Judicial Court give advisory opinions on important questions of law when requested by the governor, Senate or House of Representatives.

Sitting as the **Law Court**, the justices of the Supreme Judicial Court represent a court of final appeal. The justices hear appeals from Superior Court, final judgments, orders and decrees of the Probate Court, appeals of decision of a single justice of the Supreme Judicial Court, and appeals of decisions of the Workers Compensation Commission and other public agencies, such as the Public Utilities Commission.

The Maine Supreme Judicial Court now has seven members—the **Chief Justice** and six **Associate Justices**. The court determines the terms for its sittings, and the time and place of each term. The court ordinarily sits in the Cumberland County Courthouse at Portland for several two to three week terms each year. Justices are provided chambers in county courthouses near their homes, and there they do their opinion writing and research.

Since 1930, the **Superior Court** has been the principal trial court of the state, where both civil and criminal jury trials are held. Individual justices of this court hear appeals on questions of law from the District Court, the Probate Court, the Administrative Court, and certain public agencies. Justices hold sessions of the court in the courthouses of each of the 16 counties.

The **District Court** was established in 1962 throughout Maine to replace the Municipal Courts and the local Trial Justice system. The judges of the District Court hear misdemeanor criminal cases, traffic offenses and civil violations, and hold preliminary hearings in felony cases. The District Courts share jurisdiction with Superior Courts over civil cases involving not more than $30,000. The court offers an expedited hearing for small claims matters involving not more than $1,400. The court hears no jury trials.

The **Administrative Court** was created in 1973 with exclusive jurisdiction to hear cases relating to licensing agencies. The court's decisions may be reviewed by the Superior Court.

The **Family Court** is the newest addition to the courts, established in 1998 to hear cases of divorce, annulment, child abuse and neglect cases, paternity, child support, visitation rights and protection from abuse cases.

The **Probate Court,** dating to 1784 or earlier, has jurisdiction over the probate of wills, the grant of administration and the supervision of the management and settlement of the estates of deceased persons, including the collection of assets, the allowance of claims and the distribution of the estates. The probate courts, funded and administered by the counties, are not part of the integrated court system operated by the state judicial department. Judges and registers of probate are elected.

The **Registry of Deeds**, though not a court, is typically located in the county courthouse. Registers of Deeds for each county are the keepers of the public records of deeds, mortgages, and other instruments affecting title to real property.

Justices of the Peace remain a part of the system, with a role limited primarily to notarizing official documents.

Federal Courts

The **United States District Court** has jurisdiction over geographic areas which may include a whole state, as in Maine. This is a trial level court with very specific jurisdictional requirements. Trials are held in Portland and Bangor.

The **United States Court of Appeals** hears appeals from decisions in cases in the Federal District Court. There are eleven appellate circuits in the United States. Maine is part of the First Circuit which also includes Massachusetts, Rhode Island, New Hampshire, Connecticut and Puerto Rico. Appellate arguments having to do with appeals of Maine cases are usually heard in Boston.

---

[1] The tradition of a county court system was transferred to America by the English settlers, who brought with them strong notions that trials should be heard on the county level and that judgments should be appealable to a higher court. At the time of settlement in Maine, England had two levels of courts: four appellate, "superior" courts, which sat in London, and local or county courts called "inferior" courts, whose judgments or decrees could be reviewed by a higher court on appeal or writ of error.

[2] Counties were preceded by shires. A shire in early English history was an administrative district, ruled jointly by an alderman and a sheriff (the shire-reeve or shire bailiff). The sheriff presided over a judicial assembly—a shire-moot (or shire-mote), later called a shire-court. Members of a shire-court were often called a shire-jury. Proceedings were managed by a shire-clerk. Shire-court proceedings were held in a shire-hall, and the chief town of the shire was called a shire-town. In Maine, the use of "shire" was incorporated early into the designation of settlements such as New Somersetshire and New Devonshire. Later in the 17th century, the first judicial district set up in Maine was called Yorkshire. The use of "county" began to overtake "shire" in the 12th or 13th century to denote the meetings the sheriff held to transact shire business. The functions served by the county were the same as those of the shire and, in practice, the two terms became interchangeable. Well before the American Revolution, the use of "county" appears to have permanently overtaken "shire." In 1760, when two new administrative and judicial areas were set up in Maine, they were named counties.

[3] In Maine, a shire town is where the county courthouse is located and the Superior Court sits and hears cases from throughout its county-wide jurisdiction. The designation of county administrative and judicial centers as shire towns is a tradition that continues in Maine. The designation of a shire town officially denotes the place where the Superior Court sits, although such towns may be known more commonly as a county seat. In England, shire residents went to the shire town for normal, everyday administrative or legal functions, such as recording deeds or wills. The building where these functions were available was called a county hall. If, in addition, it was a building in which the courts of the shire or county were held, it was also known as the county courthouse. In Maine, each of the sixteen counties has a building called the courthouse, located in its shire town to house the court and county administrative offices. The Probate Court and Registry of Deeds were, in early times, housed in buildings apart from the county courthouse. Gradually, probate records were incorporated into court buildings and became an essential function housed in each building.

[4] Courts customarily hold a session—the period when judges are sitting (holding court) and are available for hearing cases (examining issues between parties to a case.) Sessions occur during a specific period of time called a term, which may be a few days, a week or longer. Terms might be held once or twice a year, or, as quarter sessions, four times a year.

Until 1760, York County was the only county in the Province of Maine.

Detail of Jeffrey's 1761 map of New Hampshire, Maine State Library

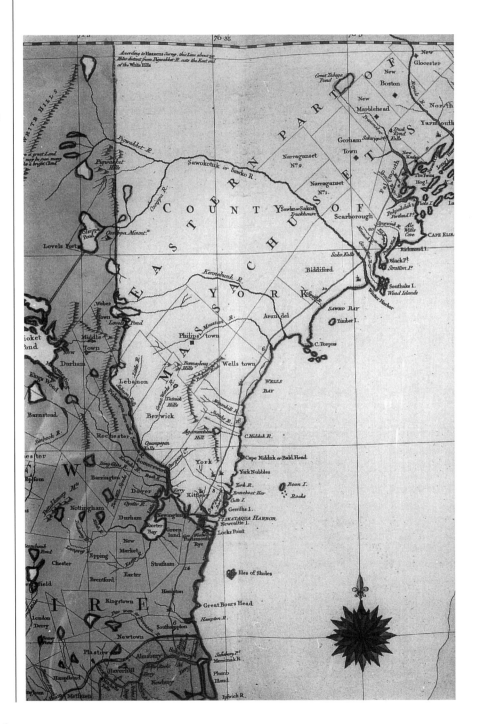

York County
1652

York County, the oldest county in Maine, is the mother of the other counties in the state. After it was established as a county in 1652, it gradually came to include the entire state. The designated shire town, where county affairs were managed and the courts were to hold proceedings, eventually became the Town of Alfred. Before Alfred became the principal seat of county government, several other locations served as shire town or co-shire town for York County—Saco, York, Kittery, Biddeford, Wells (in the part that became Kennebunk Center), and Falmouth Neck (now known as Portland).

The seat of government in the early years of the Province of Maine was the village of York (first known as Agamenticus, later as Gorgeana). The claims of other settlers to the north caused the General Court (a combined legislature and superior court) to hold its initial sessions in Winter Harbor (Saco). Lower provincial courts were held four times a year and dealt with criminal matters. In 1640, the provincial government established three sessions of these Quarterly Courts to sit at York and one session at Saco, based on a division of the province into east and west districts, or counties. The west county was informally known as Yorkshire, and the eastern as Somerset, or New Somersetshire. When the Somerset court was held on September 9, 1640 at Saco, there were 40 cases and nine jury trials.

Sessions of court were customarily held in meetinghouses at the time, and the first York meetinghouse, built in 1634, served as courthouse, town hall, and the meeting place for sessions of the provincial government. The province also built and maintained a small manor house for the Deputy Governor to use as a residence and office for conducting provincial affairs.

The First Courthouses

15

The manor house may have been used for minor hearings, and the meetinghouse provided space for more major court sessions.

The charter given to Founder Sir Ferdinando Gorges in 1641 provided for the administration of justice in the province through two courts. A court with criminal jurisdiction (called a Court Leet) was to be held twice annually during the Easter term (April-May) and Michaelmas (November). The Court Leet dealt with misdemeanors, violations of city ordinances and all crimes except those involving "life and member." Civil cases were held in another court, presided over by the mayor, the recorder, and two aldermen appointed by the deputy governor. This court dealt with disputes over amounts not exceeding ten pounds, and also acted as a probate court, settling wills and estates of residents. The town clerk acted as secretary for the proceedings.

Sitting in the first York meetinghouse, the courts heard a variety of civil and criminal actions. George Burdett, minister of York, was indicted in 1640 for adultery, "entertaining [a woman not his wife] privately in his bedchamber." He was also charged with publishing and broaching "divers dangerous speeches." Convicted and ordered to pay more the £30, he appealed, claiming the right to a rehearing in England. His request was denied and his property was seized and sold in execution of his sentence. Investigating another minister, the grand jury concluded: "We present Mr. Joseph Emerson for telling of a Ly." In 1651, a minister's wife was convicted in a trial of adultery and her sentence was to be branded on the cheek with the letter "A." This is the only known instance of the use of this type of permanent disfigurement in Maine. [1]

The courts saw certain people repeatedly. Court records show that in 1655 Sylvester Stover and his wife were presented by the grand jury "for complaining of one another on the Lords Day in the morning in saying that his wife did abuse him and bid him carry some bread and cheese...' In 1666 they were presented for "not comeing to the meeting on the Lords day [for] about six weeks." In 1667 the Stovers were charged with neglect of their responsibilities for the ferry, and "offering Mr. Hooke some abuse and for threatening to fight him." Samuel Banks was in court in 1685 for "impudently glorying in his own wickedness." [2]

The York meetinghouse was the site of one of the earliest trials for a capital crime in the courts of Maine. In 1644, Richard Cornish was found in the river, drowned with a weight attached to his body. Cornish's wife Katherine was immediately suspected of the murder. She had a reputation of being a "married hussey" and a "lewd woman," with a court record of admonishments to behave and "take heede" to end her liaisons with men other than her husband. Officials led her to view the body, which "bled abundantly," giving credence to the ancient superstition that a murdered person bleeds in the presence of the murderer. Charged with the crime and questioned, she admitted to adulterous behavior with the Mayor and another man. Further discovery was undertaken by, among others, the Mayor, who presided over the trial and never admitted to his misbehavior with the defendant. At the end of her trial, she was found guilty of homicide and sentenced to be executed. She became the first person to be hanged in York. [3]

In a subsequent trial in 1647, Charles Frost was indicted on the charge that he "...feloniously, contrary to the peace of our sovereign Lord the King, his Crown and Dignity, did, the 23d of March last, with a fowling-piece [bird-gun] murder the said Warwick Heard, not having the fear of God before his eyes...." The jury found Frost innocent, and that "...the killing was by misadventure, and Charles Frost [ac]quit[ed] by proclamation." [4]

Events in England changed the history of Maine. In 1647 Provincial Founder Gorges died, and his colony was divided by the King to form Lygonia, a province focused on Casco Bay. The Puritan victory in the English Civil Wars led to disrepute for Gorges, a supporter of the King, and weakness in the government of the province. After declaring itself an independent commonwealth in 1652, Puritan Massachusetts through its governing officials moved to seek loyalty oaths from Maine citizens. Part of the oath guaranteed protection by Massachusetts, but it led to a virtual takeover of the province. Gorgeana was renamed York, and Yorkshire was established, encompassing the entire province and allowing Massachusetts to extend its judicial system into Maine. A county court began to

York County is established

The courthouse, at right, and the meeting-house were surrounded by a high fence.
Old York Historical Society

operate, held "alternately in Kittery and … [York] at appointed times, twice a year, by such magistrate or assistant as the General Court might from time to time designate, assisted by three or five resident associates, elected for the purposes within the county. …[and] between the terms of the County Court and with the associates, hear and determine without a jury, all civil cases, or personal actions not exceeding ten pounds." Although the court sessions were held at both Kittery and York, the county records were kept at York at the residence of Edward Rishworth, who occupied the appointed position of Recorder between 1651 and 1686.[5]

With the death of Cromwell, and the restoration of King Charles II to the throne in 1660, Gorges' reputation was restored. The king established a panel of Royal Commissioners to act for Gorges' successors in governing Maine. The new appointments effectively removed control of the province from Massachusetts. When magistrates from Massachusetts arrived for the regular quarterly court, they were met by the militia company of York. Seeing the determined opposition to their presence, they protested to the Royal Commissioner for obstructing them by armed force, and retreated to Boston. The court system reverted to the control and organization of the Royal Commissioners in 1665.

But Massachusetts was not to be stopped in its quest for the Province of Maine. In 1668, the first "military invasion" of Maine occurred, when the Justices of the Superior Court of Massachusetts appeared in York, supported by an armed force, in an attempt to seize the courts. The independence of the province was permanently lost in 1677, when Massachusetts paid £1,250 for the right, title and interests of Gorges and his heirs as set forth in the original charter establishing the Province of Maine. After 1677, Massachusetts Superior Court sessions were scheduled to be held alternately in Kittery and York.

Initially, the Superior Court did not sit frequently in Maine's single county. The Superior Court sat principally in Boston for York County appeals, but in an Act passed in 1693, the Superior Court was permitted to sit annually at Kittery. The court sat only once under that provision, in May 1695. One month later, the General Court, finding that "it is hazardous for the justices of the Superiour Court of Judicature to ride the eastern and western circuits by reason of the indians lying sculking about the woods and draws a great charge to the publick for a guard to attend them for their safe passing," discontinued the York court, providing for an appeal to Boston. Although the inferior courts continued their work, the Superior Court did not sit again in York County until the May term in 1714. [6]

As the administration of justice reverted to the Massachusetts system, lower courts were held alternately in Wells and York, later in Kittery and York, and still later exclusively in York. The grand jury in Wells was given two meals a day at the expense of the court, along with one shilling for each trial over £10, and 8 pence for each trial under £10. Drummers announced the term of the court at Wells and "at the hour appointed, struck up the reveille in a most lively fashion which sent its summons far and wide." [7]

Meetinghouses Used by the Court

When county lower courts resumed meeting at York, sessions were frequently held in the town meetinghouse. The meetinghouse, constructed in 1675, was 40 by 28 feet with two stories and a turret or belfry, with walls of three-inch-thick planks, covered with one-inch planks on the outside. The building was unfinished for years, and judges noted that the deliberations in court were interrupted by chirps from birds nesting in the rafters. Periodically efforts were made to get rid of the birds and to complete the building. The building had been sufficiently completed to allow galleries [balconies] to be installed in 1680.

In this building a local resident, John Bracey, was accused in 1673 of stealing nails, but was acquitted for lack of evidence. In 1677 Bracey was sued for shooting a hog owned by Thomas Bradon, and was assessed damages and costs, but upon his petition ten shillings of the costs were remitted by the court. In 1678 he was prosecuted for stealing a pair of shoes, and when he ignored the summons, was sentenced to sit in the stocks for one hour. He escaped the penalty by paying the officers' fees. For "casting severall reflecting speeches upon the Rev. Mr. Dummer" in 1686, Bracey and Sarah Anger were sentenced to make public acknowledgment of their offense or to receive ten lashes at the whipping posts. Bracey was accused of being a common liar in 1691, and in 1698, he was found guilty of cursing and ordered to sit in the stocks for three hours. [8]

The French and Indian Wars pushed toward York from 1692 onward, at times with violence. In the first raid, Indians came to town and massacred many residents, took some prisoners, and set fire to the town. The meetinghouse escaped destruction. More vigilant, the town supplied protection and constructed "garrison houses" with high wood fences to ward off the Indians. Throughout the early part of the Indian wars, the court continued to sit in the meetinghouse, until the building became dilapidated and in need of substantial repairs.

A larger York meetinghouse was constructed in 1712, fifty feet square and "built Every way Preportionable…". Raising money for construction began with a free will offering "as Each Man Shall Subscribe." When this method became insufficient, funds were drawn from a town tax. During this period the lower courts held sessions in the building to allow wills, to hear disputes, and to prosecute crimes. Town meetings held in the new meetinghouse chose trial jurors for the upcoming sessions of the court. [9]

After the Indian Wars, the Superior Court resumed sitting in York County, alternating its sessions between Kittery and York. Residents of York and Wells petitioned in 1717 that "the Town of York be now restored to their Right and Priviledge as the Shire Town of that County." Later that year the town also petitioned the General Court that the Registry of Deeds be moved from Kittery to York. In 1718, the Massachusetts legislature ordered "that the Registry of Deeds be kept and the Superior Court of Judicaturs &c be held henceforth in the said Town of York." With this act, York began its role as shire town of York County.[10]

In one of the last Superior Court sessions held in Kittery, the court prepared for work by swearing in a grand jury and two petit jury panels. The schedule included eight appeals from the inferior courts, but only four were ready for hearing and actually decided by the court. In an appeal of the verdict in an action for horse stealing, the court reversed a judgment of £ 50 in damages, evidently because the plaintiff had failed to establish the necessary elements of the crime. All other appeals had to do with land, cases in which the court affirmed the judgments of the lower courts.

Legislation passed in 1720 confirmed the move of the site of the Superior Court session from Kittery to York and provided an extra day in the session because of the increase of court business in York County. During this period, the court heard the murder case of Joseph Quasson, an American Indian, in 1726. Quasson killed another Indian, John Peters, at Wells. Tried in York, he was found guilty and sentenced to death. On the day of his execution, he was accompanied on the one-mile walk from jail to the gallows by Parson Moody, who states that the "mile's Walk was improved in directing, encouraging & caution the Prisoner to Hope." Moody describes the gallows on Stage Neck on the sea shore: "The Gallows was fixed in a Valley with Hills on the one Side and on the other so that the numerous Spectators (they were by Conjecture about Three Thousand—there having been no such Example in the county for more than Seventy Years) had an advantageous Prospect." [11]

York town meeting voted in 1733 to give £100 toward the construction of a courthouse. A committee was appointed to do the work for the town and to "appoint a Place to set said House upon." Within a year the town took additional action by voting: "that this Town will Joyn with the County in building of a courthouse … to hold Courts in & for a Town House…to meet in on all Publick Times." The dimensions of the building were agreed to by vote: 30 by 29 feet, the lower story eight and one half feet high, the upper eleven feet and one half feet high. According to the vote, "both rooms" (presumably one room on each floor) were to be plastered and whitewashed and "well Glazed with Sash Glass" windows, and finished with "Joynery Work" to be selected by the committee. The town voted to help finance the building by assuming one half of all charges. The courthouse/town house building, built adjacent to the old meetinghouse, was placed in use in 1735. [12]

One of the first activities in the new building was the 1735 trial of an Indian woman for murder of her out-of-wedlock child. She alleged a non-Indian to be the father, but admitted to killing the child at birth. Convicted of murder, she was sentenced to death and, according to Parson Moody, was "converted" on her way to the gallows. A special court was appointed to try the case of a counterfeiting ring brought to trial in 1736 for reproducing colonial paper money. William Patten of Wells was charged with "counseling, advising and assisting in forging and counterfeiting 25 shilling bills of New Hampshire, and ten shilling bills of Connecticut Colony." Patten was tried and found guilty. On hearing the verdict, he made a motion in arrest of judgment known as "Benefit of Clergy," an ancient legal plea that was used by defendants to reduce the severity of the imminent sentence. Patten read the customary first verse of Psalms 51: "Have mercy upon me, O God, according to thy loving kindness: according unto the multitude of thy tender mercies blot out my transgressions." On this demonstration of reading ability, an official would say "legit ut clericus," ("he reads like a clerk") and sentence would be pronounced. Patten's sentence, delivered by three judges, was "...that he should be burnt in the Hand, suffer six Months Imprisonment and pay Costs." [13]

In 1734, a number of people living north of York demanded county services closer to their residences. Falmouth Neck (now Portland) was made a co-shire town. The terms of the Courts of Common Pleas and General

The 1733 courthouse, at right, was used for court sittings and for town government.
Old York Historical Society

Sessions were authorized to be held alternately in Falmouth Neck and York in January and October.

The continuing problem of Indian raids prompted the General Court to authorize extraordinary measures to protect the public records. In 1738, Jeremiah Moulton, a member of the Council, requested and received permission to construct a "fortress," for the safety of the public records housed in York. The General Court also provided three or four large guns to aid the defense.

When the French and Indian Wars ended with the English triumph at the battle of Quebec in 1759, settlement throughout the Province of Maine became safe, and immigrants took advantage of the available land. In 1760, Maine's population growth and new settlements in the northern parts of the province led the Massachusetts legislature to create new counties. York County was divided into three parts. Two new counties—Cumberland and Lincoln—were formed, and York County assumed boundaries similar to its present outline. Falmouth Neck ceased its role as co-shire town of York County and became shire town of Cumberland County. Biddeford was chosen to become a co-shire town for York County.

The Court Expands to Biddeford

Although authorized in 1760 to begin fall sessions of court in Biddeford, York County delayed the process for two years. As there was no courthouse in Biddeford, the county began the tasks of finding both space for the annual sessions of the court and methods to pay the rent for each sitting. The first court term in Biddeford was held at the house of John Gray on the King's Highway the first Tuesday of October, 1762. Gray was paid three pounds for the court's first sitting in his house, and for each of five years of its sessions until 1767. For the next two years, 1768-1770, the annual October term of the York County court in Biddeford was held in a room in Dr. Donald Cumming's house. The court paid Cummings forty shillings each term—about two pounds.

In 1771, the court sat in Nathaniel Ladd's Inn. Ladd was paid three pounds twelve shillings for the use of his tavern. The anxiety and uncertainty of the beginning of the Revolution affected where the court sat and how much rent it paid. The court paid thirty shillings to use Elisha Allen's tavern in 1774, six shillings six pence in 1775 and ten shillings in 1776. These prices may also indicate the sharp drop in legal business during the Revolution. Postwar inflation caught up with the court by 1785, when the court was housed at Marquess Myrrs for three years. Presented with their bill, the judges passed the following:

"Ordered that thirty shillings [about a pound and a half] be allowed Marquess Myrrs, for the use of his room and benches this term, of

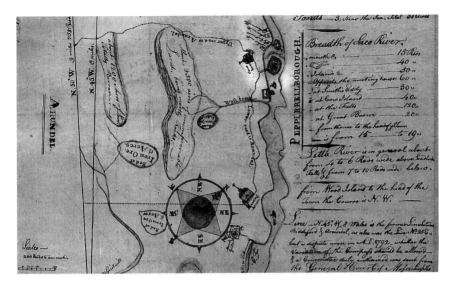

his account for Three Pounds being the full worth as thought by ye Court."

In 1786 the court moved to the residence of Capt. Seth Spring. The court once more lowered its own rent by edict:

"Capt Seth Spring having presented his account against the county for the use of a room in his house for the Court to sit in from the 13th to 21st inst., charge at Six Pounds. Ordered by the Court that he receive out of the Treasure the sum of three Pounds in full thereof."[14]

The Biddeford Courthouse and School

In 1790, Jere Hill led a group of Biddeford investors that raised forty pounds for a courthouse in Biddeford. Because court uses would occupy the building only a few weeks of the year, they planned that a school would occupy the space between court sessions. The group requested the county to pay half the costs of the structure. The court asked for title to the land on which the building would be constructed, and agreed to pay £60 in three yearly installments. Hill's associates refused the request and went ahead with the project, buying land and constructing the school. In 1792 the group invited the court to use the building and pay the costs of the finishing and equipping it for court use. In November, 1792, the Court of General Sessions of the Peace convened in the new building. The court carefully recorded the rent payment in its records and noted: "paid Daniel Hooper, Esq., the sum of Nine dollars for furnishing the Court with firewood and candles at this term." [15]

Ceremony was in favor in the court in Biddeford throughout this period. The judges donned powdered wigs and long robes in the Hooper Inn, then marched up the street behind the sheriff who held a drawn sword. A drummer on top the hill "drummed" the procession into court. The judges wore wigs until 1797.

Inside the courtroom the judges heard a variety of cases. A grand jury indictment in Biddeford, was concerned with church attendance:

> "The Jurors of our said Sovereign Lord the King on oath: do present that John Goodwin of Arrundell in the said County of York Bricklayer, at Arrundell aforesaid for the space of three months last past together hath Absented himself from the publick worship of God on the Lords days, and that he the said John was dureing all that time able of body and not otherwise necessarily prevented from attending, against the Law of this Province in such case provided and in Evil Example to others." [16]

A 1796 trial in the Biddeford Courthouse centered on the assault by three women of another woman they feared to be a witch. A newspaper account of the trial reported:

> "[I]t appeared in evidence that the defendants had threatened her life, had said that she ought to have been long ago in hell with the damned; and that they would let loose the man whom she had bewitched, John Hilton, to kill her. Whether they let him loose or not is uncertain; but it is a fact that he made his escape from the place where he was confined and ran immediately to the house of the Complainant, beat her violently with a stick, drove her out of the house, then seized her by the throat and well nigh choaked her...."
> "His honor, Judge Wells, in an address to the defendants, endeavored to convince them of the gross error into which they had fallen; and that the difficulties and dissentions among them arose rather from ignorance in themselves than from witchcraft in the poor old woman." [17]

Elisha Allen's tavern and inn was used to house visiting judges in the early years. After 1782, Hooper's Inn, with rooms for rent, a general store, a post office, a tavern, and with an attached building for doctors' and lawyers' offices, became a center of the village. Judges stayed here when in town for a session of the court. Prentiss Mellen maintained his office in the Hooper Inn when he came to Biddeford as a young lawyer in 1792:

> "I opened my office in one of old Squire Hooper's front chambers, in which were then arranged three beds and a half a table and one chair. My clients had the privilege of sitting on some of the beds. In this room I slept, as did also sundry travelers frequently, the house being a tavern." [18]

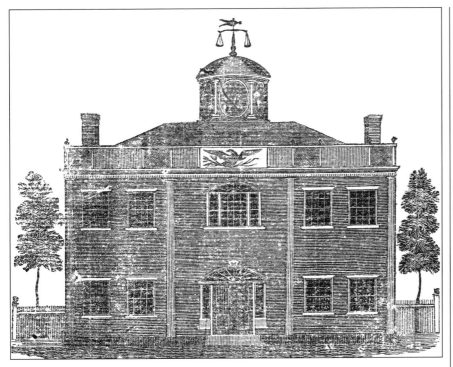

In 1824, the Town of Kennebunk advertised a design for its own courthouse.
Maine Historic Preservation Commission

The court sat for the last time in the old courthouse in Biddeford in 1806.

After 60 years of heavy use, the old town house/courthouse in York warranted replacement. By this time several towns were vying for the honor of hosting sessions of the court. For example, Waterboro residents voted on September 19, 1791 that it was "expedient to build a courthouse at the center near Phineas Colcord's by subscription." Although there is no record of the subscription or the participants, a courthouse was constructed south of the old common at the "fork of the road" for the Court of Common Pleas which held terms in Waterboro for nearly 15 years.[19]

On November 7, 1796, the Kennebunk town meeting voted unanimously that for the interest of the County the sessions of the highest court meeting in York County should no longer be held in York, but in Kennebunk as "...the most convenient place." In 1799 the Massachusetts Legislature appointed a committee to visit York, Kennebunk and Alfred to ascertain the "most eligible place for the permanent establishment of the courts." The committee, viewing the deterioration of the old building and "... the lack of accommodations for the bench and bar...." reported unanimously in favor of Kennebunk. When its report was accepted, and the Legislature ordered, Kennebunk became a half-shire town with York. The first terms of the court in the years 1800, 1801 and 1802 were held in the

Kennebunk, York and Alfred Vie for the Courthouse

meetinghouse in Kennebunk, and Kennebunk petitioned to make the change permanent. [20]

During these years, the Town of Alfred pointed out that York County was growing fast in its interior as well as along the seaboard. New inhabitants were settling well to the north of York and Kennebunk in the part of the county that extended from the early settlements to the Canadian border. The situation was ripe for expanding court services to the north, moving the shire town more closely to the center of the settled area.

In 1802, the friends of Alfred brought a petition before the Legislature to move half of the sessions of the courts from Kennebunk to Alfred. The Legislature initially decided in favor of retaining them in Kennebunk, but reversed its decision at the last possible moment. The *Kennebunk Gazette* reported angrily that the legislative action was highly questionable:

> "The subject was suffered quietly to slumber until the representatives from this part of the county had returned to their homes. The representative from Alfred then contrived to have the subject again called up and by a single vote obtained an act in favor of the location at Alfred." 21

The 1806 York County Courthouse in Alfred, right, with the fireproof public records building.

Alfred thus became a site for sessions of the court and a co-shire town with York. The people of Kennebunk and supporters from other towns apparently submitted to this extraordinary act of legislation without a fight. Yet local feelings ran high. Town meeting in 1803, was asked: "Is it

expedient that the spring term of the Supreme Judicial Court should be holden at Kennebunk and the Fall term of the same court at Alfred?" Of the Kennebunk voters, 291 voted yes and only one against. [22]

Initial sessions of the court held in Alfred were in the meetinghouse or private dwellings. The sessions of the Supreme Court sitting in York County were moved from Kennebunk to Alfred in 1803. In 1806 the first courthouse was built in Alfred on the present courthouse grounds, after the town agreed to defray the expenses of the building. It was 40 feet wide by 50 feet long, two stories high and cost $3,499.69. The gable end of the building faced the street, with simple lines suggesting a residence.

Portions of the terms of both the Court of Common Pleas and the Court of Sessions were moved to the new building in 1807. A jail became necessary and in 1808, a small log building was built to house prisoners. The office of County Treasurer was relocated to Alfred in 1813. Shortly thereafter, a building for housing court records in Alfred was proposed, and in 1815, the Massachusetts Legislature agreed on a resolution that "York County is required to erect a fireproof building in the town of Alfred for the reception of the records of the county." The building was contracted and ready to house the Registry of Deeds by 1816. Four years later, the offices of the Register of Probate and the Clerk of Courts also moved to Alfred. [23]

Residents of York were dismayed at the turn of events, and countered by gaining the support of Kittery and Berwick to construct new facilities for the court in York. The campaign was successful and a new town house/courthouse was constructed in York, using county and town appropriations, as well as individual contributions from residents of the area. The new building was opened for court use in 1811.

Competition for the court continued between the three towns. In York, with a new building available, the town selectmen sent a petition to the Legislature of Massachusetts at its May session in 1816, proposing division of the county:

> "that the town of York, together with the towns of Eliot, Kittery, Wells, Arundel, Biddeford and Saco, with such other towns adjoining them as see fit to petition for the purpose, may be divided and set off from the other towns in the county for the purpose of electing a register of deeds and erecting a building, if thought necessary, in some one of the aforesaid towns for the reception of all the ancient records of the county and those which may be hereafter made....the town of Alfred is far inland and contains a small and scattered population. ...without the Society of Shakers [Alfred] would be so inconsiderable as to be hardly entitled to representation in your hon-

orable body; the roads leading to this town are circuitous. …The petitioners also call attention to the facts that people from the interior towns necessarily seek the seaboard towns to find sale for their products and to purchase commodities needed in their homes, while business interest call very few persons from the seaboard to the interior; the mail facilities were much better on the seabord. …The towns bordering immediately on the seacost contained, in the year 1810, nearly 18,000 inhabitants and paid more than one-half part of the taxes, and it is believed have had the largest share of business to transact with the office of the register. …the records have been there [in seaboard towns] since 1647 and were always convenient…." [24]

In support of York, the Town of Lyman, immediately adjacent to Alfred, petitioned that "the law requiring the fireproof building at Alfred be repealed or that certain named towns on the seabord and such interior towns, the business transaction of the people which lead them very frequently to those on the seabord, be set off as a recording district." The petition was referred to winter session of the Legislature, and on Dec. 6, 1816 a resolve passed both houses authorizing the Register of Deeds of York County to retain its office and records at Alfred. The petitions from York and Lyman received little attention and were not supported by similar petitions from others. [25]

Under the authority of the legislature, John Holmes advertised for proposals to furnish materials and labor and to construct a fireproof building for county records. The location chosen for "the Fire-Proof" was on the northeast corner of the courthouse yard. Proposals were opened on the 18th of May and contracts were awarded immediately and specified that the whole work was to be completed by November. But construction lagged, and the building was not completed until fall of 1819, at a cost of $3,056. The county records were transferred to Alfred in 1820, and were no longer kept in the private residences of the county officers.

Terms of the Court of Common Pleas and the Court of Sessions continued to be held in both York and Alfred. The courthouse/town house in York was the site of the very first term held by the newly-formed Maine Supreme Judicial Court, in August, 1820. The Court was beginning its circuit of trial and appellate work as it sat annually for one term in each of the county courthouses.

The Courthouse in the Town of Alfred

Agitation over the "court question" continued in 1823 with a petition that all the courts in York County be located in Alfred. This action created great excitement in the towns of York, Kittery and Eliot, which claimed that it was a violation of an agreement made twenty years previously "whereby Alfred was pledged to make no attempt to remove the courts from York so long as the people of that quarter were satisfied with the existing arrangement." It was the goal of these towns to move all the courts to Kennebunk. An effort was made that year to locate new county buildings in Kennebunk. A site was offered by Joseph Storer and a several citizens gave their bond to build the courthouse. [26]

In 1824 the seaboard towns submitted petitions to the Maine Legislature asking that courts be moved to Kennebunk. To settle the question, the Legislature passed an Act requiring the voters of York County to vote at annual town meetings on this question:

> "Is it expedient that all the judicial courts and county offices shall be held at one place in the county of York? and if it shall appear that the number of votes in the affirmative exceeds those in the negative, then the inhabitants of the towns shall be required to vote in the annual election in September: Shall all the judicial courts and county offices in the county of York be located in Alfred or Kennebunk?"

The contest for the votes of the residents of York County began in earnest. An Alfred printing office put out a weekly paper called the *Columbian Star* to support its claims for selection as shire town. Kennebunk took an early public relations lead, by pointing out that the county would gain a new courthouse and a fireproof building for county offices at very little cost. Land was already given for the buildings in the center of town. The money which was being collected, together with proceeds of sale of old buildings, would be ample to pay for the new buildings

The courthouse was enlarged in the 1850s by the addition of wings on both sides.
York Institute Museum/Dyer Library, Saco

in Kennebunk. The *Kennebunk Gazette* of June 17, 1824 provided an illustration of external appearance of the proposed new county buildings. The building was proposed to be 52 by 42 feet, with two stories topped by a hipped roof. The lower story was designed to house offices of the clerk of courts and registers of deeds and probate, with proper "alcoves or safes" for the safekeeping of the records, and a fireplace in each room. "Lobbies" with fireplaces were designed to accommodate the jurors. The upper story was "to be finished off in a plain and workmanlike manner, equal at least in style and convenience to either the present courthouses in York or Alfred [and]to have four fireplaces and one lobby, with a proper number of doors and of windows of 8" by 10" glass, and all the rooms and entries to be plastered." Residents claimed that they would build a courthouse within nine months after the legislature approved. Kennebunk offered further that a jail would follow within two years.

The vote on the courthouse question took place on September 13, 1824. It was the largest vote the county had seen. Every town reported before midnight. Handbills issued from *Gazette* office gave the entire vote: 3,492 for Kennebunk, and 3,284 for Alfred. Advocates for Alfred asserted that the vote in favor of Kennebunk was obtained under an "undue excitement, growing out of the presidential election ...." The Secretary of State transmitted the returns to the Senate for confirmation early in 1825. The question was referred to a committee made up of three Senators and five House members. The committee's resolution was brought to the Senate, which initially voted to concur. But the House decided not to concur with the Senate's amendment, and when the resolution was returned to the Senate, it voted to follow the House action. Wells' 1826 petition in favor of Kennebunk was sent to a legislative committee, but the Senate voted not to accept the committee's report. The House disagreed, but the Senate adhered to its former vote, and the House voted to indefinitely postpone the matter.

Through this period York and Alfred remained as half-shire towns. In 1832, in a move toward centralizing county services and offices, the Legislature named Alfred the sole shire town of York County. All terms of the Court of Common Pleas scheduled for York were moved to Alfred. Jeremiah Bradbury, clerk of the county courts, advertised on October 28, 1833 for proposals for rebuilding the county courthouse at Alfred, with construction to be completed on or before the first of September in 1834. The seaboard towns once more went to the Legislature, which required an affirmative vote by York County towns. The towns voted against the new building, but the county commissioners had already reviewed proposals and selected a contractor, and the contractor had begun work.

After 1832, all terms of the York County courts were held in Alfred, and county use of the York town house/courthouse was discontinued. Beginning in 1859, an arrangement was made for an annual term to be held at Saco, which continued until 1931. The Probate Court was held occasionally in York during summer months up to 1863.

To cope with the demands of the courts, York County Commissioners have continually expanded the Alfred courthouse since the first building was built on its hill. The first major expansion took place between 1852 and 1854 when two wings were added on either side of the 1806 building at a cost of $29,272. These wings were well-proportioned with tall chimneys above flat roofs, rounded windows in brick insets, and vertical divisions echoing the four columns on the front. Early photos suggest that the entire building was painted or plastered in a light color that masked the brick construction.

In the summer of 1854 a "dome light" (sky light) was placed over the courtroom on the second floor at a cost of $998.50. A new jail was built in 1872, next to a heel factory in which the prisoners worked to help defray part of the expense of running the jail. The courthouse was slightly enlarged again in 1896, following a battle led by Biddeford to remove the county seat from Alfred. Biddeford's city building had burned in 1895, and the city had raised money to construct a new building to house both city and county offices and the courts. Three hundred people from Biddeford attended the hearing on Biddeford's proposal at the state house in Augusta, but support for the movement was insufficient to sway the Legislature to enact a bill that would change the shire town designation for York county to Biddeford.

Additions to the courthouse were made in 1917 to accommodate the Registry of Deeds and the Registry of Probate and to add running water and electricity. A further enlargement was made for the office of the Clerk of Courts in 1927. The most recent change was a two-story addition to the Registries of Deeds and Probate in 1964.

A disastrous fire in 1933 wrecked the central portion of the building. The two 1852 wings were damaged but not destroyed in the fire because of thick brick walls separating them from the oldest portion of the building. The style of the old building was reproduced by Portland architects Wadsworth and Boston during the 1934 reconstruction, but with modern amenities. The ancient facade with the four white columns was a centerpiece of the reconstruction and the red bricks of the original construction were exposed during the rebuilding. The entrance to the building led through the restored original facade of the building. A cupola with arched windows replaced what had been described as a "rather squatty affair." A

Changes to the Alfred Courthouse

bell, offered by the Old Congregational Church in Lyman, was placed in the belfry. [27] The total cost was $175,000.

The old courthouse stands today behind a sweep of green lawn studded with large old trees. The tall white columns of the old building with its two-story porch stand out against the old brick building. The white cupola glistens on the roof. From its hill, the structure faces Alfred's main street, ignoring the parking lot at its side and the traffic swishing past on Route 111. Two granite steps lead up to the porch and two more steps lead to the interior floor level. Marble floors gleam in a black and white diagonal pattern. Colonial pilasters and dentils are a prominent part of the interior design. Bronze chandeliers hang overhead. By heavy iron doors at one

The courthouse in Alfred was rebuilt after the fire of 1936 destroyed the central section.

side there are signs directing people to the offices of the County Commissioners and the District Attorney. The floors are spotless. A sign reminds visitors that smoking is not permitted in the courthouse. An elevator leads to the second floor. The only incongruous note is the three gumball machines standing near the entrance, well maintained, clean and full.

---

[1] Banks, Charles Edward, *History of York, Maine*, in three volumes, Cambridge, Mass.: Murray Printing Co., 1935, Reprinted by Old York Historical Society, Portsmouth, NH: Randall Publisher, 1990, Vol II, pp. 118, 121, 241. To "present" is to lay a matter concerning an indivdual before a judge, magistrate or governing body for action or consideration. *Black's Law Dictionary*, Rev. Fourth Ed., St, Paul, MN, 1968.

[2] Banks, Vol. II, pp. 21

[3] Banks, Vol. I, pp. 172-173; Williamson, Joseph, "Capital Trials in Maine," *Collections and Proceedings of the Maine Historical Society*, Second Series, Vol. I, 1890, pp. 159

[4] Williamson, Joseph, "Capital Trials in Maine," p. 160; Williamson, William, Vol. I, pp. 345-346

[5] Banks, Vol. I, pp. 192-193; Vol. II, pp. 228-229

[6] Wroth, "The Maine Connection," in *The History of Law in Massachusetts— The Supreme Judicial Court 1692-1992*, Russell K. Osgood, Ed., Boston: Supreme Judicial Court Historic Society, 1992, p. 179

[7] Bourne, Edward D., *History of Wells and Kennebunk*, Portland: B. Thurston & Co., 1875, pp. 155-156

[8] Banks, Vol. I, 269.

[9] Banks, Vol. II, pp. 105-106.

[10] *Id.*, p. 229.

[11] *Id.*, p. 242.

[12] *Id.*, p. 230; Moody, Edward C., *Handbook History of the Town of York from Early Times to the Present*, August: Kennebec Journal Co., 1914, p. 96

[13] Banks, Vol II, pp. 241-244.

[14] Biddeford, Maine, Public Library. *An Introduction to Biddeford's History and a Chronological Outline of Events*, prepared by the McArthur Library, 1944, *Stories and Legends of Old Biddeford*: Part I—1660-1747, prepared by the McArthur Library 1946, Part II—1740-1800, prepared by the McArthur Library, 1944-46, reprinted and repaginated by the Biddeford Historical Society as *Dane York's History of Biddeford*, 1980; pp. 152, 186,187

[15] *Id.*, p. 181

[16] *Id.*, pp. 136,165

[17] *Id.*, pp. 195, 198

[18] *Id.*, pp. 179-180, 189

[19] Knights, Ernest G., *Waterboro, York County, Maine*, n.p., 1954

[20] Banks, Vol. II, pp. 230-231

[21] Remich, Daniel, *History of Kennebunk from its Earliest Settlement to 1890*, Portland: Lakeside Press, 1911, p. 184

[22] Banks, Vol. II, p. 229.

[23] Banks, Vol. II, p. 229-230.

[24] Remich, p. 187

[25] *Id.*, p. 188

[26] *Id.*, pp. 188-193

[27] Pierce, Ann, "A History of Maine's County Court Houses," *Maine Bar Journal,*, Vol 1, No. 3 May, 1986, pp. 120-121; Isaacson, Dorris A., Ed., *Maine: A Guide 'Down East,'* Second Edition, Revisions prepared by the Maine League of Historical Societies and Museums and Sponsored by the 104th Maine Legislature and the State Sesquicentennial Commission; Rockland: *Courier-Gazette*, Inc., 1970.

The 1774 Cumberland County Courthouse was built at the corner of King and Middle Streets.

Detail of "Falmouth Neck, as it was when destroyed by Mowatt Oct. 18, 1775," Maine Historical Society

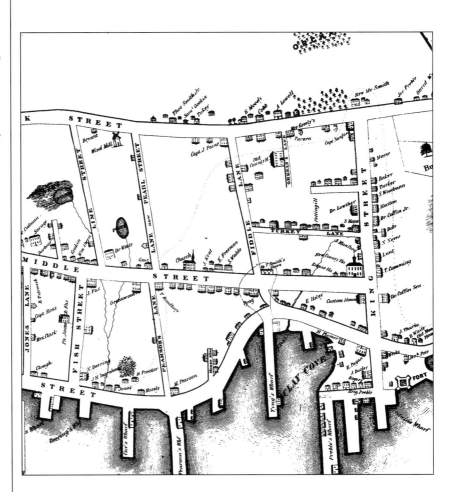

THREE

Cumberland County
1760

The courthouses of Cumberland County have a vivid history, closely intertwined with the histories of both the city of Portland and the State of Maine. The buildings are steeped in tales of early settlement on Falmouth Neck, Indian raids and fires, total destruction in the Revolutionary War, service as the state capitol, destruction twice by fire in the 19th century, and finally, service as the centerpiece of a 20th century group of government buildings.

The first settlers of the peninsula known as Falmouth or Casco Neck (now central Portland) arrived in 1637. Settlers Richard Tucker and George Cleeves built houses at a site on the south side of Casco River (now Fore River/Portland Harbor) that was technically owned by Robert Trelawney and Moses Goodyear. When John Winter, agent of Trelawney, forcibly ejected Tucker and Cleeves from the property, they moved to the north side of the river, obtained a legitimate grant to the land, and became the first European settlers on the site of Portland. In 1640, Tucker and Cleeves filed an action of trespass against Winter in the court founded in York by colonial leader Ferdinand Gorges. Tucker and Cleeves recovered damages for the trespass on their house, land, and goods in the amount of £80, with 12 shillings and sixpence for court costs.

Cleeves became governor in 1643 of the Province of Lygonia, which reached from Cape Elizabeth to Cape Porpoise. Lygonia was an ancient tract that became particularly useful to Cleeves during the English Civil War, when Gorges, the original founder of the colony, fell from favor and was imprisoned by Cromwell's Puritans because of his loyalty to the King. In 1647 the English Commissioners for Plantations agreed that the claims of Lygonia were legitimate, and Cleeves, as governor, began holding leg-

Early Settlement and the Courts

islative and court sessions. Sessions were held in Casco Neck in September and December, 1647. These sessions were held both in private homes and the town meetinghouse.

The Commonwealth of Massachusetts, sensing a disordered state of affairs in Maine in 1652, began to establish a claim to the province as far east as Casco Bay. Within six years, Massachusetts had received submission from residents as far east as Saco. In July, 1658, residents north of Saco also submitted to Massachusetts. The articles of agreement established that "those places formerly called Spurwink and Casco bay ...shall run back eight miles into the county and henceforth shall be called Falmouth." Towns had local courts to try cases involving demands up to fifty pounds. "Right trusty Henry Josselyn, Robert Jordan, George Cleeves, Henry Watts and Flavius Neale were appointed commissioners ... to hold the local court for petty causes without a jury" in Scarborough and Falmouth. Any of the appointees could perform marriages. [1]

The Indian Wars reached Falmouth in 1689. During the prior year, the English under Governor Andros of Massachusetts had attacked Baron Castin's residence in Castine. As retribution, the French and Indians settled on the destruction of Falmouth Neck. On September 17, 1689, they attacked and burned the town.

Starting Over as a Town

Falmouth was resettled in 1718. After the early families had built their homes, they agreed that a meetinghouse should be built "after the most commodious manner, for the benefit of the town in general." At a town meeting vote in February 1720, the settlers resolved "that a meetinghouse be built as soon as possible thirty-six by twenty-eight, twenty foot stud." The meetinghouse was built some 30 feet southeast of the west corner of what was then King (India) Street and Middle Street. It was destined to become the first courthouse for Cumberland County. [2]

The 1720 meetinghouse, an early focus of the town's activities, soon assumed the role of a civic center. Town meetings were held there, although the town papers and records were by custom stored at the home of the individual responsible for their preparation. A school was sited next to the building and a fire station "engine-house" joined the complex of buildings somewhat later.

The meetinghouse was gradually improved: in 1722 funding was voted for "boards plank to cover the meeting-house," and in 1723, provision was made for clapboards to cover it. A second-level gallery was constructed along with a "pew"–probably a lectern–for the minister. In 1725, the meetinghouse was the site of ratification of Lieutenant Governor Dummer's treaty with the Indians, which had been signed earlier in Boston. Governor Wentworth of New Hampshire, who was among the participants in the event, noticed the forlorn look of the building and donated glass for the windows. With some other assistance from local residents, the outside of the building was finished shortly thereafter. [3]

The King Street meetinghouse became the official courthouse only gradually. The population of the town was growing rapidly—doubling from 1718 to 1725 and doubling again by 1735. The old building came to be viewed as shabby, and was clearly not large enough to accommodate all that wanted to attend town meetings and church services. Also, the people of the Neck had begun to move west, away from the old center of town and the old civic center.

In 1734 Falmouth was made a half shire town for York County, sharing the honor with the Town of York. Now Falmouth would be the site of an annual term of the Inferior Court and the Court of General Sessions of the Peace. The court was to be accommodated in the existing meetinghouse on King Street, sharing the space with churchgoers, town meeting members, and the needs of other large meetings. But the old meetinghouse was not large enough for major events, for which other arrangements had to be made. For example, a 1739 treaty with the Indians was ceremoniously signed by Governor Shirley in a spacious tent constructed "upon the hill eastward of Long Creek, in which were placed rows of seats sufficient for the whole assemblage." [4]

The old meetinghouse eventually became the official courthouse as a result of a town vote in the late 1730s to build a new meetinghouse. In July, 1740, a new, more spacious building for a meetinghouse was completed on Queen (now Congress) Street. This new building, because of its ability to accommodate more people than the courthouse, was also destined to play a role in the history of legal proceedings in Portland. When the Queen Street meetinghouse was finished in 1740, the old King Street building was remodeled at the expense of the town for court purposes. The second story gallery and balcony area was filled in and made into a courtroom. As consideration for the remodeling effort, the town retained the right to use the space when courts were not in session.

For twenty years, the Inferior Courts of York County and the Courts of General Sessions met in the building when in Falmouth. During the same period, the Massachusetts Superior Court met in the Falmouth courthouse to hear cases once a year. Reverend Thomas Smith wrote his opinion of upcoming events in 1741: "A long Court this is likely to prove; there being about thirty actions that were continued from last Court." Smith was especially interested in the Court that year: " June 23. Our great case (for near four thousand acres of land) came on this morning and was not finished till between nine and ten at night. June 24. The Jury brought in against us."[5]

The Meetinghouse Becomes the Courthouse

Smith observed the Court at close range: "I preached p.m. and in the evening before the Court." His disapproval of their peccadilloes showed: in 1743, he wrote: "The Court this year is kept at Purpoodock [South Portland], on pretense of no tavern this side." and in 1747, "I prayed with the Court in the afternoon. Justice came drunk all day." [6]

A jail was constructed in 1753, under orders of the Court of Quarter Sessions of York County. The jail was ordered to be joined to the court-house on King Street "lean-to" fashion, with three new walls and a sloping roof attached to the courthouse. The order called for the building to be 35 feet long, 15 wide and "seven stud, with one stack of chimneys of four smokers. The building is to be of good, square, sound, hewed or sawed timber, well boarded, clapboarded and shingled outside, with a lining inside of good, sound oak plank, spiked on…." Eighty pounds was allowed as the budget for construction. [7]

One of the trials held in this courthouse had to do with the title to the territory which included Georgetown, Brunswick and Topsham. Both the Pejepscot and the Plymouth Companies claimed land at the Kennebec River and fought their claims publicly and in newspaper advertisements before the case arrived at the court. The case was heard in July, 1754. The Attorney General of Massachusetts, Jeremiah Gridley, represented the Plymouth Company, and the Pejepscot Proprietors were represented by James Otis, Jr., whose efforts on behalf of the rights of the colonies were among the most effective prior to the Revolution.

The King Street courthouse continued to be too small for large public gatherings. The Queen Street meetinghouse was used for widely-attended conferences with Indian tribes and for formal treaty-signings. The first conference was in September 1749 and the second in July 1754, when Governor Shirley and the Governor's Council, with commissioners from New Hampshire, had a long conference in the meetinghouse with the three principal Indian tribes.

Disputes with Indians were largely resolved by the end of the French and Indian War in 1759. A petition to divide York County was presented to the General Court in early 1760, arguing the inconvenience of the establishment of the courts and public offices in the southwest corner of the county. York remained the center of all but a few jury trials. The General Court responded by dividing York County into three counties—York, Cumberland and Lincoln Counties.

When Cumberland County was carved out of York County in 1760, the Falmouth courthouse suddenly gained a new status. It was no longer a branch office, used intermittently by the judges of York County. It was a place that had unique importance as the center of justice for the newly-formed Cumberland County, permanently housing the judges and records of the county. The courthouse also was used by the Massachusetts Superior Court when it was sitting to hear cases from either Cumberland or Lincoln Counties.

The courthouse became a symbolic site for celebrations; Reverend Smith notes that when the Stamp Act was repealed in 1766, "Our people are mad with drink and joy; bells ringing, drums beating, colors flying, the courthouse illuminated...." [8]

Reverend Smith described a case heard in this courthouse:

"The great case, *Jeffries v. Donnell*, was tried at this term. It was ejectment for part of the present town of Bath, in which the title of the Proprietors of the Kennebec Purchase was involved and which was decided for the Defendant. The plaintiff claimed under the Kennebec Proprietors, who derived their title from the Plymouth Company.... The most efficient legal talent of the country was enlisted to the cause: for the Plaintiff were Jeremiah Gridley and James Otis, Jr., of Boston and William Cushing of Pownalborough, now Wiscasset, afterwards Judge of the Supreme Court of the United States. On the other side were William Parker of Portsmouth, afterwards Judge of the Superior Court of New Hampshire, Daniel Farnham of Newbury and David Sewall of York. An appeal was claimed to the King in Council, but denied by the Court and final judgment entered." [9]

In 1772 the court was confronted with the first trial for murder in newly-formed Cumberland County. A man named Goodwin was charged with throwing a man overboard in Casco Bay. Many doubted his guilt; Smith writes "...he was reprieved three times." The trial, held in summer, was brief; Goodwin was found guilty and sentenced by the Superior Court to be executed. Reverend Smith visited and prayed with the prisoners, including Goodwin. Goodwin's execution at the gallows on November 12 attracted a great crowd of people. [10]

Then in 1774 the Boston Tea Party led to the British closing the Port of Boston, to dissolution of the General Court, and to alterations in the provisions of the Massachusetts Charter concerning appointments to the court. Judges, sheriffs and justices were to be appointed or removed solely by the Provincial Governor. Jury members, who had by law been selected at open town meetings, were to be selected, summoned and returned by the sheriffs of their respective counties. The new procedures drew outrage from around the country. Cumberland County responded with a series of conventions at the courthouse. At the first convention, representatives from nine towns met to determine a course of action. They asked William Tyng, Sheriff of Cumberland County, his intentions in regard to obeying the new act. Tyng responded, promising that he would not "…conform to the requirements of the act, unless by the general consent of the county…." Members of the convention asked the justices of the Common Pleas and Sessions, the magistrates, and all other civil officers to discharge their official duties as if no parliamentary act had passed. They also selected members to attend the Provincial Congress in Salem, set up to replace the General Court. [11]

The sufficiency of the courthouse was tested by the increasing number of court events and deed transactions it accommodated during a period of unparalleled population expansion. The court building and its facilities on King Street (renamed India Street after the Revolution began) remained tightly constrained and unchanged for over thirty years. It was clearly too small for the tasks assigned to it.

The 1774 Courthouse is Destroyed by War

In March, 1774 the annual town meeting took up the subject of the need for a new and more spacious courthouse for Cumberland County. The meeting, well attended by the townsfolk, became noisy and rancorous. The quarrel did not focus on the need for the new building; apparently there was consensus on the desirability of replacing the old courthouse. Rather, the arguments centered on where the new building would be located — whether the new site should be in the vicinity of the old courthouse near the waterfront or at the top of the hill, along Congress Street and near the First Parish church in an area becoming fashionable. At the end of a long session, the town meeting members resolved to use the existing large town site at the corner of King Street (now India Street) and Middle Street for the new building.

On May 25th, 1774, construction got underway. The old courthouse, school-house and engine-house were moved to new locations to clear the town lot for the new courthouse. Throughout the remainder of the year and well into 1775 construction continued. The building was sturdily framed and clapboarded, the roof was put in place and shingled, and the interior was plastered and fitted out for the court's needs. As construction was nearing completion on the courthouse but before it could be put into use by the court, events overtook it.

Following the battles of Lexington and Concord, minutemen had begun to organize in the vicinity of Falmouth. A local Tory, preparing to fit out a vessel to carry what appeared to be military supplies– masts for the King's Navy–was refused permission to complete his work in Falmouth. He called for help from the British ships and, shortly, Captain Mowatt's warship arrived in the harbor. Mowatt came ashore and went for a walk up Munjoy's hill, where he was suspected of spying on the minute-men and was arrested. Quickly released through the intervention of calmer townsfolk, Mowatt departed with an outward expression of gratitude for his safety.

Five months later, the British sent Captain Mowatt with four armed vessels and a storage vessel to punish Machias, which had captured a British ship. Because of bad weather, Mowatt could not reach Machias. Thwarted in his mission, Mowatt and his ships took positions in front of Falmouth and sent an ultimatum announcing the shelling of the town on the next day based on "the most unpardonable rebellion" of its people. Citizens were given time to evacuate and ordered to give up their arms. A delegation of town fathers went to the British ships to beg for leniency, and Mowatt, repeating his announcement, gave additional time for consideration of his demands. [12]

On Wednesday morning, October 18, Falmouth citizens met at the courthouse and "resolved by no means to deliver up the cannon and other arms," and sent the committee back to Mowatt with the answer. Half an hour after their return, Mowatt destroyed most of the town with artillery and sent his troops ashore to set buildings afire. Over 400 buildings were destroyed, including the unoccupied new Cumberland County Courthouse as well as the old courthouse which had been moved out of the way to furnish a site for the new one. Even the records of the town and county, although they were stored in private homes, were destroyed. [13]

The burning of Falmouth was not quite total: several buildings remained in place, either because of their location away from the water's

The courthouse in Falmouth, now Portland, (Upper rights, with cupola) was burned by the British during the Revolution.
Maine Historical Society

THE TOWN of FALMOUTH, *Burnt by Captain* MOET, Octr 18th 1775.

edge or because of the prudent actions of individuals. The 1740 meeting-house on Congress Street, high on the hill above the harbor, was bombed, but did not burn. Another structure still standing was the most popular and fashionable tavern of the town, kept by the legendary Alice Grele, who saved her building by remaining in it and extinguishing the flames when it caught fire. These undestroyed buildings became temporary sites for the activities of the court in the wake of Mowatt's attack and the poverty and hardships that it brought.

Alice Grele's tavern had enjoyed a reputation as a meeting spot well before the major events of the Revolution. The long, low building on the east corner of Queen (Congress) and Hampshire Streets could provide a fair number of people with space for meetings, along with continuous drink and food, if needed. The little town was expanding up the hill and around the tavern's site. A political convention responding to the Intolerable Acts which punished Boston was held at Mrs. Grele's one story tavern on September 12, 1774.

Following closely on Falmouth's stand against England, delegates were chosen to represent the District of Maine in the deliberations in Boston for representatives to the newly-formed Continental Congress. Though it was a small convention by today's standard, its business was so serious that each attendee was individually interrogated about royalist leanings. Each was then asked to pledge not to accept any commission under the recent acts of the British Parliament. In an effort to further reduce interaction with the Crown's judicial institutions, the convention resolved: "That every one would do his utmost to discourage lawsuits, and likewise compromise disputes as much as possible." [14]

After the Mowatt bombardment, taverns such as Alice Grele's became sites for civic functions and formal court activities as well. Until a new courthouse could be built, taverns were temporarily leased by the government as courtroom locations. Alice Grele was paid ten shillings and six-pence in 1776, and two pounds, eight shillings in 1777 for a room for the court's use. Samuel Freeman's "great chamber" was rented for nine pounds in 1787. Moses Shattuck's tavern was yet another site used by the court from time to time. Shattuck's tavern on Middle Street was the county-house or jailer's dwelling, which was always kept as a public house or tavern by the keeper of the jail.

Court activities continued, including trials held in Cumberland County for cases originating in Lincoln County . A case in 1776 involved the murder of Jacob Lash of Waldoboro by Andrew Cancalus, who was convicted of manslaughter and sentenced to be burned on his left hand, to forfeit all his possessions, and to be imprisoned for six months.

Essential court activities continued to be held at informal sites such as the taverns, and construction of a new Cumberland County Courthouse was put on hold until the war's end. The town was being slowly rebuilt, but it remained indefensible during the years of the Revolution and there was a continuing risk that the British might reappear. They were, after all, not far away: even after the battle of Yorktown in 1781, the British retained control of Castine and were watched closely. Until the war's conclusion in 1783, rebuilding the town took a back seat to the need to remain vigilant against further outrages from the British.

I n a single year after the end of the war, 54 dwellings, stores and shops were built. Falmouth was rapidly being reborn. In 1785, a committee of the Court of General Sessions of the Peace recommended that a new courthouse be constructed with a roof so framed that a belfry may be built upon it at some future time. Later that year, for £18, the county purchased the site for the new courthouse near the meetinghouse on Queen Street (renamed Congress Street), at the head of Court Street (now Exchange Street). In the year that Falmouth became Portland—1786—courthouse construction got under way once again.

The 1786 Courthouse

The new courthouse was designed to be 34 feet wide on the Congress Street frontage and 48 feet deep, with 24 foot tall corner posts. Its two stories were clapboarded with a hip roof topped by a belfry. This cupola was not used to house a bell, but to support a weathercock carved from wood. There was speculation that "St. Peter's testimony in denying his master may have suggested to the county fathers the propriety of surmounting the new temple of justice with a representative of the historic bird, as a caution to the witness, when he entered the portal, not to deny the truth, whatever might be the provocation from contending counsel." [15]

Perhaps as an additional reminder to tell the truth, the gallows, stocks and pillory were stored prominently in the first floor hall of the courthouse except when they were in use. In front of the building on Congress Street stood a whipping post, with bars for securing a culprit's arms and legs.

On the second floor was the courtroom. In this unadorned whitewashed room were tables for the judiciary, and a square box, raised one step above the floor for a prisoner. The box was surrounded by wooden panels with a door as high as the sides. At the top was an open railing with short balusters. Only the head of the prisoner was visible above the top rail. The courtroom was used by the Massachusetts Supreme Judicial Court, which returned to Portland in 1779, the Court of Common Pleas, the Court of General Sessions of the Peace, and, after 1789, by the United States District Court of Maine.

In 1793 Cumberland County purchased land adjoining the rear of the Congress Street courthouse as a site for a jail. The jail – built in 1797 – was the first county building constructed entirely of granite. From this jail, in 1808, Joseph Drew of Saccarappa walked to a gallows erected near Portland Observatory, one half-mile away. Drew had been convicted of the murder of a deputy sheriff. On the way to this new site for executions, he was accompanied by the county sheriff on one side commenting on the mortal sin he had committed, and Parson Caleb Bradley, of Stroudwater, on the other side, advising him of the glory of the spiritual world into which he would soon enter.

The Cumberland County Courthouse of 1786 was adorned with a carved rooster weather vane .

The separation of the courthouse proceedings from the site of punishment took place about 1800. The whipping post and the pillory were removed to the training field (near the Eastern Cemetery). In 1803, the *Eastern Argus* contained the following announcement: "George Peters, a black fellow, who broke open the shop of Abner Rogers, watchmaker, will receive his punishment on the training field between twelve and one o'clock to-day." His punishment may well have included the pillory – "a tall post about 25 feet high. About half way up from the ground was a square platform, and two planks crosswise of the post, with an opening for the neck and two below for the wrists. Two culprits could be pilloried at once. Boys were allowed to pelt them with eggs." Corporal punishment of this kind was abolished in the District of Maine in 1809. [16]

In 1792, New Gloucester became a half shire town with Portland, and the Courts of General Sessions of the Peace and of Common Pleas sat regularly here once each year. The court was held in the school house standing near the old blacksmith shop and the Farmers' Union store, just below the new cattle pound. The whipping post and the stocks, located in

The courthouse stood in the center of the Town of New Gloucester in 1794.

Detail of "A True Plan of the Town of New Gloucester… in 1794," Massachusetts Archives the western corner of the common by the meetinghouse, were used as punishment for those who disturbed the quiet of the Sabbath and the deliberations of the town meetings by their noisy and boisterous conduct. The jurors roomed at the Bell Tavern, kept by Peleg Chandler. The Common Pleas Judges frequently were the guests of Col. Isaac Parsons, and in extreme cold days sometimes held their courts beside his blazing fire. In this court as many as four hundred and fifty new cases were entered at a term. The judges who sat here in the Court were the Hons. Daniel Mitchell, John Lewis, Josiah Thatcher, William Gorham, Stephen Longfellow, Robert Southgate, and John Frothingham, The clerk was Enoch Freeman, and the Sheriff, John Waite. The Hon. William Widgery, afterwards a judge of this court, then was a judge in the General Sessions of the Peace.

When the court was scheduled to sit in New Gloucester, the village was filled with jurors, witnesses, litigants and court attendants. Important cases were tried there, and leading lawyers of the county attended the terms and took part in the trials. Lawyers whose names shine bright on the page of public and professional fame lived and practiced here. The Hon. Nathan Weston and the Hon. Ezekial Whitman, both later Chief Justices of the Supreme Judicial Court of Maine, practiced and lived in New Gloucester. Samuel Fessenden, the father of William Pitt Fessenden, came here upon his graduation from Bowdoin College and practiced here until the court was moved permanently to Portland. Simon Greenleaf, Reporter of Maine decisions and professor of law at Harvard University, apprenticed here with Ezekial Whitman. Peleg Chandler practiced law here until he moved to Bangor. All the principal lawyers in the county practiced before the court in New Gloucester, and most of the cases from the back country of Cumberland County were tried here until 1805, when Oxford county was formed and the court left New Gloucester to return permanently to Portland.

The 1816 Courthouse and Statehouse

The old wooden courthouse in Portland became inadequate for its purposes during the embargo of 1807 and the lawsuits that resulted from it. During the War of 1812, there was no thought of expansion, but when peace came in 1815, plans for a new building were revived. The new building was constructed by a committee consisting of Sheriff Hunnewell, Barrett Potter and Albert Newhall on the site of the 1786 courthouse on Congress Street, adjacent to the old county jail and jail-keeper's house.

The architect, John Kimball, Jr. was responsible for designing a Federal period building that, at 50 by 60 feet, was a "catalogue" of neo-classical elements, according to architectural historian Deborah Thompson.

"This building had two and one-half stories (with high ceilings) and was of brick construction, with a low hipped roof, surrounded by a balustrade and prominent open cupola. Its dominant architectural theme was strongly neo-classical: combinations of paired columns and pilasters extending the full two stories were spaced across the front, and the facade was broken by three projecting pavilions, the center one with a pediment. The columns and pilasters rested on large pedestals and had Ionic capitals, which, in turn, supported an elegant entablature of a sort found ever after (at least through the 19th century) on courthouses across the land. Both the entrance and first-story windows were set into shallow, recessed arches. The design was a direct import from England, perhaps via Boston. But it gave Portland what must have been one of the finest public buildings of its size in New England." [17]

The cupola had a dome with a tall finial supporting the scales of justice. It was a "very elegant" courthouse. [18]

In 1820, when Maine became a separate state, the courtroom in the brick courthouse was used by the new state House of Representatives. A new building, called the Statehouse, was built in 1820 and provided free of charge for the use of the state by prominent citizens of Portland. The Statehouse, built next to the courthouse, accommodated the Senate and state offices in a two story wooden structure with a hipped roof and high ceilings. The front was finished with a pediment supported by pilasters, sheathed and painted white. State officers had rooms on the first floor and

The 1816 Courthouse also functioned as the Maine Statehouse in 1820.

the upper story was occupied by the Senate Chamber and rooms for the governor and council. At the time, it was considered a worthy companion of the courthouse, and the start of a new civic center.

The new complex of buildings became a place for public ceremonies. At the time of Lafayette's visit to Portland in June 1825, an awning was spread from the front of the statehouse to the elm trees lining the street before it, and the general held his public reception on a platform built at the entrance. Until 1822, spirituous liquors were sold on the premises, a practice which was discontinued in that year "during the sitting of the court or legislature." [19]

The statehouse/courthouse complex was in use for over ten years. When the state capital was moved to Augusta in 1831, the state house building reverted to city ownership and was leased to private tenants until it was needed for offices of the city government. The courthouse was enlarged with two projecting wings on either side in 1831. For some people viewing the enlarged building, "the additions gave it an improved appearance." [20]

The 1858 and 1866 City/County Buildings

After 42 years of service, the 1816 courthouse with its additions began to feel cramped for county officers and court business. At the same time, the city government was contemplating a new building to house city departments that were then in separate buildings. The county offered the existing courthouse/state house lot and, in 1858, the city and the county agreed on an arrangement in which the city would lease the lot from the county and build a structure which would accommodate public offices for the city, space for the courts and county offices, and space to receive the state's legislature and executive departments if at any time they should desire to return to Portland. The old state house building still standing on the site was moved to a new location where it could provide temporary city space. The other buildings—the 1816 brick courthouse, the 1797 jail, and the 1799 jail keeper's house—were demolished.

The new building was designed of brick, under the guidance of Mayor William Willis, by Architect James H. Rand of Boston. The next city council altered the design, enlarged the dimensions, provided for a dome, and changed the material for the Congress Street facade from brick to Albert sandstone from Nova Scotia. A small additional parcel of land was purchased to allow for the expansion. The plan, perfected under Mayor Jedediah Jewett, was put under construction, and the building was completed in 1862 during the administration of Mayor Joseph Howard. The cost of the building was about $265,000.

The building was in use for only four years when the Great Fire of Portland in 1866 inflicted enormous damage. Apparently there was a mis-

understanding between people assigned to guard the building during the fire, and no one was stationed on the roof to report the approach of danger. As William Goold tells the story of the fire:

> "The burning cinders from the Natural History building … on the opposite site of the street were blown by the strong wind against the dome, and slid down on the copper sheathing, until a sufficient mass had collected at the base to melt the copper and fire the woodwork beneath. The devouring element had sought a vulnerable spot and found it here. The dome was first destroyed and then the roof, and finally the whole interior. The only public records destroyed were those of the Probate office, which was a great misfortune of itself." [21]

The city/county building was quickly replaced on the same site. A new design was provided by architect F.H. Fassett. It was based on the existing sturdy walls of the old building, which had not been wholly consumed in the Great Fire. The new building was constructed at a cost of $357,000.

This building was also destined to be destroyed by fire, after nearly 45 years of service, in January, 1908. The first alarm was sounded at 2:00 a.m. when a short circuit in the electrical system was discovered. A general alarm followed, but the fire spread rapidly. Firefighters extended ladders, and one ladder became so heavily covered with ice that it collapsed and fell across two wires on Congress Street, disrupting the fire department's entire call system. Debris and burning paper blew across the city, starting eleven more fires. The fire alarm system was out of commission for many weeks, and the event ended Portland's hazardous Tar Bucket Night (Feb. 22) with "the city fathers feeling … numerous fires in the streets in celebration of Washington's birthday would be too much of a hazard." [22]

The 1910 Granite Courthouse

The 1868 City-County Building was destroyed in fire in 1908.
Maine Historical Society

Five years before the destruction, there were clear indications of the need for more adequate accommodations for county offices and court services. The fire precipitated matters, and hastened the process of planning new buildings.

Plans were already underway for a new county building near a proposed federal building. The news was printed by the Lewiston *Evening Journal*, which scooped the Portland papers with the story:

"Within the next twelve months, Portland will gain two of the finest public buildings in the land—the one, the new Cumberland County Courthouse, the other, the new federal or U. S. Courthouse. Fortunately for the impressive architectural effect, both of these splendid edifices will almost join each other. ...these two glorious monuments of the king city of Maine will stand side by side with only Pearl Street running between them. [23]

The new building as part of a grouping of public buildings followed the City Beautiful Movement of the time. To unite the new buildings as a civic center, the county administration joined forces with the federal courts which were also planning a new building. The nearby old city/county building site was used as the location of a new city hall. The new civic center faced a central park area—the existing Lincoln Park—to frame the city, county and federal buildings. The site of the new courthouse building required destruction of "many small and diversified buildings aggregating thirty roofs ...and nearly as many separate or partially disconnected houses, shops, stables, sheds and huts which are occupied for a myriad of purposes. From their very nature, the value of these structures is small, there being but one brick structure on the lot and but one of two stories."[24]

The county commissioners retained Walter Cook of New York as an advising architect and solicited proposals for the design of the building. To review the designs, a committee of the Cumberland Bar Association was established, including Governor Henry Cleaves, Hon. Charles Libby, Hon. Seth Larrabee, David Snow, Nathan Clifford, Judge Enoch Foster, Hon. George Bird, John Merrill and County Attorney R.T. Whitehouse. They noted that the submittal by architect Pease "looked the best so far as the outside was concerned unless the high dome was to be regarded as an objection." But the interior of the Pease design was not acceptable to the committee. The architect chosen was George Burnham of Portland, who submitted a plan for an impressive four story neo-classic structure of Maine granite. The committee agreed that Burnham's designs for the interior "were better fitted to the needs of the county as explained to him by the commissioners and the Bar. [25]

The cornerstone of the new building was laid in 1906, and the building was dedicated and opened in 1910. The building was designed to accommodate the courtrooms of Cumberland County Superior Court, the administrative offices of the county and the courts, the county archives, and a two-story courtroom for the Maine Supreme Judicial Court which, the architect explained, gave "the courtroom the expression which its importance demands." A grand staircase led from the Federal Street entrance to the room housing the Supreme Judicial Court , "flanked by columns on either side of which are elevators." Special attention was paid to private rooms for judges and attorneys and to private prisoner staircases from the basement to each courtroom. Fireproofed throughout, the building had fireproof vaults for the security of county records. On the third floor, space was provided for the Nathan and Henry B. Cleaves Law Library (then known as the Greenleaf Law Library), owned by the Cumberland County Bar Association, as well as a stackroom capable of housing 50,000 volumes. [26]

The 1988 Expansion of the Courthouse

After 60 years of use, in 1970 the Courthouse was once again evaluated as to its continued usefulness to the county. Over time, the building had been renovated piecemeal, appropriating space from originally intended functions to make way for more pressing needs. A jury room was redesigned for a judge's offices. County records overwhelmed the space available to house them. The courtrooms were regarded as being attractive but in need of modernization and a new sound amplification system. The Supreme Judicial Court was making increased use of its courtroom as it expanded its sessions from one week a month to two weeks each month. Problems cited included the need for adequate hearing space, judges' offices, jury rooms, attorneys' conference rooms, detention rooms and waiting rooms for witnesses. A grand jury hearing evidence and determining whether a person should be indicted for a crime could not meet at the same time as a traverse jury, which heard the criminal and civil cases.

Following extensive surveys, designs for the new addition were prepared by Terrien Architects. The addition with a classical appearance was built in 1988. The new building nearly doubled the space available for county use. Connected to the lobbies in the older building, the new structure provided additional courtrooms, judges' and jury rooms, and clerical space. On reviewing the new design, architect Bill Hubbard reported that the original building's granite exterior is "as tough and impenetrable as a strongbox to convey the law's permanence and power—and mystery." The new building, he said, would complement the old with a screen wall of granite, and an interior with an angled corridor leading to three courtrooms in a staggered arrangement, where "each will clearly announce its presence to us." He concluded that the old building was very much like others around the country, but, with the new addition, the building would be less generic and a "building of and for Portland." When the addition to the Cumberland County Courthouse was formally opened, it was named for former Supreme Judicial Court Chief Justice Vincent McKusick. [27]

The Cumberland County Courthouse was enlarged in 1988 to add new court rooms.

[1] Goold, William, *Portland in the Past, with Historical Notes of Old Falmouth.* Portland: B. Thurston and Company, 1886 pp. 93-96

[2] *Id.*, p. 283

[3] *Id.*

[4] *Id.*, p. 267

[5] Willis, William, *Journals of the Reverend Thomas Smith and the Reverend Samuel Deane, Pastors of the First Church in Portland, with Notes and Biographical Notices; and a Summary History of Portland.* Portland: Joseph S. Bailey, 1849, p. 99

[6] *Id.*, pp 111, 131

[7] Goold, William, "History of the Cumberland County Buildings in Portland," *Collections and Proceedings of the Maine Historical Society,* 2nd Series, Vol. 9, p. 294

[8] Willis, p. 209

[9] Willis, p. 221n

[10] Williamson, Joseph, "Capital Trials in Maine," *Collections and Proceedings of the Maine Historical Society,* Second Series, Vol. 1, 1890, p. 162

[11] Williamson, William, *The History of the State of Maine,* Hallowell: Glazier, Masters & Co., two vols., 1832, reprint, Freeport, Maine: The Cumberland Press, 1966, Vol II, pp. 414

[12] Goold, William, *Portland in the Past,* p. 343

[13] *Id.*, p. 346

[14] Goold, Nathan *Falmouth Neck in the Revolution,* Portland: Thurston Print, 1897, p. 9

[15] Goold, *Portland in the Past,* pp. 498-499; Goold, William, *History of the Cumberland County Buildings,* p. 298

[16] Goold, Nathan, p. 9; Goold, *Portland in the Past,* pp. 419, 499

[17] Thompson, Deborah, *Maine Forms of American Architecture,* Waterville, Maine: Colby Museum of Art, 1976, p. 91

[18] Williamson, W., *The History of the State of Maine,* Vol. II, p. 528n

[19] Goold, William , "History of the Cumberland County Buildings in Portland," p. 305

[20] *Id.*, p. 304

[21] *Id.*, pp. 307-308

[22] *Portland Sunday Telegram*, Jan. 21, 1940

[23] *Portland Evening Express*, Sept. 22, 1979

[24] *Portland Evening Express*, May 24, 1905

[25] "George Burnham Selected to Build the New County Court House," *Daily Eastern Argus*, Jan. 2, 1905

[26] *Id.*

[27] Hubbard, Bill, "Courthouse Addition a Building of and for Portland," *Portland Press Herald*, Nov. 9, 1988, p. 13

FOUR

Lincoln County
1760

The oldest court building in Maine is a three-story hipped roof Georgian building built as the Lincoln County Courthouse in 1760 by the Kennebec Proprietors, a company of Boston gentlemen who speculated in land. The Pownalborough Courthouse which still overlooks the Kennebec River in Dresden, witnessed the first permanent settlements on the river, housed the first courts in the wilderness north of Portland, and oversaw endless arguments and suits over the ownership of the original grants to the land. The old building was used for court purposes only during the period from 1760 to 1794, but it spanned a transition through a provincial and revolutionary period that was one of the most turbulent in the country's history.

The European settlement of the Kennebec River valley above Georgetown began in earnest when the Kennebec Proprietors were organized in the mid-eighteenth century. Earlier settlements had been started under a grant from the King to the Plymouth colony in Massachusetts. The Pilgrims initially settled the area in the 17th century, and were briefly successful in fur trading. Native Americans, denied access to traditional tribal lands, began to fight back, driving the English settlers out of the valley. By 1740 the tribes were decimated by disease and in 1757 the French were driven from the region when the English gained control of Quebec. In the relatively peaceful period that followed it became possible once again to pursue expansion of English settlements into the wilderness.

During the period of Indian attacks the valley was uninhabitable for English settlers. The Kennebec Proprietors had the good fortune to begin settlement just as the British and French signed a treaty, inaugurating a peace that would last until 1754. Deserted by their French allies, the tribal

The Kennebec Frontier

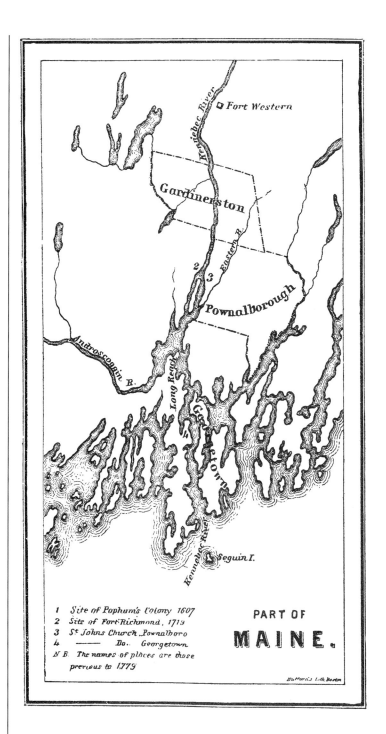

leaders were unable to continue a constant program of destablizing the region. The site of the future courthouse was initially cleared for a fortification — Fort Frankfort, later Fort Shirley, named for the Massachusetts governor. The fort was not used for military purposes during much of its existence, as the settled frontier was constantly pushed further north.

In 1749, under a newly enacted provincial law which allowed speculative land companies to incorporate, eleven Bostonians led by Silvester Gardiner, Nathaniel Thwing, and William Bowdoin, incorporated a land company known as "The Proprietors of the Kennebeck Purchase from the late Colony of New Plymouth." They took as their official seal a design of an anchor and codfish with the Latin inscription, "The King Never Gave in Vain." The Proprietors decided to build a company town, initially named Frankfort, to entice settlers from Germany. The first settlers — 54 "Germans" including Huguenots from France — were recruited by the Proprietors' representative in Europe.

The settlers arrived to find a miserable village of log huts provided by the company on a site chosen for good soil, extensive timber, and protection at the juncture of Kennebec and Eastern Rivers. The company gave each settler a standard printed form for a grant of land, requiring each to build a dwelling 18 by 20 feet and to clear 4 acres within three years. Grantees were required to live on the land for seven years to obtain a clear title. In the midst of the settlers' 20 acre lots a common area was set aside around Fort Shirley where public buildings could be constructed.

Other land claims arose early in competition with the Kennebeck Proprietors. To protect its interests, the company engaged Samuel Goodwin, whose family owned a small share in the Plymouth Colony grant of 1629, as the first clerk of Kennebeck Proprietors. He moved with his family to the Kennebeck River in 1753. He was charged by the company with the task of encouraging settlers in Georgetown and Woolwich to settle land claims with the Proprietors and of gaining their allegiance wherever possible. Goodwin busily sold off rights to land the company may not rightfully have claimed. He tried to bring the inhabitants of Wiscasset Point on the Sheepscot River to acknowledge the company's land claims and to merge with new town of Frankfort. Resentment arose when his actions led the company to sue settlers in York County Court (then covering all of Maine).

From the company's beginning the Proprietors claimed ownership through the Plymouth grant of the land in Georgetown, the largest town in the Kennebec valley, including the future towns of Woolwich, Bath, Phippsburg. Brunswick and Topsham. Each of these towns had been settled by other speculative land development companies. In 1756 the Pejepscot Proprietors sued the Kennebeck Company. The Kennebeck Proprietors, sensing a loss at court, agreed to submit the boundary dispute to a committee of referees to be appointed by the Superior Court in Boston. In the process, the referees ruled against the Proprietors claims. Undaunted, the Company laid plans to contest the decision. With this threat, they achieved a settlement of all of the coveted lands north of Woolwich. By their actions in this and other court actions, the Proprietors laid the groundwork for animosities in the region which were to cause continuing difficulty in the future.

The Origin of Lincoln County

The Proprietors were painfully aware of losing land ownership cases in the York County Court, although they were occasionally successful on appeal. There was a general feeling that the north country with its squatters and poor settlers was hostile to large land holders. As early as 1754, the Kennebeck Proprietors received a message from inside York County which fed their suspicions. The message came from Timothy Prout who had attempted to litigate with hostile settlers. He warned the Proprietors:

> "I dare venture to say to you as the Clerk of the Inferior Court said to me you will never get a verdict of Jury in this County, all the causes brought into the Court are first tryed in the Tavern and judgement passed there before its Tryed in a Court of Justice." [1]

The idea of a separate legal entity had grown quickly in the minds of the Proprietors, and through the inhabitants of Frankfort they petitioned the Massachusetts legislature to create a new county in the Kennebec valley. The first petition was assembled in 1752 by the Proprietors and had a total of 438 signatures. Its pleading was forthright:

> "...That the great Distance that Suitors, Witnesses & Jurors have to Travel from (the Proprietors' land along the Kennebec) to York together with the Badness & Dangers of the roads ...which together with the perplexity arising from Doubtfullness of such Courts Jurisdiction over them and Danger that Judgements obtained in such Courts in Local Actions arising among them may some time or other be called in Question and Reversed are a great Discouragement to your Petitioners in their Settlement and that it would very much Facilitate and Promote the further peopling and Improving said Tract and Render the Expensive Efforts of your petitioners the Proprietors to Settle the same more Successful if said district was erected into a Distinct County..." [2]

This first petition failed, as did the second in 1755. Finally in 1760, the settlers along the Kennebec succeeded in having their town of Frankfort incorporated as Pownalborough, named for incumbent Governor Pownal of the Province. They petitioned once more to the Massachusetts legislature for a new county and volunteered to construct a courthouse at their own expense. This time the effort was successful: the legislature established two new counties in Maine, one on Casco Bay to be called Cumberland County and the other, in the Kennebec River Valley, to be called Lincoln County, with the shire town at Pownalborough.

Pownalborough was selected as the shire town for Lincoln County because it was reasonably central to the property owned by the Proprietors. From the Proprietors' point of view, the building was an invaluable attraction to draw more settlers into the area. Located on the bluff commanding the Kennebec and visible for miles around, the building would be a symbol of the company's power. They voted to build it within the 200 foot square parade grounds of Fort Shirley. The building would be 45 by 44 feet, and three stories tall. One large room was planned to be fitted with boxes and benches to serve as the courtroom. A prominent Proprietor, Gershom Flagg, was given the building contract. Construction got underway in 1760.

Flagg designed the building to serve several functions: courthouse, fort, tavern, general store and residence. The courtroom occupied half of the

The Pownalborough Courthouse, oldest court building in Maine.
Jacob Sloane

second floor with windows on three sides. A jury room and a judges chamber were in the other half of the second floor. A holding room for prisoners was set up on the third floor. Around the perimeter of the third floor was a rudimentary crenellation—small holes where firearms could be pointed in any direction to protect the building if it were attacked. The ground floor had space for a tavern to serve both townsfolk and the court with food and drink. Samuel Goodwin was assigned the tavern rights and permission to open a general store. The remainder of the rooms on the second and third floors were available as quarters for the building manager and Samuel Goodwin and his family promptly moved in.

Opening the Pownalborough Courthouse

The courthouse was ready for use in early 1762. One of the first acts of the Court of General Sessions of the Peace was to adopt a court seal "...presented by Samuel Denny, Esq. the Motto whereof being a Cup and three Mullets, being the lawful Coat of Arms of the said Denny's Family...." The eastern blockhouse of Fort Shirley was appropriated for a jail and a part of the barracks was put to use as a house for the jail keeper. Gershom Flagg, the builder, reported that he "had the House well Covered and Shingled on the top and covered over the lower floor with one Ruff board, putt up Seats table etc. proper to receive the Court which enter'd the same in procession." He added that the "Chief Judge with the Rest of the Gentry Drank the Company's health and wish'd all well." With this small flourish, the courthouse was officially inaugurated. [3]

The courthouse rapidly became a center of activity in the region. As the principal tavern, general store and public hall, it became the place to hold the Pownalborough town meetings. The Massachusetts census of 1766 showed that it had six rooms, six fireplaces, one brick chimney, a stone-lined cellar, and 858 lights of glass. It also had eleven residents, but some may have been transient visitors. In 1767 a petition complained of the crowded conditions of the courthouse, and stated that strangers attending the court "have to lodge on the floor, or in barns, or sit up all night by the fire." With such intense use, the building needed continual improvements. A second chimney was added to the building in 1769 and several of the rooms were finished with plaster. The cost of the building to the Proprietors was now 546 pounds, 8 shillings and 11 pence for the original construction and an additional 101 pounds for the 1769 finishing touches.[4]

The courts that sat at the Pownalborough Courthouse served essential functions for a relatively small population. Maine in 1764 had 24,000 inhabitants, of whom 4,347 lived in Lincoln County. Most of the residents lived in Georgetown or Pownalborough, the boundaries of which covered virtually all of the land in south Lincoln County. Residents of the county would use Pownalborough for basic court services, but appeals in the

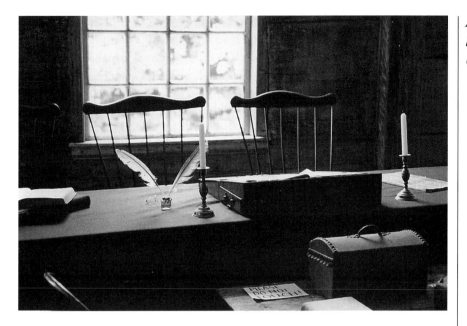

A view of the interior of
the Pownalborough
Courthouse.

early years took place elsewhere, either at Falmouth (now Portland) or Boston. The courthouse provided space for the County Court of General Sessions of the Peace and an Inferior Court of Common Pleas. Offices for the Registry of Deeds and Registry of Probate were probably maintained at Jonathan Bowman's home, not far from the courthouse.

Coming to Court in Pownalborough

With the courthouse in place, the Proprietors successfully encouraged ambitious young lawyers to settle in Pownalborough. Moving to Maine from Boston, William Cushing was appointed Judge of the Peace and Quorum and Judge of Probate for Lincoln County and his brother Charles was appointed sheriff. Both continued to do legal work for the Proprietors and received grants of land. Jonathan Bowman, a classmate of Charles Cushing at Harvard, was named Collector of the Excise, Register of Probate, Register of Deeds, Clerk of the Court of Sessions and the Court of Common Pleas, and Justice of the Peace for Lincoln County.

John Adams came to the courthouse in 1765 as an attorney for the Proprietors. He arrived on horseback, following a trail of blazed trees through the woods. Pownalborough was described as a place "...at almost the remotest verge of civilization..." He had great difficulty getting there. "After encountering the obstructions of nearly impassable roads, through an inhospitable region, and falling sick upon the way, Adams succeeded in reaching Pownalborough and gained his cause, much to the satisfaction of his client...It induced the [Kennebec Proprietors] to engage him in all their causes." [5]

continued their sessions without interruption, even though they did without juries for several terms. The Superior Court was reconstituted over a period from 1774 to 1776, but its terms were not held in Maine again until 1779. Among other reasons, the British had burned Falmouth and its courthouse in 1775.

Pownalborough remained loyal to Massachusetts and voted to raise funds for the Revolutionary troops in 1775. British General Gage begged for firewood but the town turned him down. The town was on the route of Benedict Arnold's expedition upriver to Quebec City. There was nervousness when the British attacked towns along the coast and Pownalborough feared the British would extend their efforts up the Kennebec River. The town's liberty pole was cut down in the night, and the British were suspected. Tories, those loyal to the crown, were condemned and occasionally roughed up. Loyalist properties were frequently confiscated with court approval. Pownalborough's Tory minister, Jacob Bailey, was so beleaguered by accusations that he left for Nova Scotia.

Peace between U.S. and Britain arrived in 1783. At the urging of Congress, the states gradually restored some of the confiscated Loyalist properties to their original owners. At the courthouse, Loyalists sued for restoration of their lands and the resulting cases and appeals kept local lawyers busy for several years. Maine boomed during the post-Revolutionary period, with its population growing from 56,000 in 1784 to nearly 300,000 in 1820. Massachusetts responded by extending the eastern circuit of the Supreme Judicial Court to include a term at Pownalborough in 1786. When Hancock and Washington Counties were created in 1789 the Pownalborough term of the Supreme Judicial Court heard cases from the eastern counties as well.

The brief annual terms of the Supreme Judicial Court at the Pownalborough Courthouse covered a variety of cases including several infamous cases of assault and murder. In 1787 Stephen Way of Georgetown was convicted of an assault on Lucy Sally with his fists and a saddle (a piece of wood used in the rigging of a boat). Way was sentenced to be set on the gallows one hour with a halter around his neck, then publicly whipped twenty-five strips on his bare back. He was also required to pay the costs of prosecution and to give bond of 100 pounds to guarantee that he would keep the peace. In the same term, John Brown was convicted of stealing and sentenced to be whipped twenty times, to restore the goods, and to pay six pounds, sixteen shillings, an amount three times the value of the stolen goods. A murder case in 1789 involved Samuel Hadlock of Mount Desert, who killed Eliab Gott with a wooden fence stake for one penny. Hadlock, "not having the fear of God, and being instigated by the devil," was sentenced to be hanged. Hadlock escaped and hid in a ravine near the courthouse. There is no record of whether he was recaptured. [7]

Justice McKusick tells of an incident involving Martha Ballard who recorded in her diary the proceedings of a trial in 1790 at Pownalborough:

"It was the trial of Colonel or Judge Joseph North, a leading citizen of Hallowell, on the charge of raping a young woman during her minister husband's absence from town. In this *cause celebre*, Martha Ballard's testimony was particularly strong for the prosecution because the young woman had reported the assault to Martha within ten days of the event, at a time before the woman's pregnancy was confirmed and very long before the woman made any public charge against Colonel North. The woman bore a child 8 months and 17 days after she said she had been assaulted. The jury trial was presided over by Chief Justice Francis Dana and his three associates. Martha Ballard's one-sentence journal entry drips scorn for the jury verdict of not guilty: 'North acquitted to the great surprise of all that I heard speak of it.' It was then even harder to prosecute a rape case than it is today." [8]

Minor criminal cases were also heard by the Supreme Judicial Court at its term in Pownalborough. In the 1780s Thomas Melony of Cushing was sentenced to stand in the pillory for one hour and to be whipped thirty stripes for his alleged lewdness. In 1791, William and John Malcolm and John Stevens were found guilty of stealing sheep in Georgetown. The sentence was a whipping of fifteen stripes on the naked back.

Towns themselves and their public officials were not exempt from suit. Pownalborough was indicted in 1791 for having no public grammar school, and fined £ 87 and costs, with the fine given to support the schools. In 1794, Hallowell was indicted for not having a settled minister, and for not having rails on a bridge, for bad roads and for not having a grammar or English schoolmaster. The year 1791 saw a candidate for sheriff, Lazarus Goodwin, bring a case of election fraud against the winning candidate.

Judges were also brought into court: one judge, Robert Treat Paine, successfully drafted a bill to prohibit unnecessary travel on Sunday and it became law early in 1791. In June, as a judge of the Supreme Judicial Court, he adjourned court in Portland on Saturday and hastened to get to Pownalborough to open the term there on Tuesday morning. By driving through Freeport on Sunday, his party, including another judge and the Commonwealth's Attorney General, scandalized the townsfolk for violation of the Sunday travel law. They were arrested and indicted, and ultimately forced to petition the legislature for relief, which was granted when they pleaded that they were exempt because they could not otherwise open the term of court as scheduled.

As the state's settlements reached ever further north and east, the new counties of Hancock and Washington were established and Lincoln County retained only the areas between the Androscoggin and Penobscot Rivers. Pownalborough began to lose population, in part because trade could only be continuous in a location with an ice-free harbor. Within one generation after the Revolutionary War, the ice-free harbor at Wiscasset Point in the East Precinct of Pownalborough was thriving, while the area around the Pownalborough Courthouse stagnated. Many of the most important economic activities of the area, including seafaring commerce, were focused on Wiscasset Point. But court activities remained centered on the Kennebec, even though the difficulty of overland travel to Pownalborough Courthouse was exacerbated by ill defined and rough roads. It was frequently impossible to notify citizens scattered through the wilderness of town meetings and court sessions, and great effort was required for them to attend any gathering. Pownalborough town meetings began to be held at both the Pownalborough Courthouse area and Wiscasset Point. The relative importance of the courthouse in Pownalborough began to decrease when the expanding population in the eastern portions of Maine led the Supreme Judicial Court to hold one of its Lincoln County terms in Waldoboro in 1787.

The Waldoboro Branch Courthouse

As early as 1767, people living in Medumcook and Muscongus plantations in the vicinity of Waldoboro petitioned the Governor and General Court for a change in the location of the court, because Pownalborough, in their expressed view:

> "is very near the Western side of said County & quite Remote from by far the Greatest Part of the Inhabitants of said county – that there are but a Very few Houses near said Place in which People who have necessary business at courts can have Lodging and Entertainment so that a Great Part of the People during their necessary attendance on said Courts are much distressed for Necessarys and are Obliged to lodge on a floor or in Barns or set all night by the fire during their whole stay at said Courts." [9]

Recognizing the difficulties of travel to the courthouse, the county administration agreed that some additional sessions of the Court of Common Pleas could be held outside Pownalborough. In 1786 Hallowell (now Augusta) and Wiscasset Point were selected as sites for court sessions, with Waldoboro designated as the easternmost site for a term of court. Waldoboro was chosen as a convenient location for people from the county's eastern towns—Thomaston, Camden and Rockland.

In Waldoboro, the Court of Common Pleas moved into the courthouse built on Kinsell's hill by Capt. Cornelius Turner. It was 30 feet square "...with 10 feet posts." The court was held in this building in September of 1786 for the first time. A whipping post was erected – and used; according to one account a defendant was tried for theft, convicted, and the sentence of whipping was immediately carried out—"...a method of proceeding which has not been improved by modern courts." The courthouse building on Kinsell's Hill was replaced in 1796 by a new building near a local store. When the courts were transferred to Warren in 1800, the new court building became unoccupied. In 1803 the old building was sold for $230 and moved to a new site where it became the town house for Waldoboro. [10]

The court first met at the Wiscasset Point section of Pownalborough and the meetinghouse was used for civil sessions following a vote of the congregation. The Whittier Tavern at Wiscasset Point was also the site of some court activities. Hon. Jonathan Bowman sometimes held his Probate Court sessions in the tavern, and Judge Thwing of Woolwich and Squire Davis of Edgecomb occasionally heard cases there.

Wiscasset Point residents began to develop a plan to obtain a courthouse for its growing population. The strategy was to find a way for Wiscasset to be designated as the Lincoln County seat. As a first step, the townsfolk voted to offer the use of the meetinghouse to the Supreme Judicial Court and other courts of the county. The offer was quickly rejected by the county. The citizens then joined with other settlements in the county to have the legislature designate Wiscasset as the county seat. One of the earliest such petitions came from 86 of the settlers asking to set Wiscasset off from the rest of Pownalborough. The petition was sent to the authorities in Massachusetts, but was not acted on. Another petition from Bristol, dated May 22, 1786, requested that a permanent court be held at Wiscasset Point. Petitions to the Great and General Court in Boston led to a grant that set off Alna and Dresden as separate towns in 1794. What was left of Pownalborough retained that name but its population was centered at Wiscasset Point. This residual area of Pownalborough (soon to become formally known as Wiscasset) was designated one of two shire towns in 1794, and alternated the terms of court with Hallowell, then also in Lincoln County. The first alternating term was held in Hallowell in June, 1794, and Wiscasset Point began preparations for its anticipated term in 1795 by looking for an appropriate and dignified space.

The town's principal meetinghouse and the privately-owned Wiscasset Hall were available for court use, but both buildings lacked jury rooms and space specifically for court use. County officers determined that the

The Court Comes to Wiscasset

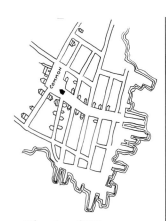

The site of Wiscasset Hall was the middle of the street at the base of the Common. Adapted from 1811 map in possession of Wiscasset Historical Society

county court's arrival in Wiscasset required a building for exclusive use as a courthouse.

Wiscasset Hall, a two story frame structure with a cupola, stood at the foot of the village common some 330 linear feet from the meetinghouse toward the river. A county committee comprised of Thomas Rice, Orchard Cook and Mark Hill, approached the owner, Abiel Wood, and made the final arrangements. The county agreed to pay $1,666.67 with interest for a "good and warrantie deed," one year from the first Monday of June, 1798 – allowing time for rebuilding the hall by the sellers.[11]

To reconstruct the building for court purposes, the proprietors of Wiscasset Hall, David Silvester, Peter Bryson and Silas Lee, in 1793 contracted with carpenters Alexander Troup, William Sellar and Robert Miller. Carpenters were hired for the varying improvements:

> "...To clapboard the said Hall complete—to make corner boards with rustic corners to said Hall—To make and put up sixteen windows in the lower story of said Hall containing each twenty-four squares of eight by ten glass -...To make two doors to said Hall, —To make a balcony in the southeast front of said Hall, said balcony to be surrounded by a complete balustrade, but not to be supported by pillars, and to make a glass door opening into said balcony,...the upper part of said door to be made and fitted to receive glass, so as to appear the same as a window ..."

The cupola on the top of the Hall was to be finished off "in a plain, neat and decent manner in the Tuscan order…". [12]

The proprietors of Wiscasset Hall agreed to pay the carpenters £72, of which £12 would be paid when the windows were installed, £12 when all of the work was finished, and the remainder within six months of completion of the work. Materials for the job were to be supplied by the proprietors. The work included a courtroom thirty nine feet long and jury rooms, "all very plainly finished, lathed and plastered". [13]

The Wiscasset Hall courtroom was used immediately by the Court of Common Pleas and the Court of Sessions for Lincoln County, and provided space for sessions of the state Supreme Judicial Court. In 1796 the court was assigned the responsibility of holding the records of the Superior Court for Lincoln, Hancock and Washington Counties -records previously kept in Boston.

Trials in Wiscasset Hall

One of the first cases heard in the Wiscasset Hall courtroom was a trial before the Supreme Judicial Court involving Father Cheverus, a Catholic missionary who later became the first bishop of Boston. Father

Cheverus was assigned to be a missionary in Massachusetts territories, including Maine. He was especially interested in the Indians along the Penobscot, many of whom clung to the faith taught by priests from Canada a generation before. Traveling through Maine, he chose a location at Damariscotta Bridge, and settled there for 10 years. Father Cheverus was accused in 1800 of marrying two of his parishioners, contrary to the laws of Massachusetts which required that marriage be performed by a minister or a justice of the peace. Cheverus had advised his parishioners to have another wedding by a justice of the peace the day after the church ceremony, but the state argued that this did not cure the problem. Attorney General Sullivan filed both civil and criminal charges against Cheverus, seeking both the pillory and a fine for breaking the law.

Slated to appear before the three Supreme Court Justices Sewall, Bradbury, and Strong, Father Cheverus faced considerable hostility. The community, which was predominantly Protestant, was unsympathetic. Justice Bradbury, the presiding judge, let it be known that he favored having the priest pay the fine. Only Justice Sewall seemed favorable to Cheverus' side. Before legal proceedings began, however, Bradbury fell from his horse and was unable to travel to Maine for many weeks. While Bradbury was recovering, interest in the case lessened and it was never tried.

Most civil cases heard by the court were land claims. Conflicts arose when boundaries overlapped or the claimants appeared to be entitled to the same concession, based on early, rudimentary surveys. Squatters took possession of lands already held under valid titles by heirs of the original grantees. As claimants and complications multiplied, the cases were watched closely by both new and old settlers. As a result of an October, 1810 decision regarding the overlapping Toppon, Drowne and Brown land claims, confusion and anger reached their peak. Judge Thacher was forced to call out the Edgecomb militia to protect surveyors running property lines. The night following muster of the troops, an open coffin was placed on the door steps of Thacher's house. Residents complained that Judge Thacher had called out five hundred men to aid in running lines that had been settled from forty to eighty years previously. The issue was settled in the General Court Resolves of June 20, 1811, which formally established a three person commission to arbitrate the issue and to award equivalent and unallocated land elsewhere in an unsettled part of the District of Maine.

Criminal cases tried in the Wiscasset Hall courthouse could result in a variety of punishments. With "gyves [leg shackles], fetters [ankle chains], handcuffs, a pillory and ducking stool all ready for use", along with a whipping post and gallows, the court had many options. In the July 28, 1795 entry in Moses Davis' diary: "A man was seen sitting on the gallows and one standing on the pillory." Peter Bobo, who assaulted Samuel Goodwin, was convicted in 1796 and died in the jail 11 years later while serving his sentence. Lemuel Lewis of Boothbay and another man were sentenced to be publicly whipped for theft in 1808, which may have been the last instance of use of the whip in Wiscasset. Moses Thorndike of Camden was convicted in 1812 for helping English prisoners of war escape. In 1817, William Campbell was convicted of "profanity and hard swearing", and sentenced to jail for fourteen days along with a fine and costs. In 1824 a fourteen-year-old boy was sentenced to a month in jail for stealing apples. [14]

The murder trial of James Sevey was held in 1816. To accommodate intense public interest and to avoid overcrowding in the courtroom, the trial was held in the meetinghouse. Isaac Parker, Chief Justice of the Supreme Judicial Court, presided with George Thatcher, Charles Jackson and Samuel Wilde, Associate Justices. Prentiss Mellon and Jeremiah Bailey were assigned to the defense. The record of the case reports:

> "James Sevey of Wiscasset, who not having the fear of God before his eyes, but moved and seduced by the instigation of the Devil... with force and arms... in and upon one John MacMasters, feloniously, willfully and with malice aforethought, did make an assault, with a certain deadly weapon called an iron crane, the said MacMasters in and upon the left parietal bone, near the coronal suture, him the said Mac Masters then and there did strike, penetrate, fracture and wound, giving a mortal wound of the breadth of two inches and of the depth of four inches, of which, the said MacMasters from the twelfth of August...until the twenty-seventh day thereof, did languish, and languishing died." [15]

The jury, "sworn to speak the truth of and concerning the premises, on their oaths say: said James Sevey is not guilty of Murder, but that he is guilty of Manslaughter." The court sentenced Sevey to a jail term of two years, with sureties of $500 to keep the peace for three subsequent years.[16]

The town added a long list of prohibitions in 1822. The 22 by-laws approved by the Court of Sessions were derided as Wiscasset's "shilling laws," because the minimum fine for each transgression was 25 cents — roughly the equivalent of the colonial shilling. With these by-laws in place, citizens of Wiscasset became liable for "incommoding" travel in the street, which meant riding horses on the sidewalk or at an "immoderate pace", throwing snowballs for sport in front of the meetinghouse, making a tumultuous noise or disturbance or violent and unnecessary outcry, injuring or destroying trees on the common, breaking or defacing any pump or injuring any well, or allowing geese to trespass on a neighbor's property.[17]

The courthouse was also the center of arguments for and against a new county formed from Lincoln County. When Kennebec County was formed from the northern part of the county in 1799, Augusta became its county seat. The shire town for Lincoln County was once more Wiscasset (still called Pownalborough), and the court held its terms solely at Wiscasset Point. Terms of each of the courts began to be held annually instead of in alternate years. Pownalborough formally changed its name to Wiscasset in 1802.

Court Terms and Half-Shire Towns

The General Court in Boston responded to Lincoln County's growth by dividing the terms of the Court of Common Pleas and the Court of General Sessions between Wiscasset, Warren and Topsham. Each was designated to be a half-shire town. At the same time, Waldoboro lost its status as half-shire town and the General Court moved its terms of courts to Warren.

Warren's representative to the Massachusetts Legislature sponsored the legislation, which was intended to bring importance and prestige to Warren by virtue of the shire town designation. He also persuaded the town to build a courthouse in 1799. In November, the first term of the court was held in a partially-finished structure. Construction work on the building was not completed until nearly two years later.

The Warren courthouse was a two story wooden structure with a hip roof and a belfry in the center of the roof. The upper story was reserved by the builders for their own use, and was later sold to the Warren Academy for use as a school room. At the construction of the courthouse, with many townsfolk present to help, a Colonel Head wore a high crowned "conical" hat, the latest fashion that was just beginning to supplant the low hemispherical hats. When a board from above fell on his hat, and the hat was crushed, Colonel Head talked loudly and rapidly of its "utility in preserving his skull from a similar fate." [18]

Warren's courthouse was used once a year for a term of the Lincoln County Court of Common Pleas. It was also used as needed for religious and other public meetings. Town meetings were held there until a town hall was constructed in 1840. The courts held their last sessions in the Warren courthouse in 1847, when the half-shire towns were given up, and all the courts in the county were transferred to Wiscasset. The building and the land were sold to the town for $751 and the lower part of the building became a school room.

In 1800 the General Court designated Topsham as the site for a term of the Court of Common Pleas. Topsham shared the shire town designation with Wiscasset and Warren. The first term of court in Topsham was underway by September of that year. The new building chosen for the court was probably not completed at that time, and the first session was held in an unfinished house nearby. Land for the new courthouse was given for a term of years by James Wilson. The building was two stories and constructed of wood with a hip roof and a belfry in the center of the roof. A bell for the belfry was purchased by subscription by the townsfolk and was the first bell in the town. The bell tolled to announce court sessions, and was also used to call people to town meeting and to services on Sundays at the First Parish church nearby.

Wiscasset Plans a New Courthouse

Despite the spread of activities of the Court of Common Pleas to Topsham and Warren, the courthouse at Wiscasset remained the principal center for superior court activities and for annual visits by the federal district court. Unfortunately, the remodeled Wiscasset Hall had no space for county offices or files. The forty volumes of the records of the Registry of Deeds were kept at the home of the Registrar, Thomas Rice. Probate records totaled eight volumes and those of the Clerk of the Courts numbered fifteen, but they initially had no permanent storage place. Within ten years, however, the County found comfortable quarters for all of its records across the street, in a two story brick building constructed in 1805 for the Lincoln and Kennebec Bank on High Street (now the public library).

Concern for the preservation of the county records nevertheless continued. In particular, there was a growing realization that the records should be kept safe from fire. It was the movement toward fireproofing that led to the abandonment of Wiscasset Hall and the construction of a county building to provide not only fireproof space for records, but also more commodious quarters for the terms of court. The impetus toward fireproofing also led proponents of a new building to derisively refer to Wiscasset Hall as the old wooden courthouse.

The Circuit Court of Common Pleas at its 1818 term in Warren appointed a committee "to consider the expediency of repairing the courthouse at Wiscasset and of erecting a fire proof building for County offices separate therefrom, or the expediency of building a new courthouse in which fire proof offices should be joined." The committee, made up of Judge Ebenezer Thatcher, Hon. Jeremiah Bailey and Nathaniel Coffin, concluded that the county should construct a new building for the court activities, after viewing "...cills & floor timbers so decayed as to require a very considerable expenditure of money to put it in a state of repair...." They stated that a new building should be fire proof for the protection of the court records, and that is should be made of brick with precise dimensions: 44 feet long, 40 feet wide and 30 feet high. But the old wooden courthouse was still serviceable, resources were limited, and no action was

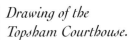

taken immediately. [19]

In 1822 the Circuit Court once again noted that Wiscasset Hall was not a fire proof building "within the intendment of the law" and that it was not worth repairing. In replacing the wooden courthouse, the Court declared "that whenever a fire proof building is erected for the public offices it will be most economical as well as most commodious to erect a new court-house in connection therewith". By January, 1823, townsfolk of Wiscasset were begging the court to build a new structure, or to purchase the Bank Building for courthouse use. Events rapidly led toward a new building.[20]

In May, 1823, at the term of the Court of Sessions. the court appointed a committee consisting of Ebenezer Clap of Bath, John Dole of Alna, and Colonel Isaac Reed of Waldoborough to determine a location and prepare a general plan for a new courthouse in Wiscasset. The court also appointed Nathaniel Coffin as its agent to build the courthouse. Later that month, the town, in its eagerness to assist in the proper location of the building, unanimously agreed to supply whatever lot of land the commit-tee might select; the townsfolk began a campaign to raise money to pur-chase the land. The courthouse committee gratefully acknowledged the town's offer of funding.

In March, 1824, a new Wiscasset site was resolved; an agreement was forged between the town and the parish to locate the new building on land which was part of the original meetinghouse lot at the top of the hill. Hon. Jeremiah Bailey agreed to sell the county some of the adjacent land so that the lot would have a frontage of fifty feet. Tileston Cushing of Bath was chosen as the Master Builder of the structure.

The *Lincoln Intelligencer*, the Wiscasset newspaper of that time, had the following news item on Friday, May 21, 1824:

> The Corner Stone of the new courthouse erecting in this town, was laid, on Tuesday last, by the Hon. Judge Mellen [Maine's first Chief Justice]. After the ceremony, the Rev. (Dr.) Packard, offered an appropriate and impressive prayer. A collation [light lunch] was prepared by the Agent, Master Builder and workmen, to which were invited the Hon Justices of the Supreme Court, members of the bar, grand and traverse jurors, citizens and strangers. The Masonic brethren and Mechanics Association volunteered as an escort on the occasion. [21]

Building the 1824 Lincoln County Courthouse

Nathaniel Coffin, Clerk of the Courts for Lincoln County, graduated from Dartmouth in 1799, and studied law in Biddeford with the Hon. Prentiss Mellen (who became Maine's first Chief Justice). Admitted to practice in 1804, by 1812 he was appointed county clerk. In December, 1823, Clerk Nathaniel Coffin invited proposals for the construction of the Wiscasset courthouse; the committee had determined that the building should be fifty feet long, forty-four feet wide and twenty-eight feet high, and would contain three fire proof offices and be constructed and finished *"nearly* upon the plan of the courthouse in Portland, "omitting, however, all the expensive ornamental work." [22]

Coffin kept scrupulous records of the construction project, including the names of every person who worked on the project and the nature of his service, as well as every bill for services and supplies. He noted that the number of bricks purchased was 289,862, of which about one-third were from John Porter's yard near Birch Point, a larger proportion from the yard of E. Lowe, who also furnished 2,596 tiles used in the floor and hearths, and that the pressed brick used on the still beautiful and much admired front (12,800 in number) were from the Cargill yard in New-castle. There was lime and 3,638 bushels of sand for plastering along with horse hair (also used in plastering) from a tanning factory. There were wood frames, sashes and blinds to be made for 25 windows, and iron doors with locks, irons for the stone stairs, railings and banisters. There were stone fence posts, stone door steps and stone stairways. There were flag

The Brick Courthouse in Wiscasset was built in 1824.

Maine Historic Preservation Commission

stones for the entry floor, and stone window caps and keystones. The bell in the cupola cost $134.04, and the front fence cost $129.78. The total cost of the building was $10,843.09, including $127.08 for rum, the beverage of choice for the workers.

In September, 1824, members of the Supreme Judicial Court were in Wiscasset for the opening of the building. The *Lincoln County Intelligencer* had this to say:

"The new and elegant fire proof courthouse in this town was yesterday for the first time occupied by the Supreme Judicial Court now in session. At twelve o'clock it was announced by John Dole, Esq. one of the Justices of the Court of Sessions, to the Court that the building was then in readiness to receive it; whereupon the Court adjourned and a procession was immediately formed, and proceeded to the new building, where a brief but appropriate address was delivered by Isaac G. Reed, Esq., which was answered by Judge Weston in his usual acceptable style, after which the Rev. Dr. Packard offered a devotional and comprehensive prayer in conclusion of the dedicatory services."

The remainder of the building was put into use on December 20, 1824, when the county officials moved into the offices. [23]

At the time of the opening of the new courthouse, Wiscasset was one of the most important towns east of Portland. The courthouse, sitting at the top of its hill and looking down the broad street leading to the wharves, was a major monument for the town. The brick facade facing the town had three arched bays with the middle bay centered on the main entrance, which had an inset elliptical dome. The arch motif was repeated in the pediment above the second floor, and the building was topped with an open belfry. The narrower side of the building became its facade, which was traditional with public meetinghouses. The windows were rectangular and plain. The dimensions of the building were 44 by 50 feet, with a porch 14 by 7 feet at the back to "form a convenient room immediately back of the

Below: Details of the 1824 courtroom at the Lincoln County Courthouse. Jacob Sloane

Judge's seats and to admit a flight of stairs from it into the yard below." [24]

Coffin described the finished building: "It is built upon a rock, its floors are solid, the foundation being levelled off with stone and floored over with hewn stone & brick, so that every room below is proof against fire." The three public offices on the ground floor were provided with fire-proof "closets" with double iron doors and "alcoves and bureaus for books and papers...[which] are sufficiently capacious to contain all the Records & Files which will probably accumulate for a hundred years to come." The ground floor also housed a Grand Jury room and an office for the County Treasurer. [25]

Upstairs the nearly square courtroom provided seats with desks for attorneys. The judge's bench and all the desktops and seats were made of varnished mahogany, and the remainder of the woodwork was "...pine well-painted...." Carpet was provided for ..."so much of the floor as it was necessary to cover on account of noise..." A balcony extended across the back of the room, and was "...furnished with shutters so as to be closed or opened at pleasure." An elegant chandelier, a gift from several "gentlemen of Wiscasset", hung in the courtroom. Outside the courtroom were a law library, a judge's lobby, and two jury rooms "...sufficiently retired for

Below left: The hall of the Lincoln County Courthouse.

Below right: Exterior of the 1824 Courthouse in Wiscasset today.
Jacob Sloane

secrecy & safety, & yet so near the Court as to be under its immediate protection & control." The total cost of the building, including land, furniture and bell was $10,293.09. Against this amount was revenue from the sale of the old courthouse ($200, less expenses of $76), and the financing of two notes of $5,000 each. The remainder of the funding came from cash on hand or the county treasurer. Used building materials were sold, as was all of the useless furniture of the old offices.

The construction of the new courthouse spelled the end for the old wooden courthouse. As construction proceeded, plans were made to move the old building to a new site. The purchaser was Colonel Hilton, proprietor of Hilton House, who chose a site for the old building behind his building at the corner of Main and Federal Streets. When the new courthouse was opened in late 1824, the old courthouse became surplus to public needs.

The old structure, like others at the time, was apparently moved rather casually and the move may have been a merry occasion; there was a saying that "any house could be moved with ninety yokes of oxen and five gallons of rum." On its new site and renamed Lincoln Hall, the building continued to serve various civic, though now more commercial, purposes. Its ground floor front room became a stationers' shop and the town post office. United States mail was delivered to the building by Colonel Hilton's stage line, and its arrival was heralded by the blast of a post-horn six feet long. The rear room on the ground floor became the location for publication of the *Citizen*. The old courtroom upstairs was used for fourth of July dinners, traveling theaters, 'slight of hand' shows, meetings, concerts and shows of all kinds. Here Wiscasset citizens saw the 'Bubble of 1825', a roaring steam engine and train of cars on a circular track – a model of a railroad train. The jury room was transformed into space for dancing and singing schools and later, a private school "taught by women". The building was in constant use until November 28, 1846, when it caught fire and was destroyed.

The Supreme Judicial Court Sits in the Brick Courthouse

The first full eight-day term of the Supreme Judicial Court was held in the new courthouse in May, 1825. Chief Justice Mellen presided, and sat with Associate Justice Weston. Maine's Attorney General Erastus Foote of Wiscasset was present, for at the time he accompanied the court as it moved through all the counties. Also present were the sheriff, Peter H. Green, the coroner Samuel Sevey, and the crier, Seth Tinkham. A reporter of decisions was not present, but the court added a reporter beginning with the term of 1827.

In the 1825 term of the Supreme Judicial Court, Attorney General Foote appeared for the state against the Proprietors of Cathance Bridge in the Town of Bowdoinham. Foote won the case for the state, and the court vacated the charter of the proprietors and declared the franchise forfeited for failure to comply with charter requirements. It was said that during his ten years in office Foote lost only a single indictment in the court and that was for "defect in form".

The criminal business of the first term in the courthouse included cases of adultery, burglary, and possession and passing of counterfeit money. Sentences included both "solitary imprisonment" and extended time in the state prison. For example, the burglary of Cushing Bryant's shop in Nobleborough resulted in a sentence of twenty days solitary confinement and one year of hard labor in the state prison. The possession and passing of counterfeit money resulted in a sentence of solitary confinement for three months.

The Lincoln County courts held all their sessions in the courthouse. In 1825 the Court of Common Pleas began sitting here and remained until 1838, when it was replaced by a District Court sitting as the Middle District of the State at regular terms from 1839 to 1852.

Sessions of the federal courts were also held in the Wiscasset courthouse. Annual terms of the United States First Circuit Court of Appeals were held in the courtroom annually until 1842. Semi-annual terms of the United States District Court for the District of Maine were also held there until 1842. In the 1830s a famous case drew Daniel Webster to appear before the First Circuit Court, with Justice Story presiding. The case, *Veazie v. Waldleigh*, involved interests of shore and water rights at Old Town on the Penobscot. Jeremiah Mason of Boston, Frederic Allen of Gardiner, and William P. Fessenden of Portland were counsel for Veazie, and Reuel Williams, "Judge" Shepley, Jonathan Rogers and John Poor, along with Webster, were counsel for the defense. Poor said, "[Webster was] in the full flush of his success and in the zenith of his power as a master of eloquence and argument."[26]

Courthouse business soared in the boom years of the 1840s. The courthouse staff and the stacks of new records and files needed additional office and storage space. In 1847, the half-shire town designations ended and Wiscasset became the permanent shire town. At the end of 1849, a committee was appointed by the County Commissioners to look into the question of court space needs. In June, 1850, the committee recommended an extension of the courthouse of about 18 feet to the west. This addition to the building, the committee argued, was needed to accommodate an expanding Registry of Deeds, and for fire-safe storage space for probate records. Adjustments behind the courtroom made space for the presiding judge's chamber, a jury room and the law library. Also, the grand jury room was to be doubled in size, and the single courtroom was to be more properly appointed, "so as to be of the same finish as that at Portland." Additional land was purchased from the adjacent First Parish Church and from Judge Bailey, an abutter. Edmund B. Bowman, Esq., the Clerk of the Courts, supervised the construction work, which was completed in 1852. [27]

The Supreme Judicial Court of Maine held its last annual session in the Lincoln County Courthouse in May, 1851. The Court Reorganization Act of 1852 increased the size of the Court to seven members and made it principally a court of appeals, so that judges who heard trials would not hear appeals on the same cases. Since that time, all Supreme Judicial Court sessions have been held in Portland, Bangor, or Augusta.

The 1852 remodeling of the courtroom was the last major change to the courtroom space. The present judge's bench was put in place, as were the enclosures for the attorneys and the jury. All have remained in use for nearly 150 years. The gallery with its original floor of 30" wide, hand-hewn pine slabs still overlooks the courtroom, but without the partitions that walled it off from the courtroom each winter to save heat. The decorations of the room are still the "same as in Portland" even though the matching room in Portland has long since disappeared. The semi-circular niches where stoves stood are visible, but the two fireplaces have been bricked up. The 1852 jury room has antique chairs and a table. Outside the courtroom, the stairway is granite with an iron stair rail. The exterior facade of the building retains its 1824 original appearance, but without the shutters which were customary at the time it was built.

Over the years, Wiscasset has remained as the shire town for Lincoln County but the rapidly growing regions between the Androscoggin and the Penobscot were gradually whittled away. Waldo County was formed partly of territory secured from Lincoln County in 1827. The entire county of Sagadahoc and part of Androscoggin County were formed from Lincoln County lands in 1854, and Knox County was set off in 1860.

The Courthouse in the 20th Century

The centennial of the old courthouse was celebrated in the courtroom on July 23, 1924. The event was bannered a "Great Gathering of Lawyers in Wiscasset" by the local newspaper, with a tag line "Shore Dinner Follows," which may explain the attendance of more than 200 attorneys. The president of the Maine Bar Association, Augustus F. Moulton of Portland, read a paper on the history of the state. Local historian William D. Patterson of Wiscasset provided an address and paper on the history of the courthouse which remains a definitive work. Following the principal talks, Judge Albert Spear, the moderator, called for remarks, eliciting from Justice Warren C. Philbrook of Waterville, the senior Associate Justice of the Maine Supreme Judicial Court, a fiery denunciation of the trend of the federal government to encroach on the state in governmental affairs. [28]

The old courthouse continued to reflect national events. During prohibition, a jury, in a celebrated trial in Lincoln County for liquor nuisance, convicted Archie Shortwell for holding cider for "tippling" purposes, rather than as a beverage. The case was appealed to the Supreme Judicial Court, where the issue turned on whether Shortwell's place was used for the illegal sale or keeping of intoxicating liquor, and whether others had come to use Shortwell's place as a source of intoxicating liquor. Shortwell failed to suppress evidence of a prior conviction for sale of cider at the same location. He was unable to show why certain evidence should not be used against him—evidence that he sold cider to an "automobile party" in the nighttime, that he had empty bottles hidden near his garage, a barrel and a half of cider, and, in cellar of his house, open barrels, pails, funnels, and a hogshead holding dregs of cider. He lost his appeal.

In 1936 a sensational murder trial in Lincoln County resulted in the conviction of Reuben Brewer for the murder of his wife. Brewer was a lobster fisherman and lived with his wife near a wharf on the ocean. One morning Brewer called the sheriff and told him that his wife was missing. When the sheriff arrived, they looked around the wharf and house. A suicide note was found. Later that morning the body of Brewer's wife was found near the surf, fully clothed in a chinchilla coat, sweater and scarf, "…and gloves, the last not buttoned." A doctor and the medical examiner were called. When the body was examined, facial wounds were found but there were no other marks of violence. The skin around the lips, nose and eyes was swollen and discolored. Brewer pointed to her suicide note and proclaimed his innocence.

The jury heard the evidence. An autopsy revealed that the blows that left the bruises on her head were received before death, and that death was not caused by drowning. Further evidence showed lividity, a discoloration beneath the skin, that indicated the victim had lain on her back for a time after death. Brewer's testimony as to what he did that afternoon was "…suggestive of his guilt." He testified that he worked in his garage, then went into the house, and saw his wife lying on her bed but did not speak to her. He next went to the local store for provisions and stayed for about two hours. He bought some coffee and lamb chops, and the proprietor twice suggested they call Brewer's wife to find out if she wanted anything. Brewer refused to call her. Brewer's statements to others on that day and the next were also troubling. Finally came the evidence of the suicide note, which the jury agreed was forged by the defendant. The motive for the murder was not determined, and, in rejecting Brewer's 1937 appeal of his conviction, the Supreme Judicial Court noted "…the jury may have found in the testimony of the respondent, who seems to have withdrawn from natural domestic life, a complete aversion for his wife."

Between 1924 and 1950, modest improvements were made to the old structure. In 1950, the building was enlarged with a north wing in keeping with the architecture of the old building. The building was again enlarged slightly in 1972. In the mid-1980s new jail facilities were completed next door to the courthouse. The old sheriff's facilities in the basement of the courthouse were converted into offices and a state-approved holding cell for murder and other felony trials. The courthouse holding cell may be the only location in the state where a criminal defendant can monitor the proceedings of his or her trial through closed-circuit television. These new facilities have made Wiscasset a favored location for removal of criminal trials from York and Cumberland Counties, which have the heaviest caseloads in the state. Criminal cases removed to Wiscasset are usually those which (1.) last longer than a week; (2.) those where a change of venue is obtained because of the notoriety of the case or when public interest makes it difficult to find an impartial local jury; and (3) those where there is concern for the safety of the defendant or that the defendant might try to escape and harm another.

Honoring the old courthouse has become a ritual. In 1990, the Supreme Judicial Court returned to the old courtroom in Wiscasset to mark the bicentennial of the ratification of the United States Constitution. Two of Lincoln County's former courthouses still stand—the Pownalborough Courthouse is now an historic museum, standing in a rural area along the

The 1799 Lincoln County Courthouse in Warren is the second oldest court building in Maine. Jacob Sloane

Kennebec. The Warren Courthouse was used until 1942 as a school, and between 1952 and 1976 as a town building, with an office and meeting hall on the second floor and the first floor acting as the town's fire house and the site of town elections. The building is now "The Village Laundry," with apartments overhead.

[1] Kershaw, Gordon E., *The Kennebeck Proprietors 1749-1775*, Somersworth, N.H.: New Hampshire Publishing Co., 1975, p. 163

[2] Allen, Charles Edwin, *History of Dresden, Maine*, Lewiston: Twin City Printery, 1931, reprinted by Jennie G. Everson and Eleanor L. Everson, 1977, pp. 215-216

[3] Maine Historic Preservation Commission, *A Biographical Dictionary of Architects in Maine*, Vol. V., No. 9, Augusta: the Commission, 1988, pamph., n.p.

[4] Allen, p. 272

[5] *Id.*, p. 242

[6] Williamson, Joseph, "Capital Trials in Maine before the Separation," *Collections and Proceedings of the Maine Historical Society*, Second Series, Vol. I, 1890, pp. 163-164; Allen, pp. 250-251

[7] Allen, p. 252

[8] McKusick, Hon. Vincent L., "The Upcoming Tercentenary of the Supreme Judicial courts, *Maine Bar Journal*, Jan., 1992, pp. 14-15, commenting on Laurel Thatcher Ulrich's book, *A Midwife's Tale.*

[9] Stahl, Jasper J. *History of Old Broad Bay and Waldoboro*, Two Vols., Portland: Bond Wheelwright Co., 1956, Vol. I, p. 499

[10] Miller, Samuel L. *History of the Town of Waldoboro, Maine*, Wiscasset: Emerson Printer, 1910, p. 94

[11] This account of Wiscasset Hall is from Chase, Fannie, *Wiscasset in Pownalborough*, Second Ed., Wiscasset Public Library, Publisher, 1967, p. 90-92

[12] *Id.*, pp. 90-91

[13] *Id.*, p. 92

[14] *Id.*, p. 111

[15] *Id.*, p. 184

[16] *Id.*

[17] *Id.*, pp. 100-103

[18] Eaton, p. 275n

[19] Chase, p. 93; Fredericks, Katherine M.E., *Bar-Bits from Old Court Records in Lincoln County, Maine*, Wiscasset: County Commissioners of Lincoln Co., 1960, pp. 39-40

[20] Fredericks, pp. 41-42; Chase, p. 93

[21] Chase, p. 94

[22] *Id.*

[23] Patterson, Hon William Davis, *Address*, Centennial of Lincoln County Courthouse, 1924, in *Sprague's Journal of Maine History*, Vol, 13, No. 1, p. 24; Chase. p. 95

[24] Thompson, Deborah, *Maine Forms of American Architecture*, Waterville, Maine: Colby Museum of Art, 1976, p. 91; Myers, Denys Peter, "The Historic Architecture of Maine," in Maine Catalog Historic American Buildings Survey, Maine State Museum, 1974

[25] Coffin, N., *Statement & Account of Expenditure of N. Coffin, Esq., County Agent for Building a Courthouse*, Text of Report (Lincoln County), 1824; Moody, Robert E. "The Lincoln County Courthouse," *Old-Time New England*, Vol. 56, pp. 61-62

[26] Chase, p. 96

[27] *Id.*, p. 97; McKusick, Hon. Vincent L., *Opening Remarks*, Law Court Session in Wiscasset, Week of May 29, 1990

[28] Patterson, Hon William Davis, *Address*, Centennial of Lincoln County Courthouse, 1924, in *Sprague's Journal of Maine History*, Vol, 13, No. 1; "Lincoln County Honored at Its Century Mark," *Kennebec Journal*, July 24, 1924

The first courthouse in Ellsworth.

FIVE

Hancock County
1789

Castine, one of the oldest and most historic towns in Maine, has a colorful past as the site of colonial battles between England and France and a role in the American Revolution. Settled as Fort Pentagoet by traders from the Plymouth colony for trade with the Indians, it was taken over by the French and became a center of French strength and leadership in the region. When the French were driven out, the British took possession of Fort Pentagoet and the settlement became part of York County, Massachusetts. Then in 1760 Castine became part of the newly-formed Lincoln County. At that time the town and its surrounding area were known as Penobscot for its location on a peninsula jutting out into the estuary of the Penobscot River. Penobscot became an independent municipality in 1787.

When Hancock County was established by the Massachusetts legislature in 1789, its boundaries were the St. Georges River, the ocean, and the newly defined boundary of Washington County. The county extended north to the Quebec border. The town of Penobscot was named as its shire town. Having a county seat in a town was thought to be an important economic stimulus, and the townsfolk were proud to have captured such a prize. The town meeting moved quickly and firmly to cement the shire town designation by providing a building in the town center to house the courts.

After the establishment of Hancock County, town meeting notes refer to the meetinghouse as the site of court activities. In the 1793 town meeting, the townsfolk voted an appropriation of three pounds for "erection of some stockes, to be placed near the courthouse on the peninsula." The peninsula was the part of the town that became Castine. [1]

Castine: the First County Seat

The Castine town house was used as the Hancock County Courthouse.
Castine Historical Society

Court activities did not bring immediate prosperity to the town, which grew slowly, perhaps because of its remote location. With only 178 residents by 1796, the town remained active in promoting the peninsula, and succeeded in having the legislature set off the Town of Castine from the older and larger town of Penobscot. Its name commemorated Baron de Saint Castin, a French military leader who was an early nemesis of the British in the Penobscot valley. Under its new name, Castine and its court building remained the Hancock County seat.

With new-found enthusiasm, Castine set about building a real courthouse. In 1798 the Court of General Sessions of the Peace (roughly the equivalent of the later County Commissioners) voted to build a one-story courthouse with dimensions of 44 by 34 feet, with 14 foot corner posts. The building was to be at least two feet above ground level, with an underpinning of stones. Work got underway through a committee of five and a budget of $600 to cover the costs of the building. But the next year the committee reported a construction deficiency of $1200.

For ten years following the 1789 act establishing both Hancock and Washington Counties, the Supreme Judicial Court continued to sit in Wiscasset as it had before. In 1799, Down East residents sponsored a statute providing for the term of court for both Hancock and Washington Counties to sit at Castine. The first term of the Supreme Judicial Court in Castine was held in June, 1801. Three justices were present: Justices Thomas Dawes, Samuel Sewall, and George Thatcher, who presided.

Warren Hall, the clerk, took and subscribed the several oaths. [2]

At the first sitting of the Supreme Judicial Court in Castine in 1801, the initial item of business was the admission of Thomas Sparhawk as an attorney of the court. Seventy-two cases followed on the docket that first term, many of them transferred from Lincoln County. One early case was an appeal from a 1791 judgment of the Court of Common Pleas—*Thomas Richard of Ipswich versus Gustavus Swan* "of a place called Condusgig Stream not in any incorporation (but now Bangor), in the county of Hancock." By the time the case was transferred to Castine, an entry was made "And now neither party appears," which meant that the case was settled. [3]

Long-time Hancock resident Justice Herbert T. Silsby, II reports that one of the first Maine cases tried on a plea of insanity took place in Castine. Here is his brief account of *State v. Seth Eliot:*

'The respondent was found one day by his wife and hired help sitting on the edge of a bed with his two-year-old son on his lap, head pulled back, throat cut, and his blood draining into a bowl on the floor. People saw the resemblance to the Bible story of Abraham and Isaac, but didn't believe God had commanded Eliot to sacrifice his son, and he was indicted for murder and a plea of insanity entered. Many witnesses, both lay and medical, testified. The State's reply to the plea was that self-induced intoxication had caused any insanity. Ebenezer Poor, a medical doctor, happened to be clerk of courts at the time of trial. Eliot, prior to trial, tried to commit suicide by cutting his wrists with a nail he had managed to draw out of the wall of the wooden jail. Dr. Poor was called to the scene and at the trial testified that he observed nothing unusual about Eliot except he showed no signs of pain when he sewed up his wrists in that day before anesthesia. …The trial report shows that the lawyers and court handled the plea in a manner remarkably similar to the McNaughten Rule, although the trial took place some 20 years before McNaughten." [4]

Justice Silsby cites an 1815 case, *Commonwealth v. Moses Adams*, in which the defendant Moses Adams, High Sheriff of Hancock County and a doctor of good reputation, was indicted for the murder of his wife. On the day his wife was found murdered with an ax, Adams had been seen leaving his house about two hours before the discovery of the body. Blood was found on his clothing. Attorneys in his defense argued that the murder was committed by a thief, that the stains were acquired in his medical practice, and that he had an alibi for the time of the murder. The evidence was conflicting. Judge Jackson, in charging the jury, noted: "…Even if it were more probable that he did it than any other person, such a probable presumption is never sufficient to affect the life of any party accused." [5]

The Castine meetinghouse where the Adams trial took place was crowded, and, during a panic which came from a fear that the balconies were collapsing, several people were injured. The jury returned a verdict of not guilty, but the verdict was not satisfactory to public opinion and Adams could not obtain a local job. He was relegated to managing a stage coach stop on the road between Castine and Bangor.

In 1817 the court scheduled a session to be held in the meetinghouse, as they expected a large attendance. An Indian named Susep was to be tried for the murder of Captain Knight, a bar keeper in Bangor. The murder happened under provocation, and public sympathy was widespread for Susep. The defense, led by Mellen, called Governor Neptune of the Penobscot tribe, who spoke eloquently, citing the peace between Indians and settlers, the precedent of a similar case in Boston where the defence prevailed, and closed with: "Hope fills the heart of us all. Peace is good. These, my Indians, love it well. They smile under its shade. The white man and the red man must be always friends." [6]

Members of the bar in Hancock County established a fee schedule for their services in 1811, based on this reasoning:

"When it is considered that the Rules of the Supreme Judicial Court require that nine years at least should have been devoted to literary

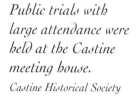

Public trials with large attendance were held at the Castine meeting house.
Castine Historical Society

and professional pursuits to qualify a man for admission to that Court as Attorney thereof; and two years' practice therein as an Attorney, to qualify him for admission as a Counsellor thereof; and that those who undertake the arduous duties of an Attorney or Counsellor at Law are bound in honor to indemnify their clients for all losses or damages which are occasioned by negligence, or want of professional knowledge, it must be evident that a reasonable and honorable compensation ought to be made, whenever professional assistance is afforded." [7]

Fees that were set included:

For advice when the property in dispute exceeds thirty dollars	$2.00
Drafting deeds and other instruments	1.00
For collecting all demands of twenty dollars and under	.50
Arguing a cause before a Justice's Court	3.00
Arguing a cause before the Court of Common Pleas	6.00
Arguing a cause to the Court or Jury, in the Supreme Judicial Court	12.00
For Naturalization	12.00
For Divorce	20.00
For Partition, exclusive of Court fees	12.00

...These rules are intended to establish the lowest compensation, and not to restrict gentlemen from receiving more liberal fees in cases of difficulty or magnitude. [8]

Castine was romantically described by William Crosby, later a justice of the Circuit Court of Common Pleas, as follows:

"Castine was the capital of all that vast territory lying east of the counties of Lincoln and Kennebec, the centre of its society and commerce, and its seat of justice. During the session of the courts there, the shores and harbor exhibited the appearance of an Indian encampment. The judge and jurors, the parties and witnesses, the lawyers, sheriffs and subordinate officers, loafers and idlers, besides not an inconsiderable number of gentlemen spectators, all arrived in open row or sail boats....There were no old men; new counties have no old men. We were all young men, healthy, hearty, and in the full flow of joyous anticipation... [9]

As early as 1800 the towns of Ellsworth, Bangor and Hampden registered complaints that Castine was too far away from the center of population in the County for convenient access. Because it was accessible

Ellsworth Tries to Become Shire Town

by water to riverfront towns in Hancock County on both sides of the Penobscot, local townsfolk were convinced that its location was accessible to all – an advantage for a county seat. Castine town meeting voted repeatedly against the removal of the courthouse to another town.

But economic growth was not taking place in Castine. Lumber mill towns, such as Ellsworth, were sources of booming economic activity and jobs and people flocked to industrial sites. Castine had its traditional seafaring occupations, but was not experiencing growth comparable to areas with lumber or other industries. Yet it retained the county seat and the activities that accompanied the honor. The town was aware of the advantages of the shire town designation:

> "The Courts and County Commissioners sat in the shire town. The county officers lived in the shire town. During term time, people with court business, jurors, and spectators came to the shire town in great numbers. Spectators were especially numerous when there was an exciting or lurid case for trial. The trial of cases was one of the foremost forms of entertainment. The shop keepers and innholders did a thriving business during term time. Thus getting or keeping the designation of shire town was important." [10]

Perhaps because of the war and the British occupation of Castine, the legislature established two half-shire towns in 1814, with court sessions divided between Castine and Bangor. Castine briefly suspended its formal court activities during the same year because of the British occupation, but apparently the court buildings were not damaged. The Hancock County Court of Common Pleas adjourned to Bangor for its November term.

Both the British occupation and becoming a half-shire town made Castine insecure of its designation as county seat. In 1816, the town regained its title to the courthouse when the county was divided and Penobscot County took the northern part of Hancock County. Within the resulting new Hancock County boundaries, Castine was once more centrally located for access to the courthouse from towns on both sides of the Penobscot River estuary. With Bangor established as county seat in the new Penobscot County, Castine returned to its role as the sole shire town in Hancock County.

Then in 1827 Waldo County was set apart from Hancock County. Waldo County took the portion of Hancock County west of the Penobscot. Castine, on the east side of the river at the new boundary of Hancock County, immediately lost its argument that it was a centrally-located town for court purposes.

With Castine on the defensive, competition for the shire town designation came again from Ellsworth. By 1830, Ellsworth was actively working with the state legislature in Augusta to gain approval to move the county seat out of Castine. Citizens from around Hancock County formally petitioned the state legislature for Ellsworth as the county seat. In 1831 Castine's residents voted in town meeting to appoint a committee to "remonstrate" against a removal of the Courts. The townsfolk assembled a rambling statement as its "remonstration:"

"…the inhabitants of Castine, believing that neither public feeling nor interest requires that the shire town of this County should at present be changed, do hereby …Remonstrate against the granting the prayer of that [other] Petition. … "…the towns of Bucksport, Orland, Bluehill, Sedgwick, Penobscot, Brooksville, Castine, Deer Isle, Vinalhaven, and other small islands in Penobscot Bay with a population of about Fifteen Thousand and exceeding the population of all other towns and organized plantations in Hancock county by about one fourth, and paying something more than four sevenths of the County Tax, are decidedly opposed to a removal of the County from Castine—that being a more convenient Shire town for them, on account of distance, and being more the center of their trade and business and of the other towns and organized plantations, … [and] …would probably prefer to have the County held where they now are, to being subjected to the burthen of increasing taxation for the erection of new County buildings again…" [11]

The petition of remonstration continued with a remarkable argument that court business was too slight to warrant removal of the county seat:

"… if litigation were extensively prevalent in this County, and our Courts were crowded with parties and their witnesses, it might be an object of importance to have the Shire town as near the centre of population as practicable—Where however the reverse is remarkably the case, where litigation is extremely limited and but few parties and few witnesses are called to attend our Courts of Law, it is believed, that for the accommodation of those few, the Legislature would not think it reasonable or just, to change the Shire town—sacrifice the property of the County, and subject its inhabitants to the weight of augmented taxation … [and] since our separation from Waldo, the average number of Jury trials of civil causes in the Supreme Court has not equalled three to each Term—and the average number of the same description of causes in the Court of Common Pleas has exceeded two only by the fraction 1/5—facts which bear more strongly upon the case when it is remembered that since 1828 we have had but one Term of the Supreme Court annually and but two of the Court of Common Pleas.

North of Castine, sentiment for moving the shire town to Ellsworth appeared to be just as strong or perhaps stronger. An editorial in Ellsworth's *Hancock Advertiser* claimed: "Ellsworth's position gives it many advantages over any other town in the county. It is the natural centre for more than half the county. The roads from every part of the county lead to the village, and daily stages run to and from Bucksport, Bangor, and Eastport." Ellsworth became prosperous based on its location at head of tide where logs from the back country were sawed in its mills, then shipped all over the world. [12]

With these commercial advantages, Ellsworth had more resources to develop a continuing strategy to become shire town. John Deane, a member of the Legislature, wrote: "We cannot calculate on success immediately, but we must worry the Legislature into a compliance with our views." [13]

People from Ellsworth worked vigorously with the residents of surrounding towns to petition the legislature to authorize the move. To strengthen its case, the town purchased land on Ellsworth's Bridge Hill for a town house and courthouse. Construction of the town house began on the land in 1834 as the beginning of a new civic center of public buildings. As further demonstration of its serious intentions, Ellsworth amended its petition to commit to construct a county courthouse at no expense to the state or to other communities if it were designated the county seat. The town added that it would turn over the courthouse to the county upon its completion.

Ellsworth Carries the Day and Builds a Courthouse

Ellsworth's package of guarantees to the state proved to be the turning point. The state legislature voted in 1836 to remove the county seat from Castine and place it in Ellsworth, provided the voters in Hancock County approved the transfer at the election in September and that Ellsworth would agree to finance and construct the county buildings. Political activities prior to the September referendum were dominated by Ellsworth, by now the more aggressive and prosperous community. The residents of Castine voted once again against the removal of the courthouse and tried to win the votes of others in the county.

Voters went to the polls in September and addressed the question: "Is it expedient that the Judicial Courts of Hancock County be established at Castine, Bluehill or Ellsworth?" Castine received 1298 votes, Ellsworth 1170 and Bluehill 23. However, 143 of Castine's votes were invalid, as they were registered by county residents who could not vote because they lived in unorganized plantations. Without these votes, Ellsworth emerged as the winner. A recount was ordered and the voter's approval of Ellsworth was upheld. In accordance with the legislative act, the formal transfer took effect on February 17, 1837. [14]

Ellsworth set out to fulfill its commitment to build the courthouse. It laid out plans for the new town house to be converted to the purposes of the courts, and designed a separate fireproof building to accommodate the county records. A resolve from the legislature allowed the county to borrow between four and eight thousand dollars to refurbish the town house for court use and to construct a jail and a records building. County records could not be moved from Castine until the new records building was completed in the fall of 1838. The first term of court held in Ellsworth was the October term of 1838.

Crowning Bridge Hill, the new court buildings were constructed in the popular Greek Revival style, facing an open green area at the intersection of two important streets leading into Ellsworth. The two county buildings were nearly identical, with colonnades on both sides. The slight difference was that the court building colonnades contained seven columns, while those at the records building had but six. At the east side of the courthouse a columned porch welcomed people into the building and multiple panes of floor-to-ceiling windows brought light into the interior. In contrast to older courthouse buildings, there was no rooftop belfry or turret, and no bell to announce important events. The roofs were plain except for slender chimneys. A contemporary drawing shows picket fences, tall trees, embanked lawns, and stairways connecting the different levels on the property.

During construction, joint use of the facility was discussed. The Ellsworth Unitarians, organized in 1837, were seeking a quiet place for services and convinced the county officials to share rooms in the structure. A contribution of furnishings was part of the agreement, and the interior of the building was furnished with "open pews, a pulpit and singing chairs." The county accepted the furnishings for joint use, although the Unitarians anticipated reimbursement by the county, which apparently never materialized. [15]

On the strength of its success in obtaining the use of the building, the Unitarians organized a weekly Lyceum featuring a lecture or debate. Justice Silsby reports a Unitarian incident:

> "On one occasion the services in the courthouse were interrupted by a drunken sailor, a frequent sight in Ellsworth's days as a port for sailing ships. The sailor, dressed in tarpaulin hat and pea-jacket, came to the services and took a front seat. He was not especially noticed until the Rev. Devens alluded, in the course of his sermon, to the moon, its distance from the earth, its circumference, and its other attributes. The sailor suddenly jumped to his feet, outstretched his arms and hollered to the top of his voice, 'Shipmates, a lunar observation.' He was promptly assisted down the hill." [16]

The Unitarians provided the first Ellsworth courthouse with minimal furnishings and few creature comforts. The courtroom had only open, backless benches for onlookers, and chairs were provided only for the most important people in the room. Complaints ensued about the lack of comfort, but it was not until the winter of 1852-1853 that a formal petition was circulated and submitted to the county commissioners to replace benches with seats that had backs.

The Supreme Judicial Court came annually to Ellsworth for a one-week term during its state-wide circuit. The circuit began in York County in April, and proceeded northward until it reached Ellsworth at the end of July. Its caseload was varied: in 1851 ten cases were argued in Hancock

County—'...four on report, two on exceptions, two on facts agreed, and one appeal from the Judge of Probate and one application for mandamus." There was no time limit on arguments. Thus the time an argument would take was impossible to judge in advance.

A statute provided that one Supreme Judicial Court justice could hold a term by himself if necessary. However, if no justice was in attendance because of sickness, accident or unforeseen cause, the sheriff or clerk was required to notify the public by oral proclamation and by public notice. To keep people up to date about court sittings, the courthouse door became a message center. A written public notice was posted on the courthouse door to adjourn the court from day to day until a justice would show up, or to continue hearings until the next term.

The Supreme Judicial Court held its last law term in Ellsworth in 1851 at the old county courthouse. The following year the court system was re-organized, and the Supreme Judicial Court sat only at Portland, Augusta, and Bangor. But the Hancock County Superior Court continued sitting in the old building.

The old Ellsworth courthouse was the site of an early battle of experts called in to interpret evidence in *State v. Smith,*, an 1872 trial of a Bucks-port man. The body of a woman was found in a building that was burning. The defendant, found with blood on his dyed jacket, claimed he had killed a rabbit and his wife had dyed his jacket to cover the stains. The jury, wavering on the question of Smith's guilt, was persuaded of his innocence by an expert from Boston who had examined the jacket for human blood. The case spurred official thinking of the need for impartial experts in trials, and a campaign to get such a rule in place was led by Lucilden A. Emory, the State Attorney General and prosecutor in the case.

The 1886 Hancock County Courthouse

As Ellsworth continued to grow, becoming a city in 1869, the modest court buildings no longer seemed adequate for the booming area. Public meeting space in the newly-built Hancock Hall was suggested as an appropriate place for court proceedings, so that the old courthouse might be used as a high school for Ellsworth. When the Free High School Act was passed in 1873, the need for a high school grew more acute.

It took almost 20 years from the time that a new courthouse was proposed until the construction and opening of a new building—the third courthouse for Hancock County. The need for a new courthouse had become more apparent because of the expanding volume of judicial work, and the County took up the movement with some vigor.

A location closer to downtown Ellsworth was found for the new court-house. Designers for a new, more spacious and modern building were put under contract. The new building would be exemplary in its Victorian

The new Hancock County Courthouse was completed in 1931 and occupied immediately by the courts. In 1933 an enormous fire destroyed most of downtown Ellsworth. During the fire, a building adjacent to Hancock Hall was deliberately blown to bits by city firemen in an effort to stop the fire. The explosion accidentally set Hancock Hall on fire. Luckily, it was no longer the site of court proceedings and the 1931 courthouse was unaffected by the fire.

One of the most celebrated cases in the present courthouse was the 1939 murder trial of *State v. Robins*, in which the defendant was accused of murdering his girlfriend, found battered to death. When arrested, the defendant sported white flannel pants that had flecks of blood. The defendant maintained that the blood came from his recurring nosebleeds, and his statement was corroborated by his sister. The case turned on identification of the evidence of blood on Robins' clothes. The case was dramatized by nationally-circulated pulp magazines. At his sensationalized trial, Robins was found guilty of manslaughter, and sentenced to 20 years in prison with no chance of parole.

Below left: The 1931 Hancock County Courthouse used the walls of the 1886 building as its framework. Right: Interior of the 1931 Courthouse in Ellsworth.

[1] Wheeler, George Augustus, *History of Castine, Penobscot, and Brooksville, Maine, including the Ancient Settlement of Pentagoet,* Bangor: Burr & Robinson, 1875, p. 60

[2] "An Act for erecting and establishing two new counties in the County of Lincoln, and declaring the Boundaries of Lincoln in future" (Passed June 25, 1789) The Laws of the Commonwealth of Massachusetts, 3 vols., (Chapters not numbered) Boston, Massachusetts: i: 476

[3] Silsby, Hon. Herbert T., II, *A Speech Delivered...before a Special Session of the Supreme Judicial Court of the State of Maine ...Commemorating the 200th Anniversary of the Incorporation of Hancock County,* Unpublished Manuscript, Ellsworth, 1989, p. 7

[4] *Trial of Seth Elliot, Esq. for the Murder of His Son, John Wilson Elliot Before the Supreme Judicial Court at Castine, October Term ,1824,* Belfast: Published by Fellows and Simpson, n.d.

[5] Silsby, Hon. Herbert T., II, *A Speech ...,* p. 8; *Trial of Moses Adams, High Sheriff of the County of Hancock, before the Supreme Judicial Court of the Commonwealth of Massachusetts, on an Indictment for the Murder of His Wife,* Boston: Printed and Published by E.B. Tileston, 1815

[6] Wheeler, pp. 106

[7] Williamson, Joseph, *History of the City of Belfast,in the State of Maine,* 2 Vols.,Vol. I, Portland: Loring, Short & Harmon, 1877, pp. 366n.

[8] *Id.,* pp. 366-367

[9] *Id.*

[10] Silsby, Hon. Herbert T., II, "Interesting History of Old County Courthouse Buildings," *Ellsworth American,* Sept. 28, 1960

[11] This account of the petition is from Little, Otis, Joseph Bryan and L.B. McIntire, (Committee) *Petition to the Senate and House of Representatives at Augusta in Legislature Assembled,* pamphl. n.p., c. 1831

[12] Silsby, Hon. Herbert T., II, "Ellsworth: A Brief History," in *Historical Record and Program: Bicentennial Celebration July 20-27, 1963,* Ellsworth, Me., Ellsworth Bicentennial Corporation, 1963

[13] Davis, Albert H., *History of Ellsworth, Maine,* Lewiston: Lewiston Journal Printshop, 1927, p. 86

[14] *Id.,* p. 81

[15] Silsby, Hon. Herbert T., II, "Interesting History of Old County Courthouse Buildings," *Ellsworth American,* Oct. 5, 1960

[16] *Id.*

[17] Pattangall, William R., *The Meddybemps Letters,* Lewiston: Lewiston Journal Company, 1924, p. 50

SIX

Washington County

1789

Washington County was organized as a jurisdiction of Maine over 200 years ago. Settlements along the Atlantic coast grew as a result of early fishing and shipping activities. As people came Down East and settled, the need for court activities began to multiply. Land claims needed to be officially recognized and recorded. Disputes needed a means for a final settlement.

Before Washington County was established, Lincoln County was responsible for administration of court and county services east of the Kennebec River. Because of the long distance from the Lincoln County seat, Pownalborough, the ordinary functions of county government were virtually inaccessible to most residents of the far northern settlements. After peace with Britain was signed in 1783, Lincoln County began to make court services more accessible to residents of the area. The first county agency brought to Machias was the Registry of Deeds, and an individual Register of Deeds was elected during a special town meeting in 1785.

The part of Lincoln County between Union River at Ellsworth and Passamaquoddy Bay became known as the Eastern District of Lincoln County. As the principal inhabited center of the Eastern District, Machias became the location of most meetings and a center for citizens to vote – for governor, lieutenant governor, senator and state representatives. Machias town meeting also initiated a movement to transform the Eastern District into a new county.

In 1786, a Machias town meeting featured, as the second item for consideration, an article asking "if the inhabitants will make application for the General court to erect this Eastern District as a separate county and

The Need for a Down East Coun[ty]

101

to make Machias the shire town." Town meeting members voted affirmatively, and invited all the residents between Union River and Passamaquoddy, to "join with them to erect this Eastern District a separate county." The group appointed a committee "to petition to the honorable General Court in behalf of this town." The committee, including Hon. Stephen Jones, James Avery, George Stillman, Capt. David Longfellow and William Tupper, was asked to "apply to Caleb Davis and Benjamin Hichborn, Esq's., to assist them in bringing forward the afore-mentioned application to effect…" and instructed the committee to apply to the Court of General Sessions, then holding its sessions in Pownalborough, for aid in the cause. [1]

It was a difficult time for Washington County residents. There were punishing expenses involved in developing the town—clearing the forest, building churches and homes, making roads, and supporting a parson. Farming had been productive, but an unexpectedly low yield on a potato crop worried the settlers. In the face of their efforts, unrest resulted from the threats and presence of the British just across the border in Canada. Topping the problems was an unresponsive government of the province, located hundreds of miles away in Boston. The issue soon expanded to include the services provided for Washington County by the courts.

As directed by town meeting, the committee developed a plan based on the need for home rule. The plan for a new county was included under the petition called "Memorial of the Inhabitants of Machias Asking an Abatement of State Tax" to the Massachusetts Legislature in 1787. After listing the problems "making it almost impossible to pay any State Taxes laid upon us …" the committee stated the case for a new county in terms of travel, crime control and distribution of liquor licenses:

> "Our great desire to support the laws renders it necessary for us to make still further applications, which is for a county to be erected in this district which if granted must be attended with very considerable expense but the necessities make us anxious for the accomplishment of it. There are many strong & urgent reasons for a County being established in this district in particular for the punishment of crimes against the public which although they are not numerous, yet there is some & among others of Fornication & Bastardy, also for granting license to persons as Innholders & Retailers of Spiritous liquors, for no person will at the expense & fatigue of travelling 300 miles & up ways through Wilderness & exceeding bad roads & when they come there, must seek friends to be bondsmen for them which perhaps as they are strangers it will be impossible for them to obtain, and the consequences will be there will be no Licensed persons in this part of

the Country. … A County Road is also exceeding wanted, which will not be obtained until a County is established here." [2]

The agitation that was developing in the Eastern District led to discussions throughout the District of Maine of separating the counties (York, Cumberland and Lincoln) from the counties of Massachusetts centering on Boston. People in and around Machias were asked to consider separation and town meeting decided that "to support a separate Government would in the opinion of this Town, be attended with much greater expense than what these Counties pay towards the present, without any real advantage coming to us." The context for the decision was pressure from the British to take land at the Maine's eastern frontier, and predictions that help might be needed from either the Commonwealth of Massachusetts or the federal Congress. Neither were expected to help against the British if the District of Maine was in rebellion while asking for assistance. [3]

The Eastern District was made into counties on June 25, 1789, when both Hancock and Washington Counties were established. Washington County stretched along the eastern frontier of the District of Maine, with a disputed boundary separating it from Canada. The boundary between Hancock and Washington counties was established at Gouldsboro Bay, and from there went directly north. Machias was designated the shire town for Washington County.

Growing Pains for the New County

People of the Machias area were disappointed that there were two counties where they had expected only one. Perhaps more important to the area, the terms of the Supreme Judicial Court were initially held only in Hancock County, and the court did not journey to Machias at all. Although the Hancock County shire town, Castine, was closer than Lincoln County, it was an unexpected inconvenience.

Washington County immediately filed a petition to the legislature, citing the unexpected "smallness of our county. …much reduced below what was expected, by a number of towns now in the Eastern part of the county of Hancock, which previous to the division of the County of Lincoln, it was always expected would be incorporated into this county and for what reason they were annexed to that County we are yet to learn as we cannot find it was by any request of the inhabitants of those towns." [4]

While waiting for a response to their petition, the residents of Washington County began to plan for housing the county functions. Machias, eager to fulfill its title of shire town, offered on June 11, 1790 to help the county find court space. The Machias Selectmen called a meeting to determine "whether the town will consent, that the Court of

Housing the Court

Common Pleas and the Court of the General Sessions of the Peace may be held in the meetinghouse at the Western Falls, till buildings are erected." Town meeting readily agreed. [5]

The Western Falls meetinghouse was more than adequate for the early sessions of the court. It was also used for town meetings, religious worship, meetings of Plantations and Proprietors, and the first school in Machias. The building had been constructed for $317 in 1774 by private subscription and was pressed into service as a town hall, school and a place to hold plantation and proprietors' meetings. When the courts began to use the structure, it was a one-story structure twenty-five feet wide and forty-two feet long, with no pews. Instead, ranges of seats were placed on each side of a narrow aisle, leading to the head of the room and centered on a small pulpit.

In July town meeting met to "choose in manner the Law directs ten persons as petty jurors in the Court of Common Pleas and the Court of the General Sessions of the Peace" and to elect six "suitable persons" as Grand Jurymen for the Court of Common Sessions." [6]

The meetinghouse, site of court sessions and town meetings, was also the center of discussions of separation of Maine from Massachusetts. In a 1791 report, Washington County residents compared the present "happy" form of government and the proposal to make Maine a separate state. Machias town meeting discussed whether separation would help alleviate the expense of travel to Boston for the residents of an area larger than Rhode Island with a rapidly growing population. One argument cited "the great distance from the office of the Clerk of the Supreme Judicial Court [in Boston] which made it difficult obtaining copies of papers". But others responded that the situation could be worse:

> "There will always be some difficulty attending business of that kind, but we are persuaded that the inconvenience is not so great as is pretended, as vessels sail daily from every part of the District [of Maine] to Boston by which such papers can be easily obtained, or they may be obtained in the three upper counties [Lincoln, Hancock, and Washington] by the post, which comes weekly to Pownalborough. It is much easier for any part of the Counties of Washington and Hancock to obtain papers from Boston than from Portland or Pownalborough, in one of which towns it is probable the Clerk's office would be held in case of a separation [of Maine from Massachusetts]. Upon the whole your Committee is fully persuaded, that the {Western Massachusetts} Counties of Hampshire and Berkshire labour under as great, if not greater inconvenience in this respect." [7]

An early malpractice case was heard in Washington County in 1822. Charles Lowell of Lubec, thrown from a horse which had then fallen on him, had a dislocated hip. The Lubec physician, Dr. John Faxon, attended Lowell, but failed to remedy the problem. Faxon called Dr. Micajah Hawkes of Eastport for a consultation. Hawkes manipulated Lowell's leg and seemingly remedied the dislocation. Four weeks later, Lowell called Hawkes to demonstrate that the leg was once more dislocated. Hawkes was unable to help, and Lowell caught a boat for Boston, where he visited physicians including Dr. John Collins Warren of Harvard Medical School and Massachusetts General Hospital. The Boston physicians were also unable to remedy the dislocation. Lowell then brought suit against Faxon and Hawkes for malpractice in their ineffective treatment. [8]

At the trial before Justice David Perham in 1822, Lowell won a verdict of $1,962, but an appeal was made immediately to the Supreme Judicial Court. At a subsequent trial in Machias before Justice Weston, the Boston physicians provided affidavits faulting the two Maine doctors. The jury acquitted Dr. Faxon and debated the responsibility of Dr. Hawkes. When one of the jurors fell ill, Justice Weston consulted with Chief Justice Prentiss Mellon. The two Supreme Court justices agreed that the probable outcome of the trial was an acquittal of Hawkes, and the could waste no more court time on the case. The result was a non-suit for the plaintiff and no costs for the defendants. Lowell bitterly attacked Justice Weston and demanded his impeachment, but the case was closed.

Court activities grew rapidly, reflecting the growth in population and the increasing need for recording and transferring land, as well as more general judicial activities. In 1798 the Court of General Sessions authorized a committee to purchase or build a separate courthouse for Washington County. Although it is unclear when the building was completed, there are notations of a courthouse on a plan of the village in 1811.

At a trial in Washington County in 1811, *Commonwealth v. Ebenezer Ball*,

> "...the issue was whether the respondent (the defendant nowadays) was justified in killing a deputy sheriff who attempted to arrest him on a defective warrant. The bench disagreed on the law of the case, which under the system at that time, left to the jury to decide both the law and the fact. Ball was found guilty and sentenced to hanging. Just before the hanging, the court announced they had reached unanimous agreement on the law, and this must have been a great consolation to Ball that he was swinging as a result of a unanimous court." [9]

Pressing for a New Washington County Courthouse

By 1822, the growth of the town at the falls of the Machias River led it to boast that it had four sawmills, one gristmill, a cording machine, eight retail stores, two wharves, three taverns, a county house and a gaol. It was a four days sail to Boston. Records show that a free-standing, spacious courthouse was built in 1826 by a consortium of private interests. The county rented space in the courthouse by the term or by the year. This rental arrangement was to proceed for nearly 30 years.

The county decided, in the early 1850s, to construct a permanent building for court and county purposes. The site chosen was occupied by the then existing, privately-owned courthouse. The new courthouse was designed by the firm of Benjamin Deane and Edwin Brown of Bangor. It was said to be primarily the work of Deane, the senior partner in the firm and a pioneer designer in Eastern Maine. The contract for construction was awarded on September 1, 1853 to Ebenezer Adams and Sons. Construction began immediately and the building, scheduled for opening in late 1854, actually opened for business in 1855.

The 1855 courthouse was built in the Italianate style, entirely of brick

The original design of the Washington County Courthouse in Machias.

with heavy wooden dentils on the cornice and gable ends. It was the first brick structure in Machias. Horizontal granite string courses marked the levels of the ground and second floors. Brick pilasters flanked the arched windows set into arched recesses on the second floor. A square wooden cupola topped the gable end facing Court Street with its arched window A pair of brass scales of justice crowned the top of the cupola. A bell was added in 1868, perhaps to notify the town of terms of court or to call jurors to duty.

In the interior of the new building a lobby or hall extended the length of the main floor. Off each side of the hall were county offices, protected by cast iron fire doors. Fireproof shutters were stationed on the inside of the windows. Four fireplaces of oversized reddish-brown brick were provided to warm the offices. The fireplace bricks were carved with a flower design.

Access to the second floor was by way of two sets of metal stairs on either side of the main entrance. Curving up to the second floor landing, the stairs led directly to the courtroom. Taking up most of the second floor, the courtroom had seating on three sides with the judge's bench at the end opposite the main door. The courtroom was rebuilt after the building was damaged by a storm in 1869. Outside the courtroom, the only other rooms on the second floor were two small rooms on either side of the landing.

The new courthouse building immediately attracted local comment. A newspaper account described the building as "economical, commodious and tasty." On the interior courtrooms, hemlock was used in the trim. One critic wrote that, although a long lasting wood, hemlock is "…inexpensive, and thus inappropriate…" for a courthouse.

Putting the Courthouse to Work

The new Machias courthouse immediately became the center of activities in Washington County. It was also the place where the first woman lawyer in Maine began her practice. In 1872 Elizabeth Nash became the first woman to pass the bar in Maine. Nash had studied law with her husband in Columbia Falls.

In 1864 the courthouse was the setting for the trial of three Confederates charged with the attempted robbery of the Calais Bank. Found guilty, the three defendants were sentenced as common criminals which caused considerable surprise since it was generally believed they would be treated as prisoners of war.

The building was also used for social occasions. At the centennial anniversary of the settlement of Machias in May, 1863, there was a grand "Pic Nic dinner", with each public building and church inviting guests to share in the celebration. The courthouse was used for a dinner sponsored by the Young America Fire Company of Machias, which entertained the

Mazeppa Fire Company of East Machias "sumptuously." It was said that it was the only place in town where fresh fruits were provided for the guests.

The interior of the building was completely remodeled in 1886, in accordance with plans drawn up by Francis H. Fassett of Portland. One purpose of the remodeling was to fireproof the building. The construction work was undertaken by Andrew R. Gilson of Machias.

The Court is Attracted to Calais

The 1854 courthouse, with building additions, still serves Washington County.

Starting in 1869, individual justices of the Supreme Judicial Court heard trials in Calais, although citizens of Machias protested any sittings outside its courthouse. In 1901, Calais pledged itself to construct a new building to permanently house its term of court. Calais appropriated

$14,000 for a new city-county building, and designs for the building were begun by H.A. Crosby. The structure was designed to be 45 feet long and 80 feet wide. The basement contained a jail with eight cells and a marshal's office. The first floor provided space for the municipal courtroom, six offices for city and county officials and a room for a law library. On the second floor was the principal courtroom, judge's offices, and jury, consultation and coat rooms. The building, completed in 1903, was immediately occupied by town officials.

The justices of the Supreme Judicial Court attended annual Washington County sessions at Calais until 1930, when the Superior Court was created to take up county work on a more regular basis. The Washington County Superior Court continued to hold several of its annual sessions at the Calais City-County Building.

John Lynch described his arrival and observation of a scene in the Washington County Courthouse in 1916:

Scenes in Court

"A day or two after the October term came in, I went to Machias and while watching the court proceedings I saw something that made a powerful impression on me. Chief Justice Appleton presided. He was a dignified, fine old gentleman. I enjoyed looking at him, and my admiration for him increased until a prisoner was brought in and put in the prisoner's box at the lower end of the bar. … "[The prisoner] had been indicted for burglary in a building in Calais in the nighttime, …after the indictment had been read he was asked to plead and he answered, "Guilty." Then the fine looking old judge said to him, "Have you anything to say before I sentence you?" The prisoner said, 'Yes, I have. I was drunk when I went into that building and did not know what I was doing …' My sympathy for him was excited…I expected if the man was sentenced it would be a very light one. Imagine my amazement and disappointment when the judge…said, 'I had made up my mind to give you three years in State Prison, but on account of your being drunk at the time you committed the crime I will add two years and sentence you to five years….' It seemed to me that I had never seen anything so cruel, but…having some experience in court, I could see that he was obliged to appear harsh and cruel and make no sign of his tender feelings for the poor man. If by his sentence he had allowed it to be understood that the plea of drunkenness had caused him to sympathize with the prisoner, and that the sentence had been lightened instead of made heavier, many men who were arraigned for crimes would have asked for mercy on account of being drunk. The judge was a noble, kind-hearted man."[10]

Additions for a law library and offices have been built on the west side and the rear of the Machias Courthouse in the mid-twentieth century. The structure was placed on the National Register of Historic Places in 1976. A tablet in the courthouse law library commemorates the First Naval Battle of the American Revolution June 12, 1775, in which local Machias people stormed the British Schooner "Margaretta" soon after the battle of Lexington and Concord.

[1] Drisko, George W., *Narrative of the Town of Machias: The Old and the New, the Early and the Late*, Machias: Press of the Republican, 1904, p. 105

[2] *Id.*, pp. 125-126

[3] "Materials for a History of Machias, Maine, from the Town Records," Excerpt from *Historical Magazine*, July and August, 1870, p. 40

[4] Drisko, p. 156

[5] *Id.*, p. 141

[6] *Id.*, p. 142

[7] *Id.*, p. 118

[8] Spalding, James A., *Lowell vs. Faxon and Hawkes, a A Celebrated Malpractice Suit in Maine*, Reprinted from the Bulletin of the American Academy of Medicine, Vol. XI, No. 1, Feb., 1910

[9] *Trial of Ebenezer Ball Before the Hon. Samuel Sewall, George Thatcher, and Isaac Parker, Esquires, for the Murder of John Tileston Downes, at Robinstown, Jan. 28, 1811,* Castine: Printed and Published by Samuel Hall, 1811

[10] Lynch, John F., *The Advocate: An Autobiography and Series of Reminiscences,* Portland: George D. Loring, 1916, p. 112

SEVEN

Kennebec County
1799

Augusta's Kennebec County Courthouse, one of the oldest and most venerable in the state, has been in constant service for more than 165 years. During this long period, it has served not only the courts of Kennebec County, but also the Maine Supreme Judicial Court, which held its sessions in the building from 1830 to 1970. The courthouse may be the earliest example of a court building in Maine designed by an architect, and it preceded by two years the work of Charles Bulfinch on the State House design. It is the first temple-fronted building in the Greek Revival style in Maine. The exterior of the building is remarkable for being largely unchanged in appearance from early times.

Venerable as it is, the present Kennebec County Courthouse is not the first building used for court purposes by the county. When Kennebec County was lightly populated, its court functions were supplied by York County. After 1760, when Lincoln County was formed, the county court functions were centered in the shire town, Pownalborough (Dresden), on the Kennebec River.

Hallowell, which at the time included the land now comprising Augusta, was made a coordinate shire town of Lincoln county in 1786, sharing the title with Pownalborough further down the river and with Waldoborough. Residents of the Hallowell area could look forward to trips to court locally, and the lengthy trips to Pownalborough could be avoided in most cases.

The first sitting of a Lincoln County court in the Augusta portion of Hallowell was at Pollard's Tavern in January, 1787, with Judges William Lithgow, James Howard and Nathaniel Thwing of the Court of Common Pleas. Judge Thomas Rice was not present. The Lincoln County Court of

The First Kennebec County Courthouse

111

Kennebec County
became the sixth county
in Maine in 1799.
Osher Map Library, University
of Southern Maine

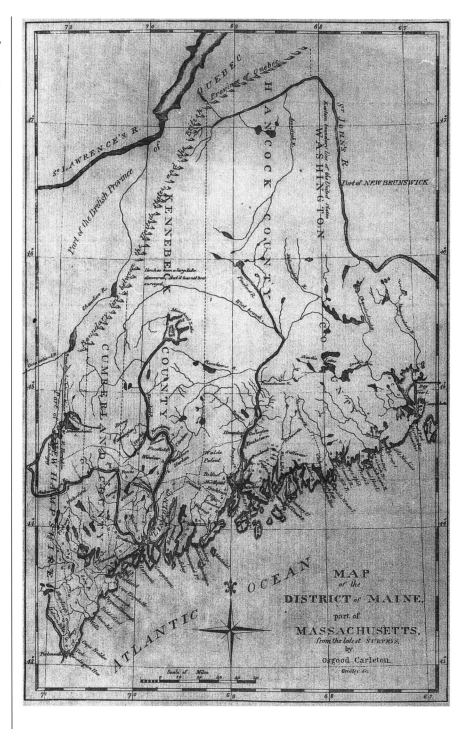

*Kennebec County
became the sixth county
in Maine in 1799.*
Osher Map Library, University
of Southern Maine

Sessions, comprised of the county's justices of the peace, initially met at the home of Colonel Joseph North.

As it became clear that court services were needed regularly in this part of Lincoln County, a courthouse became essential. A public subscription began, and private funds were raised to construct a building for the courts. A site was found on the old road to Winthrop (now Winthrop Street), laid out in 1785 as a main stem of the town. Construction got underway in September, 1790.

Progress on the courthouse building lagged; funds were insufficient to pay for construction materials. The frame of the building was empty until December, when a committee was formed to oversee finishing at least one room of the building. In January, the Court of Common Pleas was held in the framed-in but unfinished building. One room soon had lath and plaster, and the entire building was completed in December, 1791. For several years the immediate neighborhood was known as Hallowell Courthouse, reflecting the prestige brought to this part of town by the new building.

In 1793, the General Court of the Commonwealth of Massachusetts introduced more humane criminal laws and directed that jails be constructed to replace the use of stocks and whipping post as punishment for mild offenses. The jail opened in 1793, and the public stocks and whipping post set up earlier fell into disuse.

On an eventful day in July, 1794, the Massachusetts Supreme Judicial Court convened in Hallowell. Preparations had been made to use the Middle Parish Meetinghouse as court space, because the new courthouse had insufficient space to accommodate both the court and the large number of anticipated spectators. The Meetinghouse was packed with onlookers. The county business and professional leaders were all in prominent seats. Then, to the beat of a drum, a procession of officials entered the room – Justices Paine, Sumner and Dawes – newly-arrived from Boston and wearing robes of black silk, accompanied by three sheriffs wearing cocked hats and carrying swords and long white staffs symbolic of their offices. The justices were followed by a parade of members of the bar.

Court proceedings began on that day after the justices took their seats at the front of the building. Suddenly a woman stalked down the aisle, interrupting the stolid atmosphere of the court. She announced that she was the Queen of Sheba. Fearful of the woman's madness and "wild-flying hair …about her haggard face," the judges called for the sheriff to evict her. Court officials then proceeded with the business of the term.

The court term in 1794, held in Hallowell, was best known for the murder case of Edmund Fortis of Vassalborough, who , "…being moved and instigated by the devil," raped and strangled 13-year old Pamela Tilton. He pleaded guilty and was followed by "credible witnesses, by whose tes-

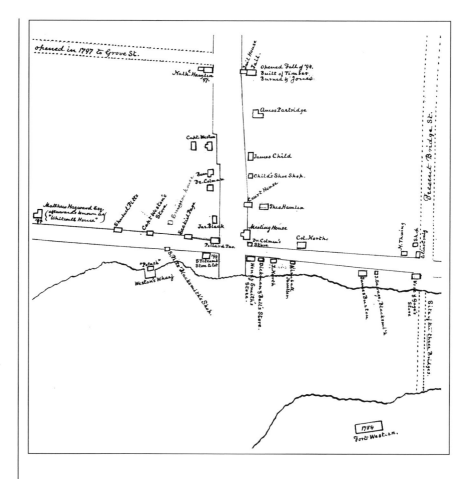

The 1791 courthouse was located on Winthrop Street (at middle of map) in the center of Augusta.
Maine Historical Society

timony the truth of his plea was abundantly confirmed." Sentenced to be hanged, Fortis endured a long speech by Judge Paine, who repeatedly addressed the defendant: "Unhappy prisoner at the bar, Edmund Fortis!"[1]

In 1797 the area around the courthouse district of Hallowell became a separate town, initially called Harrington, a name soon changed to Augusta. A year later, discussions were initiated for setting off a new county comprised of the northern area of Lincoln County. Forty delegates met in Augusta to determine how to divide the county. A plan was devised and sent as a petition to the Legislature for approval. On February 20, 1799, the new county, to be called Kennebec, was established in the northern part of Lincoln County. Augusta was designated as the shire town, and terms of court were defined: each year there would be two terms of the Court of Common Pleas and Court of Sessions and one term of the Supreme Judicial Court.

The old courthouse on Winthrop Street was soon viewed as insufficient to meet the new county's needs. Larger courtrooms were essential, and space was required for county records and administrative offices. Space was needed for the court records, which had been transferred from Boston in 1797 to the custody of the clerks of the Court of Common Pleas in Kennebec County.

The 1801 Kennebec County Courthouse

Plans were drawn up for a courthouse up the hill from the river, but still close to Market Square. The location was pristine land that is the site of the present jail. The street that passed in front was christened Court Street (since renamed State Street).

In June, 1801, construction on the new courthouse began. It was likely a wooden building, since its eventual successor was distinguished as the "stone courthouse." It may have had the appearance of a meetinghouse, without the usual tower, because available funds did not initially permit construction of a tower and belfry to house a bell to mark the time of day and to call people to court. A committee set to work to raise funds for building the tower, and managed to assemble the required amount of $150 shortly thereafter.

The courthouse building was occupied by the courts on March 16, 1802. The courthouse bell was in put in place in the new belfry and, on August 20, 1803, rang out as the first such bell in the county. Each day, it rang at seven, one and nine o'clock.

The new building became an anchor for new developments. Two new hotels were constructed nearby, to accommodate the influx of visitors to Augusta on court dates. These hotels—the Mansion House and the Cushnoc House—were especially favored by guests such as lawyers and suitors in attendance at court.

Trial of the Malta Raiders

A memorable murder trial took place in the wooden courthouse as a result of the "Malta War." The roots of the murder dated to 1802, when the courts began hearing disputes of titles to land in the town of Malta (now Windsor). Settlers in Malta had obscure or invalid deeds, and the clearest titles were held by several residents of Augusta. These landowners began eviction proceedings on people they called squatters. But many of the tenants, who had spent years improving the land, felt unjustly accused, and began an organized resistance. Disguised as Indians, sympathizers stormed the jail in Wiscasset where the tenants were being held and freed those who had been imprisoned. Threats were delivered to the landowners, who organized the Augusta Patrol with a motto *Custodia est Clypeus* (the watch is our protection.) [2]

In March, 1808, the problems escalated. An inmate set fire to the Kennebec County Jail, and the building burned down. The same night the courthouse was set afire, but the fire was extinguished before serious damage was done. The Malta "squatters" were immediately blamed, and the town was alarmed by these acts of terrorism. The Augusta Light Infantry was called out and the Augusta Patrol doubled its membership in a short time.

In Boston, the Massachusetts legislature took up the Malta dispute and quickly passed a betterment act, requiring landowners to pay for improvements that settlers made to their properties. The settlers remained unhappy. In September, 1808, Paul Chadwick, a surveyor working in the disputed area, was fatally shot. Suspects hid in the woods, but seven of them were persuaded to turn themselves in to the county authorities. To await trial, they were housed in the newly-rebuilt stone jail in Augusta. Fearing for the lives of the suspects, friends organized a raid on the Kennebec County Jail. Seventy armed men, dressed as Indians, gathered for the attack. However, a spy sent ahead as a scout was captured by civil guards stationed on the eastern side of the town. When the raiders realized the fate of the spy, they dashed to his rescue and took a hostage back with them to their camp.

Augusta was wild with fear, and rapidly made preparations for the anticipated raid. An alarm system was devised based on clangs of the bell on the courthouse, supplemented by strategically-timed gunshots. The militia was ordered to protect the jail, and companies came from not only Augusta, but also Hallowell, Gardiner, Winthrop, Readfield and Sidney. Cannon were set up to protect the approaches to the Kennebec River bridge. Women and children helped mold the necessary bullets. Martial law was in effect, and a nine o'clock curfew was established. The attack never came as the Malta settlers realized that the odds were overwhelming, but the town remained under martial law until the trial began.

The trial of the alleged Malta murderers convened on November 16, 1809, lasted eight days, and cost the state $11,000. Presiding over the trial were Supreme Judicial Court Justices Sedgwick, Sewall, Thatcher, and Parker. The courthouse was crowded every day, as curious onlookers gathered to watch the proceedings. The evidence brought against the accused by the prosecutor was overwhelming. The final arguments and the charge to the jury left little doubt about the seriousness of the crime. The public expected that the jury would find the seven defendants guilty.

Deliberating for two days, the jury paused only to inquire if they could find some defendants guilty and acquit the others. The judges responded that they were bound to find the same verdict for all seven defendants, and the jury retreated to its discussions. To the surprise of everyone, the jury then found the entire group of defendants not guilty. A great many Augusta residents were vocal in their disappointment with the result of the trial. However, this unlikely verdict had the effect of settling the dispute, and the Malta War abruptly ended.

The 1801 building served court purposes for 30 years. The activities within it changed dramatically during this period as Maine became a state with its own courts and administrative jurisdiction, and the courts themselves evolved to meet Maine's special needs. In addition, the town used the courthouse for town meetings until 1811, preferring it to the old town meetinghouse.

One of the earliest Maine legislative actions provided for terms of the Maine Supreme Judicial Court to be held annually in each county in the state. A majority of the justices were required to be present. The first term of the new Maine Supreme Judicial Court to be held in Augusta was in September, 1820, with the Court hearing cases for both Kennebec and Somerset Counties combined. All three of the newly appointed justices were in attendance: Chief Justice Prentiss Mellen and Associate Justices William Pitt Preble and Nathan Weston, Jr.

An additional term for jury trials was to be held annually by one of the justices of the Supreme Judicial Court in Kennebec County in September. Capital cases were to be tried by a majority of the court. The office of Court Reporter was established in 1820, to follow the sittings of the court

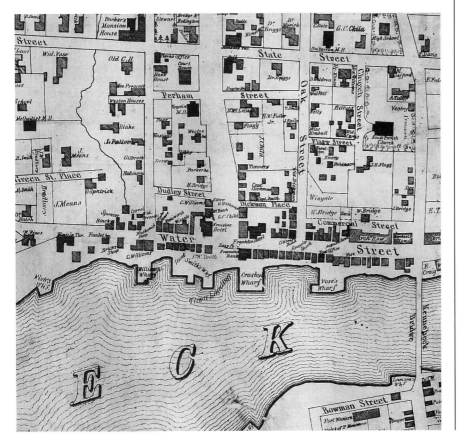

The 1801 Kennebec County Courthouse (here designated as "Old C.H.") was located on Court (now State) Street.
Maine Historical Society

and to document its proceedings. The reporter has recorded the decisions of the Supreme Judicial Court, sitting as the Law Court, since that time.

In 1822 a new Court of Common Pleas was established by the Legislature of the State of Maine. Its jurisdiction extended over the entire state and its terms were to be held by a single members of the court who travelled to each county, and received a salary instead of fees for compensation. The first judges on this court were Ezekiel Whitman of Portland, chief justice, and Samuel Smith of Wiscasset and David Perham of Bangor. Although abandoned for several years, the Court of Common Pleas was the predecessor of the present-day Superior Court.

The Kennebec Court of General Sessions of the Peace—the county court—also held its sessions in the 1801 courthouse. The Court of Sessions comprised all the justices of the peace in the county, with powers to hear and determine all matters relating to the "conservation of the peace and the punishment of offenders," to lay out highways, to superintend the house of correction, and to have charge of the financial affairs of the county. The court continued in operation until 1831, when it was replaced by three county commissioners elected by the people.

A Probate Court was established in 1799, with a judge appointed by the governor and council. The Register of Probate, first appointed in 1799, kept the records of the Probate Court. Clerks of court were provided in the 1799 legislation establishing Kennebec County.

Use of the courthouse became routine and well-scheduled. In 1822 the annual term of the Maine Supreme Judicial Court in Kennebec County was set for the fourth Tuesday in May. Terms for the Court of Common Pleas in 1822 began on the second Mondays and Tuesdays of April, August and December. The Kennebec Court of General Sessions of the Peace were set for Augusta on the second, third and last Tuesdays of each month.

Building the 1830 Kennebec County Courthouse

The Court of Sessions at the December term in 1827 voted to build a larger and more spacious building for the county public offices. A committee was appointed to arrange for construction, and it chose architect James Cochran to design the new building. Robert C. Vose was selected as the builder. Master builder Berry was chosen to supervise construction.

Granite was the material chosen for the Greek Revival building, an unusual choice because most buildings of the era were constructed from the plentiful supply of Maine wood. With Maine becoming a state and advancing rapidly in population and economic development, the builders expected that the stone would represent permanence and endurance during an exciting period of growth.

Design and construction of the Kennebec County Courthouse began before builders could get the state house underway. A good-natured race began to finish the courthouse before the state house could be completed. The courthouse was designed in 1828 and completed in 1830, while the state house was built between 1829 and 1832. While the state house was a transitional design reflecting the older Federal period, the courthouse became the first building in Maine with the temple front motif of the new Greek Revival style. Its facade was designed to include columns, portico and pediment reflecting its ancient Greek roots.

On May 29, 1830, the building's cornerstone was formally put into place by General Joseph Chandler, in the presence of a few witnesses and some workmen. An engraved plate was placed in the cornerstone with the date, the names of the Governor, the Justices of the Supreme Judicial Court and Court of Sessions and the master builder of the courthouse.

The newly-completed building faced State Street with a prominent por-

This panorama of Augusta in 1823 shows the 1801 Courthouse with its tower.
Maine Historical Society

tico or porch with a high triangular pediment above a double level gallery of columns. On the first level six plain square piers support the second floor lintels. On the second floor, six Doric columns form a colonnade. An architectural historian remarked, "An elegant cast-iron railing between the columns contributes the only light touch to alleviate the forceful severity of the building." As initially constructed, the building had no belfry and no bell. To remedy the situation, a small bell tower was initially added at the rear of the lot. Residents scornfully referred to it as the tower of a sunken church. In the late 1830s, a great square wooden belfry was added to the original building. [3]

Within the building, space was provided for the Supreme Judicial Court, which first convened in the building in 1830. At the first session of that court in the new building, Chief Justice Prentiss Mellon prefaced his charge to a jury by remarks on the convenience of the new building.

The 1830 Courthouse Comes of Age

In 1835, Joseph Sager of Gardiner was convicted of poisoning his wife. Sager was condemned by the court to be hanged. A gallows was erected near the courthouse and jail, and Sager was brought to the scaffold still protesting his innocence The minister in attendance read a manuscript that the murderer had prepared "partly by narrative and partly by exhortation." Between 8,000 and 12,000 people attended the execution. There was much jeering and throwing of stones, and "liquor flowed freely and was disposed of by the barrel." The trap that was sprung under Sager was retained for years for viewing by the public in the basement of the courthouse. [4]

In 1848 the trial of Dr. Valorous Coolidge for the murder of Edward Mathews was heard by the Supreme Judicial Court in the Kennebec County Courthouse. Coolidge was indicted for administering prussic acid (cyanide) to Mathews in a glass of brandy, and then striking Mathews with a stick of wood to avert suspicion from the poison and make it appear he had died from violence in the street. The motive appeared to be Coolidge's pressing need for money, shown by his pattern of extravagant offers of interest for short-term loans. Mathews had $1500 and a gold watch that he was loaning to Coolidge on the day of the murder. Coolidge was in possession of a large supply of cyanide, and was seen with the victim on that day. The jury found Coolidge guilty of murder in the first degree and he was sentenced to solitary confinement in the state prison and at hard labor for one year, and then to be hanged. The report of the trial noted: "Though there was apparently no motive for the commission of this monstrous act, many of the convict's necessities, it is said, can be traced to habits common to youth, and against which young men cannot be too much on their guard." [5]

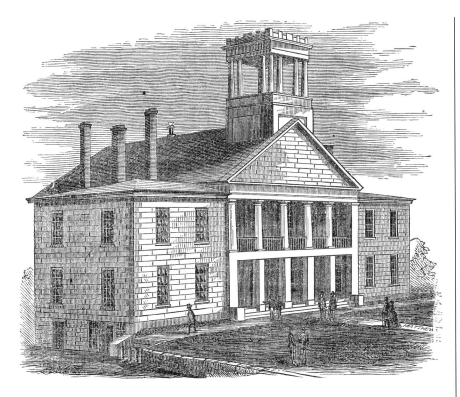

The 1830 Kennebec County Courthouse attracted artistic treatment.
Maine Historic Preservation Commission

The 1830 courthouse was enlarged in 1851 by two identical wings to flank the original building on both sides. Emphasizing the new construction, the architect designed the new wings to abut the existing Greek Revival portico; the result is an unique facade that is all on one plane. Both wings have tall, deep-set windows that march across the memorable State Street facade, adding to its strong design. Crenellations were added to the belfry and to the roofs on the two wings. At the ends of each two-story flat-roofed wing, three chimneys served the fireplaces and, later, the wood stoves inside the building. The building was also expanded in 1851 by a separate wing to the rear. Construction of this wing, on the southeast corner of the building, required the taking of a brick building which served as headquarters of the Kennebec Bank.

The interior of the oldest portion of the building was organized with a wide central hall leading to court offices on the first floor. The hall was remodeled later, with decorative tin panels added to the walls and ceiling to cover the plaster of the original building. A private rear stairway leads to the judge's rooms. Second floor space is allocated to the court, jury rooms and judges quarters.

Space was added to the south side of the courthouse in 1907 for several purposes: to house the Probate Court, the law library, and the office of the resident justice of the Supreme Judicial Court. In the Probate Court wing,

high ceilings characterize the space with transom doors and oak paneling. The Clerk of Courts' office has a prominent fireplace. The vaults have become cramped with existing documents, many of which are still parchment tied with ribbons.

The Supreme Judicial Court sat in annual sessions the Kennebec County Courthouse from 1830 to 1970. The Court sat in the courthouse for both trial and appellate work from 1830 to 1852. After 1852, with the state divided into three districts for Law Court purposes, the building in Augusta served as one of three courthouses used by the Court to hear appellate cases. Single justices were available to conduct trials until 1930, when the statewide Superior Court was established. Throughout the

1950s and 1960s the Supreme Judicial Court held three terms annually in Augusta and four in Portland, largely for appellate work. In 1995 a public-spirited individual donated a building on the east side of the Kennebec River, within sight of the 1830 courthouse, to be used as the headquarters of the Supreme Judicial Court.

The court room occupied by the Kennebec County Superior Court and, until 1970, by the Maine Supreme Judicial Court.

Jacob Sloane

[1] Nash, Charles Elventon, *The History of Augusta, Maine*, Augusta: Charles E. Nash & Son, 1904, p. 333n

[2] *Trial of David Lynn, et al., for the murder of Paul Chadwick at Malta, in Maine on Sept 8, 1809*, taken in short hand by John Merrick, Esq., Hallowell: Ezekiel Goodale, 1810

[3] Thompson, Deborah, *Maine Forms of American Architecture*, Waterville, Maine: Colby Museum of Art, 1976, pp. 98-99

[4] Nash., pp. 558-559

[5] Trial of Dr. Valorous P. Coolidge for the Murder of Edward Mathews at Waterville, Maine, *Boston Daily Times* reprint, 1848.

Anteroom for lawyers in the South Paris Courthouse.
Jacob Sloane

Oxford County

1805

T he village of Paris Hill is idyllic New England with a unique twist. Its black-shuttered white residences surround a community church and a grassy open common. But the view from the village, atop a high hill in Oxford County, is a White Mountain vista that stretches from Mt. Chocorua to Mt. Washington. It has been called the finest view in Maine.

Sitting on the rim of the hill is a small group of buildings that served as the Oxford County court and administrative center between 1805 and 1895. These buildings, built shortly after Oxford County was established, include the old courthouse, the jail, the jailer's house and the registry. When the county was set off in 1805, Paris was designated as the shire town, and the courthouse buildings were constructed in the village of Paris Hill. The original Paris Hill courthouse and county buildings built in the early 1800's that are still in existence were preserved through renovation for use as private homes and a public library/museum.

O xford County was organized in 1805 with land set off from parts of York and Cumberland Counties. A site committee was appointed of justices of the peace to review the options. The committee recommended a site in Paris Hill and it was affirmed at the August, 1805, term of the Oxford County Court of General Sessions of the Peace. The deed for the land for the county buildings was executed in October of the same year. The land, known as the county common, abutted the south side of the town common.

Until the completion of arrangements to build a courthouse in Paris Hill, the first sessions of the courts were held in the Baptist meetinghouse on the common. It was clear that the meetinghouse was not designed for

Oxford County Builds in Paris Hill

use as a courthouse. There was no raised dais for the judge, and no special boxes for either a witness or a jury. A gallery ran around three sides of the interior and a high pulpit with a sounding-board above it was provided for the minister. Most of the main floor was occupied by square pews with high sides and half doors to combat drafts in winter. Nevertheless, it was fine for the initial courthouse sessions: there was plenty of seating for the public and the building was well-supplied with natural light. Two tiers of multi-sashed windows let light into the building's two and one-half story auditorium.

For early court terms, judges usually stayed in private homes, such as that of the Hamlins facing the common. Each court day, judges and court officers were escorted across the town common to the meetinghouse in a procession headed by musicians playing the fife and drum. The court procession passed through the front door of the meetinghouse under a lofty tower with a double-tiered belfry topped by a weathervane.

Meanwhile, the process of building the county structures got under way. The first county building built on the common was the jail, constructed of sturdy hewn logs. At the midwinter term of the court in 1813, a courthouse was authorized. A committee which included attorney Albion K. Parris was appointed to select the site and design. Captain Jonathan Bemis contracted to build the courthouse.

Despite a controversy about whether Paris would share a shire town designation, the new courthouse was completed in 1815. The two-and-a-half story brick building with its front facing east toward the main street repeated the style of the churches of the period, but without a bell tower. The building's proportions were based on "bays": it was three bays wide and four bays long. Each bay contained a window on both first and second floors. The central bay on the front of the building contained the main double doors, capped by a broad, elliptical wooden fan. The courtroom was located on the second floor. Administration, court records and offices occupied the first floor. The heating for all the rooms was provided by fireplaces on the outer sides of the building, marked by tall chimneys.

Fryeburg, settled prior to Paris Hill, was an economic center exceeding Paris Hill in vitality. In 1799, a York County Judge of Probate was authorized to hold court in Fryeburg each year. After Oxford County was organized Fryeburg continued to serve as a branch location for the probate court of the county. The first building constructed for the Oxford County Registry of Deeds was built in Fryeburg in 1820. The brick building held deed documents transcribed by Daniel Webster, the orator and statesman, among others. Webster, a preceptor of Fryeburg Academy, interrupted his law studies at age 20 to come to Fryeburg on his first job, to earn money partly so his brother could continue college. He "moonlighted by copying deeds for the registrar at 25 cents each, managing two deeds per night and so earning his $2.00 weekly board, thus leaving his salary [from the Academy] clear." One local historian claimed his conduct in Fryeburg did not presage his later flamboyant reputation:

> "I've searched in vain for the source of the statements that he drank rum, played cards and showed little promise of his future remarkable

The Registry of Deeds Opens in Fryeburg

A separate Registry of Deeds building was constructed in Fryeburg in 1820.
Fryeburg Historical Society

career.... While here he ran a charge account at the local store, which totaled $33. No rum appears in the entries (though it often does in other people's charge accounts) but he bought "segars" and raisins several times.... [One] fifth of the expenditure was for writing equipment (pencil, paper, quills, ink, powder to blot ink). His letters show he was careful to be reserved with "the misses" because many were his pupils."

"Much of his spare time was spent in reading, in writing letters and verse, and conversing with a local young lawyer. Evidence shows he was energetic, diligent, prudent and successful. Deeds were copied with care. He was an able inspiring teacher. School performances during the semi-annual exhibition were so good the trustees gave him an extra $10. He began studying the government history of the U.S. He wrote and delivered an oration for the 4th of July observance (the original manuscript is at the Academy). Its closing works were the same as the last words he spoke in the Senate in 1850. Someone present at the 1802 oration was so impressed that he prophesied Webster would become the New Hampshire governor." [1]

The Registry of Deeds at Paris Hill.

Ben Conant, Paris Cape Historical Society

In 1823, the brick courthouse was expanded toward the street; the upper part of its facade was extended forward, and placed on four square piers. The first floor overhang protected people entering the building from the weather. On the second floor the wooden addition allowed county facilities to expand adjacent to the courtroom. The large center window on the new facade suggests that the middle room on the second floor was the most important, perhaps reserved as a judicial chamber.

In spite of the new courthouse, the Baptist meetinghouse on the common, with its tall belfry, retained a county function. In 1821 the County Court of Sessions appropriated $130.00 for a bell for county use, to be "swung" in the belfry of the "centre meetinghouse …in Paris." The court order encouraged the use of private funds to buy the largest bell possible. The court allowed private use of the bell "…so long as they may keep it there swung or in such other place as may be equally convenient for the use of the County in such manner and at such times only as shall not interfere with such use of said County…." [2]

To match the county appropriation, a private subscription raised $297.25 towards the purchase of a bell. The bell was ordered from the Revere foundry in Massachusetts. Cast by Joseph Revere, son of the famous Paul Revere, the 906 pound bell was first positioned, or "swung," in the meetinghouse in late 1821. It was rung for the terms of the county courts, for public and patriotic occasions, for thanksgiving, for funerals and for the services of the church.

The Paris Hill Court Complex Expands

The Law office of Albion Parris at Paris Hill.
Jacob Sloane

Adding to the growing county facilities, a new jailer's residence was constructed between the jail and the courthouse around 1822. The house was built to be part of a package to encourage recruitment of a family man as jailer. The jailer was carefully selected: he would need to be a married man, for a wife was essential to cook the prisoners' meals.

In 1823, the old wooden jail was replaced by a new two-story granite building. Its walls were sixteen inches thick and its floor was the living granite of the hill. Long granite blocks spanned the upper story, supporting a stone floor for the upper cells. Because of the solid stone floor, the upper story was reached by an exterior wooden stairway. There were four cells, two on each floor, separated by cast iron bars. Each cell could hold up to 8 prisoners at a time. The building cost the county $5,000.

The registry building was the next to be added. County records had been kept in a variety of places during the early years of Oxford County. Registry records were kept at Morse's Tavern in South Paris Village by the first register of deeds. In 1826, a building constructed for registry purposes was erected diagonally across the road from the courthouse. "The

Registry," as it is still known, contained two large fire-proof vaults in the basement to house the records of the registry of deeds and the registry of probate. Built of brick with large chimneys on both ends of the building and gables facing away from the road, the registry had an appearance not unlike a two-story private home. Four windows flanked a center entrance with double doors, and, like the courthouse, a semi-circular wooden fan topped the doorway.

The first law office in Oxford County was located across the road from the county common, where Albion K. Parris, Esq. set up shop in 1811. The small building housed Parris as a state representative, a senator from Oxford and Somerset Counties, and a Congressional representative between 1815 and 1819. Parris left for Portland when he was appointed judge of the United States District Court. He was subsequently elected Maine's second governor. The Parris Law Office was later used by Enoch Lincoln, Maine's third governor and by Congressman Rufus K. Goodenow.

Judges and lawyers lived near the county buildings. Thomas Crocker, a member of the governor's executive council, built a large brick residence about 1809 across the road from the county common. Directly in front of the courthouse but across the road from the registry building, Judge Stephen Emery (father-in-law of Hannibal Hamlin) built a large residence in 1818. Judge Emery was a judge of probate, and later the attorney general of Maine under Governor Fairfield. Judge Joseph G. Cole built a house nearby around 1845. Further up the street was the house of Rufus Goodenow, first clerk of the judicial court and later elected to Congress. Later the Goodenow house was occupied by Samuel Rawson Carter, lawyer, county register of probate, and owner/editor of the *Oxford Register*.

Court and county politics became the center of life for residents of Paris Hill. Persis Sibley Andrews, wife of Charles Andrews, state representative, speaker of the house, and congressman, was a keen observer of county political and court events. She reported in her diary entry of 18 October, 1846:

> "The past has been 'Court Week' S.J. (Supreme Judicial) Court – Judge Tenney on the bench. Portland Att'ys practise much here – eight & ten of the most talented have been here all the week – not a very interesting term, however – as most of the important business is delayed until the next sitting. Judge T is deservedly popular. The week has been rather agreeable to me… several very agreeable calls from various members of the Bar etc have served to cheer & enliven… & kept me informed of the doings of Court…." [3]

In 1894 a sensational murder trial gripped the community. Abner Thorne was put on trial for the murder of a young man involved in a county undercover operation. Thievery had been discovered at the local general store, and the Sheriff of Oxford County placed Jailer Chandler Garland and an assistant, Harrison Whitman, in a nearby building for nighttime surveillance of the store. Around 2:00 am, Garland noticed a flash of light at the store and sent Whitman to fetch store owner Newell. Upon his arrival, Newall entered the building while the other men stood on the sides of the building to intercept anyone who might attempt to leave. Behind the front door, Newell found the intruder who escaped by bludgeoning Newell. Shots rang out. Outside the building, Whitman fell, crying, "I'm shot!" The intruder got away, but Whitman died ten minutes later.

Jailer Garland suspected Thorne because of a series of prior thefts. Proceeding to his residence, they found Thorne in bed, fully dressed under the covers with a .32 calibre revolver in his hip pocket and enough stolen goods in his room to make him a suspect. Thorne was arraigned before Justice Herrick Davis, and pleaded not guilty to the charges of larceny and murder. Defense counsel James Wright asked that he be bound over for appearance at the February term of the Supreme Judicial Court. Unable to meet bail, Thorne was put in jail to await the trial.

In March, the trial of Abner Thorne began. Witnesses were unclear on the circumstances of Whitman's death. Newell, Thorne and Garland were at odds over when the shots occurred. An alleged confession by Thorne was declared inadmissible when it was discovered that it had been extracted with threats and published in the local newspaper as an actual confession. The bullets had been carelessly handled by a coroner's jury, and had been dropped as they passed through the jurors' hands.

But a firearms expert testified that Whitman died from a .32 calibre bullet. Thorne was the only person known to be in possession of a .32. Jailer Garland's wife testified that his .32 calibre revolver was in his drawer at home the night of the shooting. The defense attorney challenged the prosecutor to prove that the shooting involved malice aforethought and to show beyond a reasonable doubt that Thorne was guilty of murder.

Despite the efforts of the defense attorney, the jury found Thorne guilty of murder in the second degree. He was imprisoned at hard labor for life. When the court clerk read the sentence, the *Oxford Democrat* reported:

> "...almost everyone (including the defense attorney, James Wright) was in tears, and the judge was the most deeply affected of any. The prisoner showed no sign of emotion, and resumed his seat without a tremor. After a pause of utter silence the jailer led him back to his cell." [4]

Paris Hill, with its fine view and beautiful hill, was destined to lose the county buildings to South Paris, but it took 90 years. After the railroad arrived, South Paris became a vigorous center for business and industry. Oxford County's first railroad, the Atlantic & St. Lawrence Railroad, was located along the easy grades of the valley of the Little Androscoggin River, and avoided Paris Hill which is located on one of highest points in the county. Instead, the railroad company located its station in South Paris, a promising site about halfway between the village of Paris Hill and the Town of Norway. The station was about three miles from the court buildings in Paris Hill.

In 1848, a year after the railroad arrived, the first attempt to move the court was made by business people from the Town of Norway. Paris Hill used its considerable political clout to retain the court functions in the existing buildings. Proponents of the move were so thoroughly thwarted that it took thirty years for their next attempt.

The court buildings continued to serve the residents of Oxford County, with only a few minor mishaps and changes. In 1857 the jailer's house burned, and was replaced on the same site by a new two-story house for the use of the jailer and his wife. In 1864 the courthouse was enlarged with a 25 foot long wooden addition on the rear of the building. In addition to the sessions of the courts, social gatherings were held in the courthouse, ranging from the Union Temperance Society of the County of Oxford to a showing of a panorama of Dr. Kane's Arctic Expedition.

The Court Leaves Paris Hill for South Paris

The next effort to move the court came in 1877, when Norway's business people offered $75,000 toward construction of new court buildings and circulated a petition in all the towns of Oxford County. About 2,300 residents signed the petition. But Paris countered with a petition that had 2,700 signatures against the project. In the state legislature, the matter was referred to the Judiciary Committee which considered the matter and decided that the petitioners should withdraw their petitions. The courthouse stayed in Paris Hill.

Norway persisted in trying to move the court buildings, and by 1885 had lined up support for the move from the business people of South Paris. They proposed a location on the Norway Branch Railroad between South Paris and Norway, on a lightly serviced railroad—unfortunately inconvenient to both towns. The opposition to the relocation was fierce, and the politically adept forces of Paris Hill won the day before the legislature.

The next attempt to move the court buildings was in 1892. This time preparation was more thorough. Political support was gathered prior to petitioning the legislature for the change. The county commissioners and the legislature were carefully approached. Proponents of the move got help from Albert Andrews of Norway, known throughout the county as a dramatic spokesman. Speaking before the county commissioners, Andrews laid out the advantages of the move: 1) the county buildings in Paris Hill were deteriorating and needed expensive repairs; 2) county records were not being protected by up-to-date methods and thus were subject to destruction; 3) the jail had been condemned by the Maine Jail Commissioners; 4) the county did not own the land where the buildings stood; and 5) the probate courtroom was not suitable for the demands on it. The proponents asked the county commissioners to select an appropriate site near the South Paris railroad station, to hold a public hearing on the proposal, and to submit the proposition to a vote throughout the county. The commissioners agreed to the requests.

At the public hearing, heated arguments on both sides of the issue were heard. Representatives of both Norway and Paris Hill heaped allegations of misconduct and spreading of misinformation about each other. Both sides made light of the state jail inspection. The county commissioners, hearing the arguments, voted their agreement with the plan to move the court buildings, but declared a referendum on the proposal.

With the commissioners' decision, fund raising and the campaign for votes began. Norway and South Paris business people guaranteed that the buildings and property would not cost over $30,000, and Paris Hill representatives maintained that the old buildings could be repaired for $1,450. Those in favor of moving the court buildings solicited votes from the town residents in Norway and South Paris; those against the move concentrated on rural voters. Neighborhood residents as well as farmers were canvassed for their votes.

The county commissioners set up the vote in two parts: 1) whether there should be new buildings constructed at a cost of $30,000 or less; and 2) whether the county should issue bonds to pay for the construction. Voters marked either "yes" or "no" on the double-headed question. The voting was heavy. This time the proponents of the new court buildings were the winners by a vote of 3,297 "yes" votes to 3,147 voting "no." There were only six negative votes in the Town of Norway. Paris Hill residents sued, claiming fraud in the voting in Norway and other places. They also claimed that the simple "yes" or "no" vote on a complex questions was unorthodox. The Law Court considered the arguments. In January, 1895, it rendered its decision that the election was not fraudulent and that the unorthodox method of requesting a simple vote was allowable.

Construction of the new county buildings began right away on a site selected by the county commissioners across the street from the railroad station in South Paris. The architect was G.M. Coombs of Lewiston, and the construction contract was awarded to Joseph Philbrook of Lisbon. The court buildings included a jail and sheriff's residence, and a carriage house. The court complex was located across the road from the railroad station, so that judges and lawyers from Portland and elsewhere would be able to get to the new buildings rapidly with the new mode of transportation. A railroad freight shed was removed to make the county buildings more visible.

The cornerstone, laid on a "perfect" day in July, was the center of a celebration described on July 9, 1895 in the *Oxford Democrat:*

> "A large delegation of Masons from near and far was on hand for the ceremonies. At 11:30 A.M. the procession was formed in Market Square. …The Grand Officers marched to the site and assembled at the northeast corner of the building, around the corner stone, which was supported by a temporary derrick. The rest of the Masons gathered around in as favorable situations as possible, while hundreds of spectators clustered around the open cellar and took stations upon the hillside, to witness the impressive ceremonies of laying the corner stone in the usual form…."

The cornerstone surrounded a box containing an 1895 calendar for the Supreme Judicial Court, an official register of Oxford County, a court directory and county officers, copies of the *Oxford County Advertiser,* the *Oxford Democrat,* the *Eastern Argus,* and the *Masonic Journal,* and United States coins of 1895. [5]

The Grand Lodge of Maine presided over the cornerstone placement in

The South Paris court room mural of Justinian, by Harry Cochrane.   Jacob Sloane

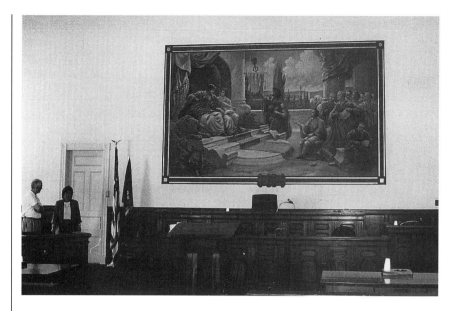

1895, following the tradition originated in the middle ages by associations of builders and masons. Commenting on this history in 1895, the Honorable James S. Wright said:

> "It has long been the custom of the [Masonic] order to be present and assist in laying the cornerstone of important public buildings…not to use the trowel in spreading the cement that is to unite the several parts of this building into one great mass and structure, but to use it in …spreading the cement of brotherly love and affection…" [6]

The buildings were completed in late 1895, and the county records arrived from the old buildings at Paris Hill in December. The three-and-one-half story brick and stone building featured a bracketed cornice, a hipped roof and a domed cupola. In the courtroom, Maine artist Harry Cochrane painted a large mural behind the judge's bench. The structure was inaugurated during the regular session of the county commissioners in December, 1895.

Famous Cases in Oxford County

One of the cases to be heard in the new courthouse involved the death of Edgar Radcliffe in 1907. A dynamite shack in a molybdenite mine exploded on a summer night, killing Radcliffe. Wallace Everett, who reported the death, had found Radcliffe intruding in a mine shack and placed a plank against the door so that Radcliffe could not escape. Shortly thereafter, the shack exploded, killing Radcliffe. [7]

Under the direction of Charles Barnes, the Oxford County Attorney, Radcliffe's body was closely examined and a deep cut was found in his neck. Barnes suspected Everett may have had something to do with the death. Barnes knew that Everett was a suspect when a well had been dynamited a few years earlier, and Radcliffe had testified against Everett at the time. Although Everett was acquitted for lack of evidence, he might have a motive for killing Radcliffe.

A detailed autopsy was performed. Death was declared to be due to the neck injury and not from the explosion. Everett was placed behind bars. Insurance policies on Radcliffe's life were found, taken out two months before his death, with premiums paid by Everett; the only beneficiary was Everett. At the trial, Everett testified that he paid the premiums because Radcliffe had no money to pay them, and that Radcliffe's mother needed money if her son died. The judge charged the jury that they must find the defendant guilty of murder and did not offer them the alternative of manslaughter. The jury deliberated for 25 hours but could not agree on a verdict of murder. A second trial was scheduled.

At the trial in early 1908, new witnesses took the stand. The fellow employees who found the bloody knife recalled that Everett picked it up despite their warning not to touch the evidence. Everett had wondered aloud what Radcliffe could have been doing with it.

Radcliffe's mother testified that she had never heard about the insurance policies, but that Everett had offered her $25 to leave town and take her son with her. Everett was quoted as saying that revenge was his and that he'd "get" the fellow who got him arrested. Others also testified that he was seeking revenge against Radcliffe for his testimony during the well dynamiting investigation. After four days of court testimony, the jury deliberated for four hours, and found Everett guilty of manslaughter. Everett was sentenced to thirteen years in the state prison.

A second notorious murder trial occurred in 1937. Paul Dwyer, aged 19, was found asleep in a car in New Jersey with two bodies in the trunk. He denied, then confessed, to murder of Doctor and Mrs. Littlefield and was extradited to Oxford County, the site of the murders. At the arraignment he pleaded innocent. After three days of trial, he changed his plea to guilty. He was sentenced to hard labor for life. [8]

Three months after he was sentenced, Dwyer wrote a statement of the course of events that he said he was terrified to reveal at trial. He said he had confessed to the murders because of threats to his life and to his mother and girlfriend. He named Francis Carroll, a former deputy sheriff of Oxford County, as the murderer.

Carroll was indicted for murder. Dwyer appeared as the star witness, telling the story of his love for Carroll's daughter, and of her letters accusing her father of sexually molesting her. Dwyer testified that he had told Dr. Littlefield of Carroll's incestuous relationship with his daughter and that Carroll claimed that she was pregnant with Dwyer's child. Doctor Littlefield was summoned to examine her at Dwyer's house. Unfortunately, Carroll was present when Littlefield and Dwyer arrived. Littlefield said Carroll should be run out of town, whereupon Carroll attacked Littlefield and killed him. Carroll threatened Dwyer that he would be next if he did not give him his daughter's letters. Terrified, Dwyer complied, and was ordered by Carroll to place the doctor's body in the car.

Dwyer feared for his life and did not return to his house to see Carroll. Instead he went to see Mrs. Littlefield, and told her of her husband's death. He took her to Carroll's house. Carroll came out to drive away, and Dwyer followed him. He succeeded in stopping Carroll, who got out of his car. Someone produced a gun, and Carroll used it to hit Mrs. Littlefield over the head. Carroll told Dwyer to keep driving, and during the next few miles, Carroll strangled Mrs. Littlefield. Dwyer's mind went blank and he drove south—anywhere to get away from Carroll. He stopped in New Jersey to sleep.

After ten days of trial, the jury deliberated for five and a half hours, and found Carroll guilty. Carroll was sentenced to prison for life. Twelve years later, Carroll charged that he had been convicted without due process, and a public hearing convened by Justice Albert Beliveau resulted in a grant of habeas corpus to Carroll. He was later pardoned by Governor Payne in 1950. Dwyer, however, served twenty-one years of his sentence before obtaining parole in 1959 for the crime to which he had confessed but for which he was never tried.

The Court Expands to Rumford

In 1915 legislation was passed authorizing the town of Rumford to construct a public building "to be used by the county of Oxford for court purposes and by said town for municipal purposes." It provided for a courtroom, jury room and judges' chambers, intended to be used by the Supreme Judicial Court for one or more of its sittings in Oxford County. The movement which led to this legislation was inaugurated by the local chamber of commerce, which formed a committee to examine the issue. At the time the town and county were paying $3,000 a year for office space, court facilities and jail space. Judge Spear of the Maine Supreme Judicial Court was heard to say "I will never come to Rumford again until adequate provisions are made for court facilities."

Costs of constructing the building were shared by Rumford, which voted to pay $45,000 at a special town meeting, and Oxford County, which paid $25,000. The building was designed in colonial revival style, with columns gracing the main entrance and a cupola which housed the town clock. A great mural was painted by Harry Cochrane behind the judge's

bench in the courtroom on the main floor. The mural depicts Moses coming down from Mount Sinai carrying the Ten Commandments.

The set of buildings completed by 1896 served Oxford County for nearly 75 years without substantial change. The South Paris Courthouse, Jail and Carriage House were from the beginning the focus of county activities. In more recent years, the original buildings have seen several changes. In 1965, the old carriage house was torn down to make room for a new District Court building. In 1979 a new sheriff's department and jail was built at the rear of the property. In 1983 the Registry of Deeds was expanded to make room for additional research space for attorneys, title searchers and the public, along with added shelves for storage of documents. The offices of the District Attorney, the County Commissioners and others were renovated in 1983. Security measures have been installed around the judges chambers. In 1986 an elevator was added to comply with state regulations regarding access to all people. The cost of the new elevator is noted in *Paris, Maine: The Second Hundred Years, 1893-1993*, as $108,000—"...more than four times the amount paid for the original courthouse and grounds." [9]

Today, the court buildings stand remarkably unchanged after 100 years

*Modernizing the
Court Buildings*

of use. A minor change was the removal of the white balustrade around the edge of the roof during World War II. The courtroom has been restored, including the large mural of Justinian delivering the code of justice covering the wall behind the bench, painted by Harry Cochrane. The witness and jury boxes have dark wood panels dating from the original construction. Behind the courtroom, the law library retains a large fireplace and high ceiling, with tiers of elaborately framed pictures of Oxford County judges lining the walls.

In 1995, bagpipes, kilts, top hats and white gloves were evident at the July reenactment of laying the cornerstone of Oxford County's courthouse 100 years ago. Members of the Paris Masonic Lodge #94, Blue Lodge of Masonry, led the ceremonies—some in kilts and others in full regalia of dark suits, gold chains, white gloves, and Masonic aprons. The leader of the ceremony, Harland Hitchings, Grand Master of Masons in Maine, wore a silk top hat, and Chaplain Edward Fenderson carried his bible on a table supported by a cord round his neck and pressed against his belly. The ceremony was held on the lawn in front of the Oxford County Courthouse in South Paris. Frederick Kennard and Steven Merrill, County Commissioners, welcomed the guests and thanked them for the interest in the history of the building and for their support of county services. With the great arches of the courthouse entry above him, Mr. Hitchings recounted the history of the building.

---

[1] *Fryeburg Webster Centennial, celebrating the coming of Daniel Webster to Fryeburg 100 years ago*, Fryeburg, A.F. Lewis, 1902

[2] Dibner, Martin, *Portrait of Paris Hill*, Paris Hill Press, 1990, p. 78

[3] *Id.*, p. 113

[4] *Id.*, p. 131-134

[5] Paris Cape Historical Society, *Paris, Maine: The Second Hundred Years, 1893-1993*, Camden, Maine: Penobscot Press, 1994, pp. 4-5

[6] *Oxford Democrat*, July 9, 1895

[7] Dibner, p. 134–138

[8] *Id.*, pp. 139–145

[9] Paris Cape Historical Society, *Paris, Maine: The Second Hundred Years, 1893-1993*, Penobscot Press, 1994, pp. 7-8

NINE

Somerset County

1809

Somerset County was formed on March 1, 1809 from the northern part of Kennebec County, largely through the legislative efforts of John Ware, then a Maine representative to the General Court in Boston. The new county included eighty-three unorganized townships, twenty-six towns and seven organized plantations within its boundaries. The county was allowed two sessions of the Courts of Common Pleas and General Sessions. All matters for the Supreme Judicial Court would be heard in Augusta.

The shire town designation was settled on Norridgewock, one of the oldest settlements and the most important town in the new county. The choice of shire town was made after canvassing the merits of towns competing for the title: Anson, Canaan and Norridgewock. As a principal founder of the town, John Ware made strenuous efforts to have the courts sit in Norridgewock. He offered to donate a building for the county's use if the county administrators chose to locate the shire town there. His donation of space for the court was for "as long as they choose to occupy the building." Ware said that he would agree that the other contenders for shire town should have all that belonged to them. Asked what that was, he replied, "the gallows rope to Anson, and whipping post to Canaan." [1]

The first sessions of the court in 1809 were held in the town meeting-house while the building donated by Ware on the banks of the Kennebec was being converted from a residence to a courthouse. When it was completed it housed most of the county functions and appointees. Norridgewock residents staffed the courthouse positions. William Jones was appointed Judge of Probate and Clerk of the Courts, Richard Sawtelle as Sheriff, John L. Prescott and Samuel Searle as Deputy Sheriffs, John

Norridgewock as
Shire Town

ever, were somewhat rare. Nevertheless, the county remained ready to house and tend suspects and criminals. A residence for the keeper of the jail and his family was built of brick in 1826. The new building extended over the attic story of the jail to which it was attached. One of the rooms in the building served as the jailer's office.

The jail was soon occupied by suspects in two of the early murder cases in Somerset County. The earliest capital trial was in 1827, when Gridley T. Parkman of St. Albans was tried for poisoning his wife. He was acquitted. Adaline Taylor of Mercer was tried in 1828 for the murder of her infant son, Warren. She, too, was acquitted. Nearly twenty years later, in 1845, John Ferguson of Haverhill was tried for the murder of Jefferson Spalding. Ferguson was also acquitted.

The 1820 courthouse was refurbished and updated in 1847, using a county appropriation of $296.57 A new slate roof was added.

The County Moves to Skowhegan

In the latter half of the century, Skowhegan rapidly grew to become economically more powerful than Norridgewock. Skowhegan residents and business men began to look at the possibilities of moving the county seat to their town. Using their new-found power, the Skowhegan state representative was able to convince the legislature to favor his town with a redesignation as shire town.

On Feb. 15, 1872, Governor Perham approved "An act to change the place of holding the Supreme Judicial Court in the County of Somerset, and to change the shire town of Somerset County." The legislative act contained three sections:

- The first section of the act provided that the several terms of the Supreme Judicial Court "now required to be holden in Norridgewock, shall after the first day of March 1872, be holden in Skowhegan."
- The second section required the county commissioners, within five years from the date of passing the act, to build a courthouse in Skowhegan, "suitable for the accommodation of the courts and offices of said County, and to procure a loan of money for that purpose and assess taxes for the payment of the same."
- The third section specified that the town of Skowhegan, by the first day of March, "provide suitable room and other accommodations for said court and officers to the acceptance of the majority of the county commissioners." [6]

After the passage of this act there were only 14 days for the town to find accommodations for the court before its first term. Residents of Skowhegan immediately began to reconstruct two stores in the Williams building at the south corner of Elm and Madison streets into offices, along with

Norridgewock thought that moving its courthouse was as likely as a locomotive flying.
Maine Historic Preservation Commission

two brick vaults to accommodate county records. At the same time, they moved to transform Coburn Hall, a private meeting space, into a court-room.

The time was short and when the first day of March arrived, attorneys representing Norridgewock claimed that the vaults prepared were not in suitable condition to receive and safely preserve the records and that the law had not been complied with. By the provisions of the act, remaining issues were left to a majority of the commissioners and their decision was final. As expected, the commissioners decided that their preparations had been adequate.

Despite the commissioners' decisions, residents of Norridgewock continued to press for relief. The Honorable Stephen D. Lindsey and John J. Webster, Esq. prepared a petition for a writ of prohibition against the County Commissioners. Honorable Joseph Baker of Augusta, and Honorable David D. Stewart represented the county commissioners. The petition was brought in the name of Sylvester Walton who was state's attorney for the County of Somerset.

The Norridgewock petition was heard in the March term of the Supreme Judicial Court on the third Tuesday of March, 1872, with the Honorable Edward Kent of Bangor presiding. The county commissioners' counsel filed a motion to dismiss, a motion to remove the temporary prohibition that had previously been entered and an answer. After a hearing by Justice Kent, the petition was dismissed. Exceptions were filed and allowed. Immediately after this decision, Kent adjourned court to convene at Skowhegan on the fourth day of the term.

The exceptions were heard by the Law Court at which John H. Webster, Esq., argued for the petitioners and Honorable David D. Stewart for the respondents. The court sustained the ruling of Justice Kent, thereby deciding that Skowhegan was the lawful shire town of the county of Somerset.

The New Somerset County Courthouse

Yet the designation of shire town seemed tenuous, because Skowhegan had not made arrangements for a permanent courthouse. The issue divided the county politically for the next few years. Norridgewock supporters nominated candidates for county commissioner at the next election, and nearly all of them were elected. They were determined to restore the shire town designation to Norridgewock.

In a dramatic last-minute action, before the newly elected officials could act, ex-Governor Coburn, a Somerset County resident, offered to donate a sufficient amount of money to build the county a courthouse at Skowhegan. The offer was immediately accepted by the county commissioners. As the shire town designation passed to Skowhegan, according to one historian, "Norridgewock, much to her sorrow, was bereft of her favorite child." [7]

Plans for the new building were drawn under the guidance of architect C.F. Douglas. In 1873 construction of the courthouse on the corner of Court and High Streets began, under the supervision of John Russell, S. B. Walton and E. G. Pratt, the county commissioners. Foster & Dutton were the builders.

At the formal dedication on Feb. 5, 1874, Ex-Governor Coburn explained in simple terms his purpose in offering "to build a suitable building for a courthouse. I have been wanting for some time to do something for the citizens of the county." At the exercises in Coburn Hall, later in the day, one of the several speakers, Honorable J. C. Talbot of Machias,

The elegant new courthouse in Skowhegan was placed in use in 1874.
Somerset County Commissioners

described the "whole secret" of Governor Coburn's life: "he proposes and then sets about to carry out the purpose. As long as this beautiful court-house stands, it shall stand as a monument to an honest and noble-hearted man." A life-like bust of Governor Abner Coburn has stood since 1875 in the Somerset County Courthouse. [8]

In the county commissioners' records for 1876 were the following expenditures:

For jurors	$3,800
Sheriffs bills	1,200
Jailer for support of prisoners	500
Constables for serving	125
Clerk of Courts compensation	275
County Commissioners' bills	675
For Judge of Probate salary	250
Register of Probate salary	400
County Treasurer, compensation	275
Books, stationery, blanks and printing	500
Fuel	300
Fencing Courthouse	100
Record damages and cost	80
Costs of committees and posting notices	200
Bills of costs in criminal cases	2,000
Repair of roads in unincorporated places	100
Furnishing Courthouse	100
TOTAL	$14,000

Similar expenditures for furnishing and upgrading the courthouse occur over several years in the commissioners records. [9]

Updating the Courthouse

In time, the business of the county outgrew the 1874 Skowhegan Court-house, and in 1904 the building was enlarged and remodeled under the supervision of John Metcalf, M.L Merrill and L. C. Williams, county commissioners. John Calvin Stevens was architect and R. J. Noyes, the builder. The existing site, purchased from Rev. Samuel Bickford and L. L. Morrison, was enlarged by buying land on the east side from the Morrison family. The building's original chimneys and roof outline were considerably altered from the 1875 design. In addition, the landmark cupola with its tall flag staff was removed.

In 1937, as the accumulating volume of records and documents once again outgrew the capacity of the filing rooms, it again became necessary to enlarge the courthouse. The remainder of the Morrison lot was purchased and in 1938 a large fireproof annex was built, with corridors connecting it with the courthouse. The Registry of Deeds and grand jury rooms occupied the first floor of the annex, with the law library, district attorney's room and a hearing room on the second floor. The newly vacant space on the first floor of the old building was taken over by the Maine State Police Detachment until the completion of the police barracks in 1950. After 1950, it was used for additional filing space by the Probate Court and Clerk of Courts. The space on the second floor was converted into a jury room and consultation rooms. All construction was under the supervision of Lee W. Foss, Simeon J. Whitney and Henry Crowell, County Commissioners. Bunker & Savage were the architects and H.P Cummings Construction Company, the builder.

When the municipal court system was changed to state-run district courts in August, 1965, the east end of the courthouse was remodeled to provide a site for the district courtroom and attendant offices. In the early part of the 1970s, the entire courthouse was renovated with a new heating system, carpeting and modern lighting.

In January, 1975, the county attorney system was changed by the state to the district attorney system. In place of one county attorney serving Somerset County, the new system had a District Attorney and several assistants serving a district made up of Somerset and Kennebec Counties. In July of 1976, administration of the Superior Court was taken over by the state. All court personnel became state employees and the position of Clerk of Courts was removed from the county ballot.

Social programs were gradually added to the county budget and were housed in the county courthouse building. These included food stamps, County Soil Conservation, extension service, Association for Retarded Children, Mental Health Association, Northern Kennebec Regional Planning Commission, Kennebec Regional Health Agency, Northern Kennebec Community Action Council, Central Senior Citizens, Human Relations and Skowhegan Area Industrial Development Commission.

In 1986 the District Court moved from the courthouse into separate quarters. The Somerset County Courthouse was added to the National Register of Historic Places. Old county buildings in Norridgewock still stand in a quiet location along the Kennebec—the Probate Court building (extensively altered), the Clerk of Courts building, the building John Ware provided for the first county courthouse, the Danforth Tavern and the jailer's residence. Unfortunately, the 1820 courthouse and the jail are missing from this group of early county buildings. The old jail at Norridgewock was used until 1895 when property opposite the Skowhegan courthouse was purchased for construction of the present jail. Granite from the jail was used in part for tombs in the nearby old cemetery. The old 1820 courthouse in Norridgewock. was sold and became a coat factory. It burned completely in 1890.

1 Hanson, J.W., *History of the Old Towns of Norridgewock and Canaan, comprising Norridgewock, Canaan, Starks, Skowhegan and Bloomfield from their early settlement to the year 1849*, Boston: published by the Author, 1849, p. 346n.

2 *Id.*, p. 346

3 Allen, William, *The History of Norridgewock*, Norridgewock: Edward Peet, 1849, pp.138-139

4 Hanson, J.W., *History of the Old Towns of Norridgewock and Canaan, comprising Norridgewock, Canaan, Starks, Skowhegan and Bloomfield from their early settlement to the year 1849*, Boston: published by the Author, 1849, p. 346

5 Coburn, Louise H., and Henrietta Wood, "Taverns and Stage Coaches of Skowhegan & Norridgewock," in Daughters of the American Revolution, Maine Chapter, *Trails and Taverns of Maine*, 1932, Vol. 2, p. 120

6 Coburn, Louise H., *Skowhegan on the Kennebec*, 1941, Skowhegan: Independent-Reporter Press, 1941, pp. 772-773

7 Wood, Henrietta D., Early Days of Norridgewock, Skowhegan: The Skowhegan Press, 1933, Reprinted, 1941, p. 47

8 Coburn, pp. 966-967

9 Records of the Somerset County Commissioners, Vol. 6, p. 133, 1876

TEN

Penobscot County
1816

Three courthouses have been constructed in Bangor to serve Penobscot County. The rapid growth of the county and its logging industries required construction of two substantial courthouses in the nineteenth century and one in the twentieth. The last to be constructed still stands proudly on the site of one of its predecessors.

The first courthouse in Penobscot County was built on speculation, several years before the county was incorporated and on the probability that a courthouse would soon be needed. According to a 100-year-old account in the *Maine Historical Magazine*, the first Penobscot County courthouse was built "as a house of Public Worship, and for a courthouse when wanted." The builders were "an association of public spirited gentlemen," who formed the Bangor Courthouse Corporation. The group included Capt. Charles Hammond who arrived in Bangor in 1805 and became a leading citizen, store owner and real estate developer, from whom the group purchased a half-acre lot bounded by Columbia, Hammond and Main Streets. [1]

The location of the courthouse on the west side of the Kenduskeag Stream was apparently no accident. One explanation is found in a story told in 1870 by an elderly early resident:

> "Two well known citizens, A and B, purchased together a pipe [barrel] of brandy, which by mutual consent was stored in the cellar of B. When they came to divide it, A charged B with having watered it, for which B pulled the nose of A, and C interfering as the friend of B, called A a rascal, whereupon A sued C for defamation of character, and recovered some five hundred dollars damage, which … C had to

The First Penobscot County Courthouse

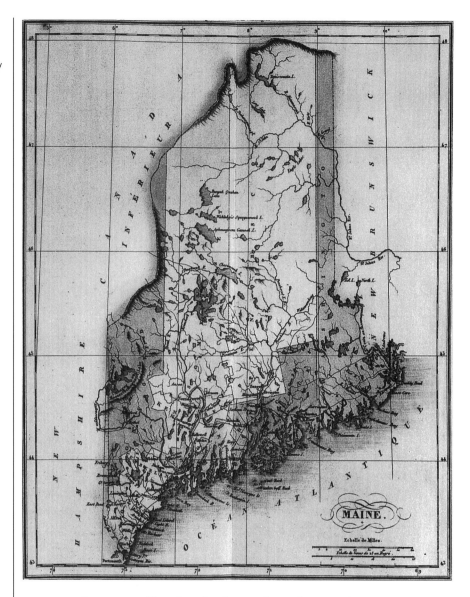

pay. A, however, offered to discharge the judgment if C would apologize, but blood was up and loss before dishonor the motto, and the offer was refused. A sort of truce was afterwards patched up, but it was only an armed neutrality. The store of B was on the east side of the Kenduskeag, and that of A was on the west side. From this day forward every effort was made by A and his friends to build up the west side and depress the east side. Neither time, nor money, nor arguments, nor persuasions were spared to accomplish the end. The courthouse, the town house, the jail, the work house, hotels, stores and dwelling houses all went up on the west side under this influence, nay, even the grave yards were on the west side...."[2]

The new building was built to face Market Square near the corner of Main and Hammond Streets. A crew headed by Rowland Tyler, a local carpenter, began construction in 1812 and work was completed in 1813. It was put to immediate use for town meeting and the religious worship services of the First Congregational Society. Architecturally, it was a handsome structure—an early design in Greek Revival style. The building was 40 feet wide and 60 feet deep, and three stories high with a gabled attic and a cupola above the front entrance. Tall wooden pilasters emulated Grecian columns on the facade of the building, both at the corners and between the sets of windows. Above the double front doors were two tiers of palladian windows with shutters, and in the uppermost gable a crescent-shaped window ranged between the tops of two pilasters. A circular space for a clock was located in the squared-off portion of the cupola, which was topped by a railing with banisters and decorated newel posts. A hexagonal belfry and peaked roof completed the cupola's composition.

Sitting on its hill, the new building was approached by three flights of

The 1813 Penobscot County Courthouse in Bangor.

steps through a steep, terraced lawn, enclosed by a fence. Wooden posts stood at the corner of Hammond and Main Streets through which a pathway led to the building. A visitor entering through the front doors would find that the principal meeting room was on the second floor, in the custom of the time. Offices for clergy or court officers were on the first floor, under the grand room upstairs. The meeting hall, a two-story space with a balcony—a "gallery" on three sides of the room, was designed from the beginning by the corporation to become a courtroom at a later date. Sunday school classes gathered in the gallery which extended around three sides of the courthouse, then the only place of worship in the town.

Before the building was put to use as the courthouse for Penobscot County, it was "occupied" in a very different sense by the British in the War of 1812. Bangor's vulnerability in the war was extremely significant to residents, who lived through moments when the whole town might be destroyed. Looking back after the war, a resident remembered the "…battle and the taking of Bangor by the British troops, the burning of the shipping and the fright of the women." Another resident remembered that he shed "…the first and last blood for my country, being knocked over by a kick from a horse, in front of a British regiment." [3]

British troops arrived in the defenseless town on September 2, 1814, intending to occupy all of Maine from the Penobscot River to the north. They commandeered the courthouse building as a barracks for the soldiers. The British didn't stay long in Bangor—two days during which Bangor was forced to give a bond to assure the delivery of certain vessels, then under construction, to the British at Castine. Because of the town's bond, the courthouse and most of the town emerged intact.

After the war, in 1815, when the affairs of the town were once more back to normal, Benjamin Bussey, who owned land around Bangor, gave the First Congregational Society a bell, cast by Paul Revere, which was placed in the belfry of the courthouse.

Penobscot County was formed by the General Court in Boston in 1816, before Maine was officially separated from Massachusetts. The first term of court held in Bangor was the Court of Common Pleas on July 2, 1816. In March of 1817, the proprietors of the courthouse building voted to sell it to the county, and the Court of Sessions accepted the sale in principle at the March term in that year. Negotiations for the sale were not completed, however, and during the July term of the court, the proprietors proposed "to lease the courthouse for ten years, free of expense, reserving the use of said House for Public worship during the term aforesaid." Accompanying the proposal was an offer for land as a site for the county jail on the west side of Kenduskeag Stream and north of Hammond Street. The court officers accepted the proposal willingly. [4]

Over the next few years, court activities expanded. By 1822 the Congregationalists moved from the courthouse into their own church building. During this period, the proprietors of the courthouse who had received no financial return from their land used by the county, subdivided the site into building lots. Promoting these building sites for their proximity to the courthouse, the proprietors were able to profit from their initial investment in the land and building. As they sold off lots facing Main Street over the next few years, the courthouse lot was shaved from a half-acre lot to one that was forty by sixty feet. In 1825, when all the lots were sold, the proprietors authorized their treasurer to deed the courthouse and its lot to Penobscot County for $2,000. A ten-foot passageway to Main Street was retained in the deed, subject to its being "arched over" as a condition of the deed. The court accepted and the first courthouse became county property.

The Maine Supreme Judicial Court held its first term in Bangor in this building in October, 1821. All of the newly-appointed members of the Court—Chief Justice Prentiss Mellen and Associate Justices William Pitt Preble and Nathan Weston, Jr.—were present for the session. The court at that time performed both its trial and appellate functions when sitting in the courthouse in Bangor.

By the 1830s, Bangor was in the midst of a lumber boom, growing at such a rapid rate that the population tripled in four years. The boom brought country loggers and deep water sailors and boat builders to Bangor, with the accompanying taverns, grog shops, lodging houses and brothels. The dozen lawyers available in 1825 quickly grew to forty. The townsfolk agitated for more law enforcement—a more up-to-date and fire-proof courthouse as well as a separate building for town law enforcement officials, town records and offices. In February, 1831, the county appointed a committee to receive proposals for a brick courthouse. A site for the building was found on Hammond Street. Anticipating the successful conclusion of the work of the committee, the Court of Sessions authorized the sale of the old courthouse to the town of Bangor for use as a town hall. The sale price was $3,260.00. The terms of the deed reserved the use of the building for court purposes until the new building was ready for use.

Planning for the new building proceeded under the direction of a building committee (Thomas Hill, John Godfrey and Thornton McGaw), authorized to procure "a quantity of seasoned boards for the courthouse which is to be erected next year," for no more than $1000, and to assemble the 100,000 bricks "already purchased of J. and J. Hellier." Charles H. Pond, the builder-architect selected for the work, submitted his plans and specifications for the building in December of 1831. The contract for the

The Second Courthouse

building went to Pond, along with Otis Small, mason, and John Brown, housewright. [5]

An article in the *Penobscot Journal* of April 10, 1832, describes the interest that the new building generated in the town, along with a critique of its proposed placement and architecture:

"The new courthouse will be situated for convenience, but badly for show. This is the more to be regretted as, if executed according to the plans we have seen, it will be one of the most ornamental buildings in the place. With one or two exceptionable defects, which could not well be avoided, its external proportions and design are accurate, and its interior finishing will be unusually neat. It will be the handsomest courthouse in the State." [6]

Construction of the building began in 1832 and it was completed and occupied in 1833. Mirroring the first courthouse, the new building was also built in the Greek Revival style that was sweeping the country in these years. It was two and a half stories high, with a simple second floor courtroom. There were no balconies in the courtroom. Court offices, including those for the judges, were on the first floor. The new building retained the symmetry of the old building but had no pilasters or palladian windows decorating its facade. Directly above the front entrance was a cupola and bell tower, topped by a small domed roof, a lightning rod and

The 1833 Penobscot County Courthouse in Bangor.

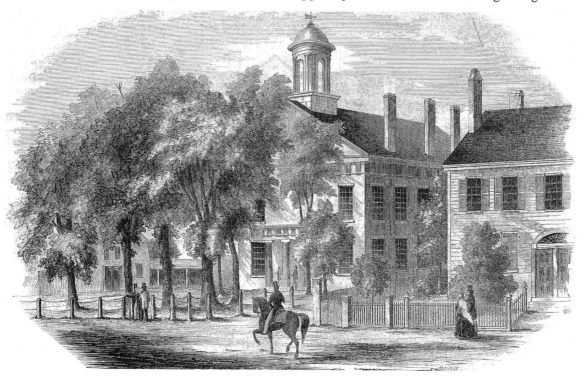

an arrow-shaped weathervane. The entrance was grand: a portico supported by simple Doric columns to form a porch for citizens entering or leaving the building. The new building sat behind a small fenced front lawn, situated close to the street for easy access from the community. Its crowning feature was that it was made of brick and stone, and was thus less vulnerable to fire; native granite served as a basic foundation and embellished the brick at the windows and doors in the exterior brick walls.

The new courthouse was constructed just in time for the land speculation boom which reached its height in Maine between 1834 and 1836. In these two years, land that sold for a few cents an acre in the morning might bring a price of several dollars in the afternoon. Townships and lots were sold repeatedly "sight unseen." Brokers' offices were established and a courier line was set up to bring the news to and from Boston. The town was full of speculators and gamblers. It was said that two paupers who had escaped from the Bangor almshouse and were caught early the next morning had made $1800 each by speculating in timber lands."

The boom subsided when people began looking more closely at the lands they purchased and the network of dishonest surveys and swindlers fell apart. The court became a beehive of activity in these years—both as the site of recording of deeds and as the main source of remedies for the dishonest activities.

Bangor's fame in handling timber reached its peak in 1850, when it was probably the leading lumber port in the world. Lumber production continued through the years of the Civil War, but slowed with the depletion of the north woods' stock of white pine. When other woods became commercially useful, Bangor witnessed a second boom in timber production.

After 1850, the population and growth of Penobscot County led to a discussion of a new building to replace the aging and inadequate 1833 structure, but resulted only in a modest wing being added to the building. The Bangor Daily Whig and Courier of October 19, 1859, describes the newly constructed addition:

> The improvements at the courthouse in this city, by which the building is extended about 22 feet on the rear, are now nearly completed and the new part will be in readiness for occupation in the course of a couple of weeks. The extension affords two large and handsome rooms on each floor, one upon each side of the central hall leading from front to rear and also two rooms in the second story, reached by a flight of stairs in the new part. …

The new extension provided room for the probate office and for the meetings of the county commissioners on the first floor, ". . .those officers

Expanding the Courthouse

having had their official quarters heretofore, in common with the Grand Juries, in a sort of dog-kennel in the attic excellently well calculated to bake their honorable bodies in the summer, and either to freeze or suffocate them in the winter as they might prefer."

On the second floor was a room for the grand jury, "light, pleasant and well ventilated ", and an ante-room "...for the use of ladies who may be obliged to attend court, either as parties or witnesses," in a location which did not require ladies to climb or descend the stairs just prior to testifying. Total cost of the new rooms was between $2500 and $3000, including the improvement of warming the whole building with a new steam heat "apparatus." [7]

The courthouse was used for sessions of the Supreme Judicial Court serving Penobscot County until 1851, when a court reorganization act divided the state into three districts for appellate or "law" court sessions. The Eastern District was focused on Bangor, and the courthouse became the place for holding the terms in June and July of each year.

The building was known for its judges. Probate Judge John Edwards Godfrey, commenting on his reputation while writing to his sons at mid-career, noted that "Some money-worshippers told you Aunt Mary that I am very popular as a judge, but that I favor the widows too much."

John F. Lynch tells a story of Judge John Appleton:

"...when courthouses were lighted by kerosene lamps, he [Judge Appleton] was holding court in the old courthouse in Bangor, and during the trial of an important case, two lawyers, Mr. B and Mr. M., after the lamps were lighted, became so violent in a legal contest that they began to fight with their fists. Mr. B was the stronger man, and soon had Mr. M down on the floor and was hammering and choking him severely. Judge Appleton, seeing that no one showed any disposition to part the combatants, took his lamp in his hand, went down into the Bar, and leaning over the fighters said, 'Mr. B, you have hammered and choked Mr. M long enough. I order you to let him get up.' Then a weak voice from the floor was heard to say, 'Judge Appleton, that is the first honest, just ruling you have made in this case since we started the trial.' ... Judge Appleton was a great lawyer and a great judge, respected and beloved by all who knew him, yet like all other men he was not perfect, and had one weakness which caused him to be criticized by other lawyers. He was inclined to take sides in cases tried before him, and sometimes leaned strongly in favor of one side or the other in his charges to juries. The tendency was so strong that Judge Kent, ...on a tour of Europe, after visiting the leaning tower of Pisa, …wrote…that it reminded him of one of Judge Appleton's charges to a jury." [8]

When he became Chief Justice of the Maine Supreme Judicial Court, Appleton, according to Penobscot County Judge John Edwards Godfrey, was:

"probably the most generally intelligent man on the bench, yet he has quite a desultory mind. He is very fond of books, has read Jeremy Bentham excessively, has adopted his views in regard to evidence and has been the chief instrument in [changing] the laws of the state so that all parties may testify. …The judge in court has only one object in view apparently to get action off the docket. His law is not always well-considered in trying cases. He gives an offhand opinion, sometimes to the detriment of justice.… He is a little odd, but, withal, is a good judge…" "Chief Judge Appleton was in my office last week, and says that he thinks it is a pretty good thing to have money to do with in this world." [9]

Judge Godfrey was well acquainted with the Supreme Judicial Court justices with roots in Penobscot County. He described Justice Kent, former governor and Mayor of Bangor as "versatile," adding:

"Judge Kent…will tell stories and smoke and smoke and tell stories until they strangle all those hearing with tobacco smoke and laughter.… He is quite a literary man,…used to be quite slovenly in his habits, but since he married this young wife, he has picked up… Judge Kent enjoys a good supper and a good story equally well." [10]

The 1903 Penobscot County Courthouse

The 1831 courthouse with its 1859 additions continued in use to the end of the century, when the county commissioners authorized the construction of a new building. The new structure to be designed by architect Wilfred E. Mansur was to be on the site of the old courthouse. Mansur's design called for a three-story classical style structure. The front entrance was made with granite Ionic columns and pediment rising above the three evenly spaced arches that lead to the large front doors. On the exterior of the massively scaled building were brick walls above a smooth ashlar foundation. Granite was used extensively to highlight the structural elements of the building and was "rusticated" by leaving the stone in a roughened form. Granite quoins marched up the corners of the building, and a granite belt defined the first story. Windows were outlined with granite. Above its copper cornices, the new building was capped by a hipped roof accompanied by a shallow gabled wing on each side.

Construction of this building, the third Penobscot County Courthouse, began in 1901 with the demolition of the old building. The May, 1902, *Industrial Journal* described the building during its construction, highlighting its dimensions, which were massive compared with those of its predecessor:

"Architect Mansur's plans call for a structure of rectangular shape with a central section projecting from either side, the extreme dimensions of which will be 94 x 131 feet." [11]

Dimensions of all rooms in the building were detailed, together with the purpose for which they were designed: the registry of deeds, a witnesses' room, a copying room, a grand jury room connected with the county attorney's room, the probate courtroom, the commissioners' room, the sheriff's room, the treasurer's room, and rooms for the court records, the library, the clerk of courts, the jurors, the judges and the attorneys. The principal courtroom in the building, fifty feet square and thirty feet high, was located on the northeast corner of the second floor. The *Industrial Journal* article makes special note that toilets were provided for the staff in probate records, and for the commissioners, the sheriff, the clerk of courts, the attorneys' and the judges. Fireplaces were reserved for the library and the attorneys' and judges' rooms.

The Penobscot County Courthouse was completed in 1903. With virtually no alterations to its exterior, it remains in service to county residents

and officials. The interior has been modernized over the years to keep up with county needs. A major and dramatic visual change is the magnificent mural depicting the history of Penobscot County which rises through the building on the grand interior staircase.

In addition to the use of the building by the Penobscot County Superior Court, the courthouse provided space for terms of the Maine Supreme Judicial Court until the 1950s. A reorganization of the courts in 1930 resulted in the institution of the statewide Superior Court system. The statutes specifying the time and place for holding terms of the Law Court were repealed, and the specification of those times and places were left to the Chief Justice.

The building was renovated in 1961 and an addition was added to house the Probate Court. In 1963 the first floor was altered to provide rooms for the District Court. The courtroom used by the Superior Court and also used by the Supreme Judicial Court, was significantly altered. The ceiling, more than 50 feet high, was lowered to make way for rooms above it, and space was taken from each side of the courtroom to house a jury room, four consultation rooms, rest rooms and a judge's office.

[1] "The First Courthouse in Penobscot County, Now the City Hall in Bangor", *Maine Historical Magazine*, Vol VII, July, 1891-June 1892, pp. 33-35, Bangor: Glass & Co, 1892, pp. 33-34

[2] *Centennial Celebration of the Settlement of Bangor*, 1865, Bangor: Benjamin A. Brown, 1870, p. 137

[3] *Id.*, p. 92

[4] *Id.*, p. 111

[5] Thompson, Deborah, *Bangor, Maine 1768-1914: An Architectural History*, Orono, University of Maine Press, 1988, p. 191

[6] *Id.*

[7] *Id.*, pp. 353-354

[8] Lynch, John F., *The Advocate: An Autobiography and Series of Reminiscences*, Portland: George D. Loring, 1916, pp. 112-113

[9] Godfrey, John Edwards, *Journals: Bangor, Maine, 1893-1869*, Rockland, Maine: Courier-Gazette, Inc., 1979, pp. 104-105, 201

[10] *Id.*, p. 107

[11] Thompson, pp. 472-473

Waldo County

1827

Waldo County celebrated the 140th anniversary of the construction of its courthouse in 1993. The courthouse, a modest brick building standing on a slight hill above High Street in Belfast, is in active use serving the court needs of the county. Though construction was completed on the bulk of the building in 1853, modifications over the years have been made to update the building and to meet county needs. The history of the building and its forerunners tell part of the story of the pioneer period in the history of Maine.

The area now included within Waldo County originally looked to York County for court-related legal services. In 1760, near the end of the colonial period, Lincoln County was established with a seat at Pownalborough (now Dresden). Pownalborough, accessible initially only by water, dealt with legal business that could not be handled by a local justice of the peace. Jurors for Lincoln County (which was also the easternmost district of the Massachusetts Supreme Judicial Court until 1801) were drawn from a population scattered throughout the eastern half of the state from the Kennebec to the St. Croix River. There were few demands for juries for trials at the Lincoln County Courthouse, and it was not until 1791 that the first jurors traveled from Belfast for a sitting of the Supreme Judicial Court at Pownalborough. These jurors were paid the legal compensation of ninety cents for each day attending court, and four cents per mile for travel.

After the Revolution, population increases led to a division of the large area included in Lincoln County. In 1789, Hancock County was established by the Massachusetts Legislature with a shire town at Penobscot (now Castine). Two terms of the Court of Common Pleas and the Court

Forming Waldo County

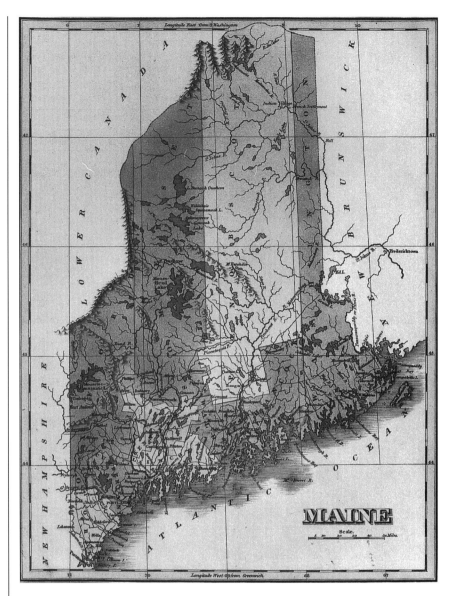

of General Sessions were held annually in Castine—one term in June and one in September. Three Justices of the Common Pleas were appointed and two Special Justices. None of the appointees were lawyers. One of the Justices acted as Judge of Probate, and a Special Justice served as the Register of Probate. Other citizens were appointed Clerk of the Courts, Treasurer, Register of Deeds and Sheriff.

The jurisdiction of the Court of Common Pleas included all civil actions where amounts involved four pounds sterling or more. Appeal was available to the Supreme Judicial Court. Even after Hancock County was formed, the Supreme Judicial Court continued sitting once annually at Pownalborough, which was the seat of its eastern district.

The Court of General Sessions initially comprised all the justices of the peace in the county. Its jurisdiction focused on criminal matters, with the authority to summon juries. The court carried out the management functions for the county that would today be administered by county commissioners. In 1807 a fixed number of justices was established, with six set for Hancock County. Each justice was appointed by the Governor.

Castine on its peninsula was isolated and inconvenient for many of the county's residents. As early as 1792 there was a movement to move the courts to a more accessible location. But citizens in the area of Belfast voted "not to have the courts removed from the peninsula where they are now held." In 1811, a proposal to create a registry of deeds on the western side of Penobscot Bay was opposed by the Belfast people, and two years later, a plan to divide Hancock County was also voted down, as "inexpedient at present." [1]

Following the War of 1812 Castine was eclipsed by growth elsewhere in the eastern region of Maine. Belfast grew rapidly between 1810 and 1820 and support increased for its designation as a half-shire town to share the county court activities with Castine. At the annual town meeting in 1818, Belfast voted to establish a committee to petition the General Court for one term of the Supreme Judicial Court to be "holden" at Belfast. The petition was not granted, for Massachusetts was not easily moved to make such changes.

Setting up Court in Belfast

After Maine separated from Massachusetts in 1820, its new legislature was presented with a plan to have sessions of the court in Belfast. Meeting with little success, local people shifted to a scheme to establish a new county. A significant effort was mounted among the towns of the region at their town meetings, and a petitions were presented to the legislature in 1827. An example of the petition from each town appeared as follows:

To the Legislature of the State of Maine, January, 1827.
The undersigned, a Committee of the town of ____ in the County of ____, legally chosen at the Annual Meeting on the second Monday of September, 1826, for the purpose, beg leave to represent that the counties of Hancock and Lincoln comprise long and extensive territories, and many of the towns are situated a great distance from the Shire Towns in each of said Counties, which renders it very expensive and inconvenient for those to attend who have business with our Courts and Public Offices, that the public good and the interest and convenience of your petitioners will be greatly promoted by the formation of a New County, consisting of the following towns and plan-

tations, viz.: Belfast, Brooks, Jackson, Thorndike, Monroe, Northport, Islesborough, Swanville, Knox, Belmont, Waldo, Lincolnville, Vinalhaven, Searsmont, Prospect, and Frankfort in the county of Hancock; and Camden, Hope, Montville, Montville Plantation (now Liberty), Appleton, Palermo, Thomaston, Warren, Cushing, St. George, Union, and Washington in the county of Lincoln; and Freedom, Unity and Joy (now Troy) in the county of Kennebec be erected into a new County. The above towns probably contain about thirty-six thousand inhabitants.

We therefore …ask your honorable body to incorporate us, together with the towns and plantations above mentioned, into a County, bearing the name of Knox and that Belfast and Warren be the Shire Towns for years, or such other town or towns as the Legislature may direct; as in duty bound will ever pray.[2]

The Maine Legislature, in deliberating the petition, assigned the initial work of investigating the proposal for a new county to a joint standing committee. The towns appointed their own committee to lobby for the measure in Augusta. One of the arguments for the new county was the difficulty and inconvenience of crossing the bay from Belfast to Castine in some seasons of the year. This committee resorted to many tactics to achieve their goal. Humor was a tool they used rarely, but an tongue-in-cheek instance was noted in which a whole term of court was lost because the sloop in which the judge was sailing had become becalmed.

Action on the measure in the joint legislative committee was swift. The committee removed several towns from the proposal and reported a new bill establishing a new county with Belfast as the sole shire town. The name of the county was left blank; the proposal for a Knox County was deemed inappropriate because the actual homeland of General Knox in and around Thomaston had been deleted from the boundaries of the smaller new county. At the suggestion of Representative R. C. Johnson, the name of Waldo was inserted in the bill to honor the name and memory of General Samuel Waldo, who had once owned nearly all of the land within the limits of the new county. After two days of deliberation, despite opposition from Castine, the House of Representatives passed the bill with a majority of twenty-three. In the Senate, little opposition was made, and Governor Lincoln signed the bill on February 7, 1827. The county would go into operation in July, with officers appointed by the Governor. A principal feature of the bill was that one term of the Supreme Court would meet annually in the county, along with three sessions of the Court of Common Pleas.

A place to hold court was clearly needed. In 1825 the citizens of Belfast had voted to furnish and prepare the town hall for use by the courts, if Belfast became the shire town of the new county. In 1827, with Waldo County a reality, the town spent $600 in finishing the second story of the town hall for a courtroom and other "apartments". The courtroom was about forty feet square and had no chairs. Instead it was furnished with wooden benches with no cushions. All attendees used the benches—the attorneys, jurors, court officers, and spectators. Attorneys had to lean on desks similar to those found in an old-fashioned schoolhouse. The floor was lightly covered with sand or sawdust. A long bar or prisoner's dock, guarded at each end by court officers, was at the rear of the room.

The Court of Common Pleas for the new county first met in July of 1827, in the remodeled town hall. The old building was badly ventilated and cramped. It had no offices for the judiciary separate from the courtroom. Thus, the judge worked at home, and was accompanied to and from his private lodgings by the sheriff bearing his official staff. The jury rooms were small and had no communication with the courtroom except through its main and only entrance. In 1829, to partially remedy the lack of room, the court rented offices in a store-front building. The probate office occupied the street floor, with the offices of the clerk of the courts and the Registry of Deeds and Treasurer on the second floor. There were fireproof vaults for the court papers and county records. In 1841, the attorneys' schoolhouse desks were removed from the courtroom at the old town hall and tables were provided.

In 1844 Waldo County established a Town Court, and became the only county in the state to do so. Legislation authorizing Town Courts established Justices of Trials, with one justice allowed in every town, and two

By the time of the next murder trial in Waldo County, grisly crimes were viewed as sensational events. As a result, the Belfast courthouse was packed with the spectators who had arrived to view the proceedings. The trial of John Gorton took place in November, 1873, before the Supreme Judicial Court, with Chief Justice Appleton presiding. Gorton was alleged to have used an ax on his brother, his sister-in law and an infant niece, mangling their bodies and setting the house afire. The trial lasted eight days. The jury deliberated for one hour and returned a verdict of guilty. Gorton, sentenced to death, was executed at the state prison.

Physical changes to the courthouse came gradually as the county officers saw new needs for the building. In 1856 a cupola was added to the roof with a bell to announce events. Stone steps leading up from High Street were constructed at the eastern entrance to the building in 1876. Steam heat and running water were added to the building in 1887. The law library was moved from the clerk's office to a room on the second floor in 1888; practitioners of the local bar provided the furnishings. Electric lights were substituted for gas lamps in 1889. A new ceiling for the court-room was also provided in 1888.

Updating the Courthouse

The building was considered cramped by the mid-1870s. In 1898 the Waldo County Bar Association called a special meeting, and voted to petition the county commissioners to enlarge the courthouse, stating that the building was too small to meet current needs, and that the records of the Probate and Register of Deeds Offices were endangered by not being properly protected from fire. The commissioners took no action on the petition, and in 1899, three local attorneys petitioned the Supreme Judicial Court to issue a mandamus compelling the county commissioners to expand the courthouse. The three noted that the county had $21,000 available in the treasury to pay for the addition to the building. At the April term of the court, an order of mandamus was issued, commanding the county commissioners "to provide in the shire town of the county, a fireproof building of brick or stone, for the safekeeping of the records and papers belonging to the offices of the Registers of Deeds and Probate and the Clerk of Courts, with separate fireproof rooms and suitable alcoves, cases, or boxes for each office." [3]

Following the mandamus, the county commissioners enlarged the court-

The granite stairways in the Waldo County Courthouse.

thouse with an addition toward High Street. The architect for the addition was E.F. Fassett. The cost of the construction contract was approximately $20,000 for the structure and its fittings and furnishings. The addition was completed during the winter of 1900 and the county records were moved into the new space.

The courthouse has seen little change in its physical dimensions since 1900. Its additions and modifications have served the county well. Inside the 1853 portion of the building, the courtroom is largely unchanged in size, although modern lighting has been added and up-to-date furniture has been installed. On the first floor of the building, office fixtures have been repeatedly replaced to keep the old structure up to date. In recent times modernization has been more dramatic—one recent addition is the computer network that serves users of the Registry of Deeds.

[1] Williamson, Joseph, *History of the City of Belfast, in the State of Maine*, 2 Vols., Vol. I, Portland: Loring, Short & Harmon, 1877, p. 369

[2] *Id.*, pp. 369-370

[3] Williamson, Joseph, *History of the City of Belfast, in the State of Maine*, 2 Vols., Vol. II, Boston: Houghton Mifflin Co., 1913, p. 122

TWELVE

Franklin County
1838

Franklin County was formed through the efforts of residents in and around Farmington. In July, 1832, a group of representatives of the area assembled to draft a petition to the legislature to "erect a new county." Initially, the legislature did not support the effort, but the idea was compelling to local residents. In the mid-1830s, Dr. Josiah Prescott was elected to the House of Representatives from Kennebec County on a platform of forming a new county with the shire town at Farmington. Prescott succeeded in raising the question for consideration early in the 1838 legislative session, with the help of Hon. Hiram Belcher, a state senator. The bill encountered strong opposition from the representatives of areas that were to lose part of their territories—Kennebec, Oxford and Somerset Counties.

To counter the opposition in the legislature, Farmington volunteered to furnish a courthouse for ten years free from expense to the county. The offer of a courthouse helped move the act forward, but the legislature was still wary. The legislature called for a referendum on the act by the legal voters in the towns included in the new county, stipulating that a majority vote would ratify the act. At the election of April, 1838, the votes were cast by residents of the proposed new county and returned to the Secretary of State's office. When the Governor and Governor's Council tallied the ballots, a majority were in favor of establishing the new county.

Governor Kent issued a proclamation on May 10, 1838, formally establishing Franklin County. He was quick to fill the appointive offices, naming fellow Whig party members as sheriff, clerk of the court, judge of probate, register of probate, county attorney, and county commissioners. The county treasurer was appointed by the county commissioners. Because of

Farmington Finds a Courthouse

173

the importance of proper recording of land transfers in the early settlement period and to ensure responsiveness to the community, the Register of Deeds was to be elected. The clerk of court acted as register of deeds until the election was held in September, 1838.

At the time the county was established, Farmington leaders had been negotiating with the proprietors of the Center Meetinghouse for court space. These meetings bore fruit in June of 1839, when the proprietors offered to give their building and land free of charge to the county for courthouse use, subject to a few provisions. The first provision allowed the proprietors to retain the use of the lower floor of the building for the purposes of church services and town meetings, "so long as the building shall stand." Secondly, the proprietors reserved an access way 45 feet wide to the burying ground. Third, they required a full discharge of all claims of the county on the proprietors arising from their furnishing a courthouse. As part of the arrangement, the proprietors allowed the county to "alter, repair or fit up" the building "in a proper manner" to hold court sessions there. [1]

John Church, treasurer of the proprietors, executed a deed of the Meetinghouse and site to the inhabitants of Franklin County. The county commissioners made acceptance of the deed contingent on a bond to indemnify and hold harmless county residents and officers from damages arising from defect of title and "actions or suits that may be commenced by persons holding or claiming pews in said house." The bond was executed on June 26 by 18 local residents. On July 6, 1839, the county commissioners accepted the property.

With the execution of the deed, Franklin County received title to the Center Meetinghouse. The county commissioners appropriated the funds

The courthouse, at left, forms part of the Farmington skyline.
Richard Mallett; Farmington Historical Society

to remodel the second floor into a courtroom. The first session of the
District Court was held in the new courtroom in 1840. The new courtroom and courthouse were to serve Franklin County for nearly 50 years.

The building became insufficient to house the rapidly expanding staff
managing the new county services, and a new brick building for county
offices was constructed at the intersection of Broadway and Main Street
in 1843. The new building burned in the great downtown fire of 1850,
which did not affect the Center Meetinghouse used by the court.

Butler's 1885 *History of Farmington* refers to the years between 1862 and
1869 as a "carnival of crime"—an unusual period for Franklin County
because of the significant number of sensational crimes that took place

A "Carnival of
Crime"

during those years. In 1862, on a Sunday morning in September, a brutal murder took place in the town of Strong. Lura Vellie Libby, nine years old, left her home alone to go to the village to church. When she did not return and could not be found, the citizens of Strong and adjacent communities formed a search party. Her body was found 24 hours later buried in the edge of a wood a short distance from the highway. It was sheer luck she was found: "...so ingeniously was the concealment of her body effected that the merest chance revealed the grave." [2]

As investigation of the crime began, Lawrence Doyle, employed by the family and living in their home, came under suspicion. He was arrested and taken to the Farmington jail. Local feelings against him were strong. The evidence against him was almost entirely circumstantial. He was not brought to trial until the fall term of the Supreme Judicial Court in 1863. The trial began October 28, with Hon. Charles W. Walton presiding. The prosecution was undertaken by Attorney General Josiah Drummond and County Attorney Samuel Belcher. Justice Walton appointed Eben F. Pillsbury, Joseph A. Linscott and Oliver L. Currier as counsel for the defense.

Doyle was about 30 years old and had lived in several families' homes as hired help. He was "ignorant and illiterate, [he] had always been regarded as a quiet and inoffensive man." The testimony against him was made up "of the most minute bits of evidence, all appearing to fit together to form a chain to fasten the guilt upon Doyle." During the trial he appeared stunned and dazed. The final summations were made and the case was given to the jury on November 5. After 25 hours of deliberation, the jury found it could not agree. Seven stood for conviction and five for acquittal.

Because of the hung jury, a second trial began in April of 1864. Justice Walton again presided. The prosecution added John A. Peters, and the remaining attorneys were not changed. This time the defendant testified in his own defense and his testimony "... was generally regarded as prejudicial to his case." Presentations and summations of the case were concluded on May 10. The jury deliberated for one hour and returned a verdict of guilty. On the same day the prisoner was sentenced to death.

In 1863 a quarrel over sheep wandering away from their owner resulted in another death. Jesse Wright, a farmer in the town of Phillips, argued with his neighbor, Jeremiah Tuck, about Tuck's sheep trespassing in Wright's fields. Wright, "in the midst of high words," raised his gun and shot Tuck, killing him instantly. Indicted by the grand jury for murder, Wright was brought to an October trial before Judge Walton. Josiah Drummond and Samuel Belcher appeared for the state, and J.H. Webster and H.L. Whitcom for the defense. The trial lasted only two days and resulted in a verdict of guilty. Wright was sentenced to death and taken to state prison at Thomaston. Because he was more than 70 years old, Wright received both sympathy and efforts to gain him a pardon. The pardon was refused, but he was allowed to return to the jail at Farmington. After four or five years, Governor Chamberlain pardoned Wright, and he died not long afterwards. [3]

A third death in 1863 resulted from an argument over a farmer's fence. Joseph Edes, accompanied by his son, went to the home of Samuel Richardson to discuss his suspicion that Richardson had removed the fence. Richardson became excited, grabbed an old sword and attacked young Edes, breaking the sword. He then grabbed a gun, and in the resulting confusion, the two Edes men succeeded in disarming Richardson. As they backed away, Richardson grabbed an ax and plunged it into Joseph Edes' chest. Edes died about four hours later, and Richardson walked to Farmington, where he turned himself in. Richardson's trial began in April, 1864, before Judge Walton. Samuel Belcher appeared for the state and Robert Goodenow for the defense. The jury returned a verdict of guilty and Richardson was sentenced to death by hanging. The sentence was never carried out, and Richardson died as a prisoner at Thomaston.

The old county office building itself figured in a criminal event. In 1869 three "gentlemanly looking" strangers arrived by train in West Farmington and walked toward the center of town. Each carried a large valise which appeared to be heavy. At about 11:00 that night, Joseph Bangs, a watchman, was passing the county building where the Sandy River National Bank was located. Hearing an unusual noise, Bangs gave an alarm, and the burglars, who were at work inside the bank, immediately fled down a back stairway. Inside the building, elaborate preparations for the burglary were found in place. On the floor was a kit of burglar's tools, "of the most ingenious construction," and rags "used to deaden the sound of the blows upon the cold-chisels." Also in the room were "dark-lantern," a bottle of brandy, heavy window draperies, and wires from the room to the back door ("evidently for the purpose of communication with an outside party"). A four-inch square hole in the safe was cut, but the interior was not reached. A search was initiated from Farmington, and the next day a railroad handcar was found pitched over an embankment in Livermore. The burglars were not apprehended and townsfolk shuddered to think of the "professionals." Within a year, the bank moved to a new and safer building. [4]

In 1870 a death occurred in New Sharon. Deputy Sheriff Brown went to the farm home of John S. Tolman to collect a payment of a debt against Ezekial Tolman, a brother who lived with the family. Ezekial refused to pay, and was aided in resisting arrest by his brother John. A warrant was issued and Constable John Fletcher was charged with the duty of making the arrest. On going to the house, Fletcher and Brown found that the whole Tolman family was in a "...state of great excitement, and determined to resist to the last." After calling for assistance, Brown and Fletcher began a siege, which resulted in violence. In the semi-darkness of a winter night, Fletcher shot at John Tolman and inflected a groin wound, causing Tolman's death. The grand jury indicted Fletcher, and the case came to trial in March before Judge Rufus P. Tapley. Philip Stubbs and Nathan Webb appeared for the state. The trial lasted six day, and the jury, deliberating for one hour, returned a verdict of not guilty. [5]

The Brick Courthouse of 1885

The Franklin County Courthouse was open for use in 1885.

Maine Historic Preservation Commission

In the 1850s the neighborhood of the Center Meetinghouse began to deteriorate, and vandalism was noted. Lafayette Perkins, secretary of the proprietors of the Center Meetinghouse, noted that damage had been done to the meetinghouse, the burial grounds, the fences and the trees. The proprietors of the building were apparently not receiving remuneration from the county for the upkeep of the building and grounds.

The arrangement with the proprietors of the Center Meetinghouse was never quite satisfactory and remained somewhat unsettled. Joseph S. Craig, treasurer of the Center Meetinghouse, brought suit against the

Franklin County Court House, Farmington, Me.

county by "writ of entry" in 1867 to test the validity of the county's title to the courthouse property. After nearly two years of argument in the courts, the case was tried before the Supreme Judicial Court during its January, 1869, term. The court ruled in favor of the county, confirmed its title to the building and grounds.

The growth of Franklin County led to discussions of the need for a new courthouse in the early 1880s. The proprietors of the Center Meetinghouse again questioned the county's title to the building and land. In a final effort to settle the question of property ownership, the county purchased any remaining interest of the proprietors of the Center Meetinghouse in 1884 for $750.00. The building was sold to the town of Farmington and removed from the site.

With the property ownership settled, the county commissioners— Franklin W. Patterson, Isaiah Chick, and Samuel K. Wellman—sought a design for the new building. They chose George McCoombs of Lewiston as the architect, and M. C. Foster & Son as the builder. The second Franklin County Courthouse was built and opened in 1885.

The new building was a sophisticated design that did not have the pretensions or the complexity of other Victorian buildings of the time. The building, a 3 1/2 story brick building with a centrally-placed cupola, was designed as a simple rectangle. The limitations of the shallow site led the architect to place the long side of the rectangle facing Main Street, and the principal entrance on one of the short ends of the building, facing away from the Common and Main Street, but toward the business section of Farmington. The architect included a slated, hipped roof, interrupted by

Administration of court affairs was centered in the county building in downtown Farmington.
Richard Mallett; Farmington Historical Society

the gables and roofs of the pavilions accenting each door. To emphasize the courtroom functions of the second floor, windows were extended vertically and given rounded tops. Decorative terra-cotta panels graced the pavilions above the doorways. The cupola contained a clock and a metal dome, from which sprouted a weather vane.

The new courthouse became a prominent feature of Farmington, an anchor of the downtown area, and a place of pride for the county. Over the years, the building continued to be embellished. In 1904, the Franklin County Civil War Memorial, a stone obelisk, was raised across the street from the courthouse in the Common. The water trough for horses, originally in front of the courthouse, was moved across the street to the Common. The town bandstand was also located in the park. In 1917 the courthouse was enlarged by County Commissioners Herbert Landers, Charles Gay and Fred Lace. Harry S. Coombs, son of the original architect of the building, was the architect for the addition, and Joseph W. Matthiew was the builder.

Court Cases in the Brick Courthouse

The celebrated Bean case of 1923 lives on in the legends that surround the courthouse. Otis Bean, a summer guide for tourists coming to the Rangely area, was murdered on October 6, 1922. Bean was caring for the summer camps owned by Toothaker at the time. In the morning, Bean brought Toothaker to Haines Landing in a boat, then drove him to the train station at Oquossoc. That night, he made the same trip, to meet the train and pick up the mail. Bean was alone as he walked through town to his garage. At the slope leading to the garage he was shot and killed.

At first it was thought that two lumberjacks were responsible for the murder. These two men, Wheaton and Mawson, were in the vicinity when Bean was killed. Subsequent investigations cleared them of the crime. Attention then turned to the murdered man's wife, Ethel Bean. The motive was thought to be rage over another woman involved in her husband's life. She was charged with the death and brought to trial by the prosecutors, Attorney General Ransford W. Shaw and County Attorney Currier C. Holman. Attorneys for the defense were Cyrus Blanchard, W. R. Pattangall, and James G. Perkins. Pattangall was a well-known figure in Maine bar activities and state politics A prominent Democrat, Pattangall was renowned for his sense of humor and his witicisms.

Selecting jurors proved to be a major task when the prosecution and defense could not agree on a twelfth juror. After spending a considerable amount of time on the selection process, Pattangall rose and announced that the defense would consider using only eleven jurors. But Judge Dunn would not be deterred from the number 12, describing:

"…the mystical quality of the number twelve in Anglo-Saxon history with twelve knights in King Arthur's Round Table, twelve months in the year, twelve hours of darkness and twelve of light, and he wound up his dissertation on the number twelve by saying that even the Lord Saviour had twelve apostles. Pattangall arose and pointed out the Saviour would have been better off with eleven apostles. Even so Judge Dunn refused to forsake his mystical twelve." [6]

The trial got underway with the prosecution's case. The two lumberjacks were called, but were able to provide little evidence against Ethel Bean. "Mawson stuttered, and when he was excited stuttered even more. The result was that few answers to questions were understandable." The other woman was also called, in a largely unsuccessful effort to support the prosecution's claim that Ethel Bean had been jealous of her. [7]

During the trial, the prosecution realized that its case was flimsy, and gave up. Ethel Bean was freed. Later it was revealed that a defense expert had been prepared to testify that Mrs. Bean could not have fired the fatal shot because of the difference in the couple's height and the conditions of the death.

In June, 1941 another sensational murder trial claimed the attention of the court. Fred G. Wheeler, a prosperous cattle dealer, was accused of killing his lover Florence Buzzell of New Sharon with a .22 pistol. Apprehended in Boston, he was held without bail until the beginning of the trial in October. Wheeler was represented by Cyrus Blanchard, Currier Holman, and David and Benjamin Berman. Attorney General Frank Cowan and county attorney Ben Butler represented the state.

The Franklin County Courthouse dominates the view on Farmington's Main Street.
Richard Mallett; Farmington Historical Society

A contentious jury was empanelled on November 25. As the trial began, Florence Buzzell was presented as a bright and promising woman who met Wheeler to obtain a loan to attend the Augusta Business College. A love affair characterized as torrid followed, and Wheeler was seen frequently at Buzzell's apartment in Augusta. The affair cooled off, but both Buzzell and Wheeler visited Buzzell's family in June. Witnesses disagreed about the behavior of the two on the fatal day. Attorney General Cowan summarized the case as one with jealousy as the principal motive. Berman in his summary claimed that Buzzell either killed herself accidentally or committed suicide. The jury deliberated for two hours, returning a verdict of not guilty.

Midway through the Wheeler trial, during the identification of the photographs taken at the scene of the murder, the proceedings were interrupted by the bark of a dog. "Is there a dog in the courtroom?" asked Judge Beliveau. Several seconds later, a young woman left the courtroom carrying a tiny dog in her handbag. The sheriff followed closely behind and she was apprehended and told to appear the next day. At her appearance, the judge reprimanded her for disruption of court decorum, and fined her $10.

The Franklin County Courthouse still sits on its hill overlooking downtown Farmington. It was remodeled in 1958 under the guidance of County Commissioners Ralph C. Hall, B. Warren Dodge, and Richard A. Childs. The architect chosen was Alonzo J. Harriman, and K& H. Foster, Inc. was the builder. In this remodeling, a new entrance at street level leading into the basement of the building was provided on the Main Street side. In the interior, new offices in the basement and an elevator to the upper floors were added. In 1983 the Franklin County Courthouse was nominated for the National Register of Historic Buildings.

[1] Butler, Francis Goule, *History of Farmington, Franklin County, Maine, from the Earliest Explorations to the Present Time, 1776-1885*, Farmington: Knowlton, McLeary and Co., 1885, Reprinted in 1983, p. 172

[2] *Id.*, pp. 241-242

[3] *Id.*, pp. 243-244

[4] *Id.*, pp. 249; Mallett, Richard with Paul H. Mills, "Crime and Punishment "(1843-1922) in *The Early Years of Farmington, 1781-1860*, Wilton: Wilton Printed Products, 1994, p. 31

[5] Butler, pp. 254-255; Mallett, p. 31

[6] Mallet Richard P., *The Last 100 Years: a Glimpse of the Farmington We Have Known*, Wilton: Wilton Printed Products, 1991, p. 34

[7] *Id.*, p. 35

THIRTEEN

Piscataquis County
1838

The people of Piscataquis County, on the early frontier of settlement in Maine, have been served by seven courthouses—only three of which were located within the county. Although settlers reached Piscataquis County in 1794, it took over 40 years for the services of the court to be located in a convenient local courthouse within the county.

Prior to settlement, the land that became Piscataquis County was part of Lincoln County, with a courthouse at Pownalborough (now Dresden), and later a part of Kennebec County, with a courthouse at Augusta. By the time the first settlers arrived, the area had been made part of Hancock County with a shire town at Castine, nearly 75 miles away on a route comprised of a lengthy footpath and a river. Built in 1790, Castine's courthouse was used by settlers of the land that became Piscataquis County for county courts and, perhaps most important, the registry of deeds. The courthouse stood opposite a stone jail where residents were detained if necessary and where lawbreakers would have been held in the stocks for public punishments.

To get to the courthouse in Castine or the Registry of Deeds took a three day walk from Dover and Foxcroft through the wilderness to Bangor, followed by a 35 mile sail on the river (or another 2 or 3 day hike on the riverbank). Few lawyers were willing and able to make the trip for their clients. For appeals to the Supreme Judicial Court, residents of the future Piscataquis traveled to Boston, since Maine was then a part of Massachusetts. A trip to Boston required the settlers to walk the three days to Bangor and there to obtain passage by boat for the remainder of the 240 mile trip.

The Need for a Courthouse

Access to the court was clearly a problem for the residents of small settlements throughout Piscataquis County. When Hancock County was partitioned in 1816, the newly-formed Penobscot County incorporated the area that would later become Piscataquis county. Bangor was named the shire town and the county court began holding sessions in the Bangor Courthouse.

Even though Bangor was less than 40 miles from Dover and Foxcroft, the distance was a challenge and roadways were not passable at all times of the year. Meanwhile population was growing, and prosperity was on the horizon. Foxcroft had only 65 residents in 1810 but in the 1820s both towns rapidly added new industries and population.

The vast distances between the outlying Penobscot county towns and its shire town may have hindered a county-wide determination of common goals. In early records, the Court of Common Pleas of Penobscot County appears active in monitoring publicly-sponsored improvements. For example, in 1822 a summons was sent to the Town of Foxcroft to appear

The Piscataquis County Courthouse built in 1844.

before the justices of the Penobscot County court in Bangor to answer allegations that the town was delinquent in repairing a town road. Unhappy with the town's response, the court fined Foxcroft $600 for its inaction. Significantly, the towns and the county sparred continuously over alleged neglect of the maintenance of the bridge over the Piscataquis River. The contentiousness between officials of the towns and Penobscot County, along with the county's lack of understanding of local issues and its persistence in enforcing public improvements, may have been factors in hastening the process of setting up Piscataquis County.

Local residents went to the new state house in Augusta to petition for the establishment of a new county to be made up of a portion of Penobscot County. In the winter of 1838, when the bill establishing Piscataquis County was before the Maine Legislature, objections were registered regarding the expense of constructing and maintaining buildings for the proposed new county. Anxious to assure a favorable result, the proprietors of the Universalist Society of Dover and Foxcroft sent a message to the state house in Augusta proposing a unique arrangement: in return for the State's establishment of Dover as the shire town for the new county, the church proprietors would permit the use of the five-year old church building as a courthouse during the week (reserving the use of the building on Sunday as a place of worship). The church proprietors offered to sign a written contract for the use of the church as a courthouse so long as it might be needed, free of expense to the state. With this offer, the legislative battle was won, Piscataquis County was formed, and Dover became the county seat.

The Universalist congregation went to work to prepare the church for the court's use. Inside the church, the pulpit was cut down to make a more convenient judge's desk. Two of the front pews were removed to make space for attorneys' presentations and arguments. Behind the main hall, a room was converted for the use of the jury. On June 25, 1838, the courthouse was ready for the first sitting of the court, which was a session of the Supreme Judicial Court. Chief Justice Nathan Weston presided, having driven the long trip to Dover with a team of horses. The first term of the Court of Common Pleas was held in the Universalist meeting-house on September 18, 1838.

When the county was formed, lawyers were scarce. Early practice in Dover and Foxcroft was dominated by J.S. Holmes and Charles Chandler. With Holmes having an office in Foxcroft and Chandler in Dover, the two attorneys controlled the practice of law in the county for a time. Chandler, according to one historian, came to be known as the "honest lawyer of Piscataquis", which leaves some question as to the honesty of his colleagues and the other attorneys in the county. Holmes and Chandler spent private time debating public questions. Their 1828 correspondence includes discussion of whether it would be expedient to abolish imprisonment for debt.

The First Piscataquis County Courthouse

In 1839 the Court of Common Pleas was replaced by the District Court, and six years after the founding of the county, the need for a permanent building became apparent. The courtroom was called make-shift and the jury room was called a "little den between the entrance doors, so dark that we had to keep the door open during the day to see anything." Another writer, identifying himself as "Foxcroft," said, "Having recently visited the clerk's office in this county, I could not but notice the exposed situation of our records. The office is kept in a wooden building in which there are no less than four fires." With these criticisms, it was clear that the makeshift arrangements for the courts and the Universalist church building were soon to be abandoned. [1]

Foxcroft entered the contest for a new courthouse building, and succeeded in having the state legislature put the designation of shire town to a vote by county residents. The vote was taken in September, 1841. Dover received 1,097 votes—mostly from residents of the southern part of the county—and Foxcroft received 1,067—mostly from the north. The margin of victory was too close, and county officials decided to hold another election. This time Guilford decided to offer itself as a site for the shire town. The result was a split of north county votes, and Dover emerged as the winner.

Public spirit was roused in Dover, and the first courthouse built specifically for Piscataquis County courts was erected in 1844. The 40' by 55' building was constructed by T.H. Chamberlain at a cost of $2,900. Furnishings for the courtrooms and the county offices were included at an additional cost of $800. Two stories and built of wood, the building was surmounted by a bell tower. No jail was included in the first Piscataquis County Courthouse; prisoners were detained in Bangor.

The town was proud of this sturdy courthouse. It was used for special occasions, including seasonal use by church congregations needing housing. The walls of the building still exist as part of the present courthouse.

The Supreme Judicial Court sat annually in the Piscataquis County Courthouse from 1839 to 1851. In that year the reorganization of the Maine courts separated the trial cases from the appellate cases and established three districts for the Court to hear appellate or "law" cases—one each in Bangor, Portland and Augusta.

The old courthouse served well into the early Victorian era, but after 40 years the building needed expansion and modernization. The roof was leaking and rot was detected in the supporting timbers. Furthermore, fireproof court buildings were required by state statute as protection for personnel and the public as well as for the archives of the county.

In 1885 the Piscataquis County Commissioners obtained help from the legislature, providing $12,000 in state money for courthouse expansion. Adding some $2,000 of county money, the commissioners developed a thrifty plan to use the walls of the 1844 building as the basis for the new building. The plan called for gutting the interior and enlarging the building with jury and meeting rooms, offices, and a law library under a new peaked slate roof. Although the width remained the same as the old building, the new building length was extended to a total of 80 feet. The second floor ceiling was raised 6 feet. Decorative woodwork came from local forests and slate was quarried within the county. The bell from the older courthouse was installed in the new cupola.

On the ground floor of the new building were rooms for the clerk of courts, county treasurer, county commissioners, grand jury, Probate Court, Register of Deeds and three fire-proof vaults to store the county archives. Inside the main entrance, stairs led to the main courtroom on the second floor, entirely finished in yellow birch, cherry, and white wood

The Second Piscataquis County Courthouse

The Piscataquis County Courthouse, opened in 1886, incorporated the walls of the prior county building.
Maine Historical Society

including the judge's chambers and library at the back of the building. In the basement an area was reserved for a jail. When completed, the Piscataquis County Courthouse was reported to be one of the most convenient and attractive courthouses in Maine.

The formal opening of the new courthouse was a major civic occasion. On Thursday, February 18, 1886, the new building was dedicated with celebratory exercises. The building was opened to the general public for inspection and "poking about" at 2:00 p.m. For the evening's entertainment prior to the ceremonies, Dyer's Band was scheduled to play. The Hon. Alexander M. Robinson presided over the ceremonies, and music was furnished by Taylor's Military Band of 24 pieces. Before a large assemblage of citizens from throughout the county, letters were read and speeches were made, with reminiscences of the old courthouse, the county and the Piscataquis bar. The new courthouse was extolled as a structure with "no equal in Maine" and "no superior" in convenience and safety. The *Piscataquis Observer* reported a "...Large Attendance, And a Highly Interesting Affair." [2]

Updating the Courthouse

Since 1886, the "new" courthouse has remained the focus and location of Piscataquis County administration and court activities. In 1901 the jail and a residence for the "turnkey" or jailer was added on the south side of the building. At about the same time, electricity was added to replace the kerosene lamps. A central heating plant was constructed to provide steam heat, replacing the wood-burning stoves and warming the cold stone floors.

Little was changed in the courthouse for the next 50 years. Dover and Foxcroft were united as one town in 1922. In 1930, the Superior Court took up its business in the building. In 1956 a $200,000 wing to the east of the building was added to the courthouse as new space for the cramped county offices. In 1975 the commissioners renovated the courtroom, incorporating acoustical walls, installing wall-to-wall carpeting and adding new seats. Between 1988 and 1990, further renovations and additions were made to the jail. The buildings have been made accessible to disabled people. The cupola on the courthouse has been enclosed, but it is uncertain whether the bell is still in place.

During the 1975 period of renovations, the former residence of Joseph B. Peakes was remodeled to provide a separate building for the District Court adjacent to the courthouse in Dover-Foxcroft. This building has become a courthouse annex, with space for a courtroom for the District Court, the judge's chamber, the clerk of courts, law library, and District Attorney's Office. As the most recent courthouse for Piscataquis County, this building becomes the seventh building used for court purposes.

The Piscataquis County Courthouse sits gracefully in Dover-Foxcroft.
Louis Stevens

[1] Stevens, Louis, *Dover-Foxcroft – A History*, Somersworth: New Hampshire Printers, 1995, p. 143

[2] Stevens, Louis, *Booming! Dover and Foxcroft from 1881-1892*, Newport, Maine: Newport Print Shop, 1996, p. 43

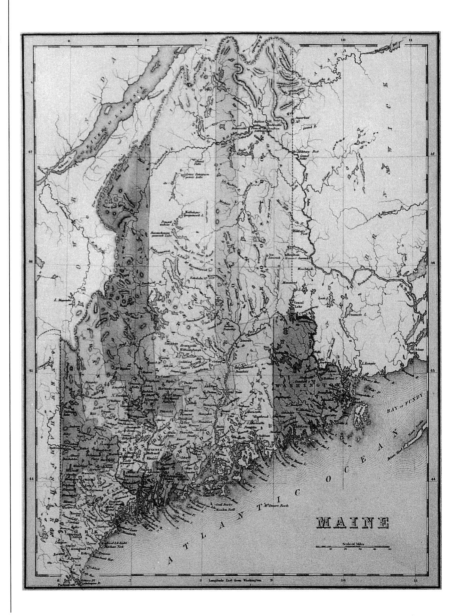

The 1839 map of Maine shows the newly added Aroostook County.
Osher Map Library, University of Southern Maine

190

FOURTEEN

Aroostook County
1839

Aroostook County is the only county in Maine with two court-houses in current use. The principal courthouse—the "head office"—is located in Houlton, but a second courthouse became necessary because of the size of the county and the sheer distances that must be traveled to Houlton. The second courthouse is located 55 miles away at Caribou, with offices for judges and rooms for court sessions, and a northern Registry of Deeds.

Houlton captured an early edge as the principal town in the county because it was settled on one of the first grants of land within Aroostook County. The town occupies land given by the Massachusetts Legislature to the people of New Salem for income to establish an academy in their Bay State town. Soon after the legislative grant, thirteen residents of New Salem purchased the land from the town, with a deed dated in 1810. These thirteen proprietors looked for a surveyor to lay out lots for sale in their half township.

The proprietors contacted Joseph Houlton who was appointed in 1808 to become the first Register of Deeds for the Northern District of Washington County by Governor Sullivan of Massachusetts. Houlton became their agent, surveying the land and cutting a path to the new townships which would later be named for him. The part of Maine that eventually became Aroostook County was initially part of Lincoln County, then part of Washington County in 1789, a part of both Penobscot and Washington Counties in 1815, and a part of Piscataquis County in 1838. The eastern boundary between the United States and Canada remained in doubt for over 50 years after the Revolution. During the War of 1812, the British

The Court Comes to Houlton

191

unabashedly contended that Maine north of the Penobscot remained part of Canada.

After the War of 1812, with the boundary issue still unsettled, new settlers began to arrive. Houlton and much of the surrounding area remained part of Washington County. Except for the Registry of Deeds, county administrative and judicial services were available only in the Washington County seat at Machias. In 1828 Houlton became a military outpost. The Hancock Barracks were constructed on Garrison Hill for Company C of the Second U.S. Infantry which had arrived by way of the Penobscot and Mattawamkeag Rivers, and rough roads into Houlton. As other soldiers arrived, the commander of the post, Major N.S. Clark, decided to build a military road direct from Houlton to Mattanawcook (Lincoln), where a state road led to Bangor. Constructing the new road took three years. Completed in 1832, Military Road was to become the address of the Houlton courthouses. During an incident of the "Aroostook War," the road was extended to the Madawaska settlements in the disputed territories.

In 1833, Houlton residents proposed the organization of a new county with Houlton as the shire town. The town clerk, Alpheus Felch, wrote to Shepard Cary, state representative in Augusta, to urge him to advocate for the establishment of the new county. Despite his efforts, Cary failed to move the Legislature to action.

Four years later, the initiative was renewed. A formal petition was sent to the Legislature by 26 Houlton residents, arguing: "…the inhabitants of the Northern District of the County of Washington are subjected to numerous inconveniences in consequence of their connection with the Southern section of that County." They listed the inconveniences:

- being so far distant from the shire town, parties cannot attend court with their witnesses without incurring great expense;
- jurors have the fatigue of a long journey, and do not draw fees sufficient to defray their expenses;
- county officers are subjected to risks in conveying prisoners to jail, requiring aides and large disbursements which are not repaid in full by the county.
- sums allowed for these expenses are a "heavy charge upon the County." [1]

This second petition also failed to pass the Legislature, perhaps because the proposed area did not include some portions of the disputed territories in the Madawaska area. A third petition appeared, written by some of the residents not involved in the second petition, and calling for the new county to be named Aroostook. Houlton residents acted quickly to amend their second petition to include the missing territories around Madawaska.

In January, 1839, the amended petition was submitted, but the name of the new county was left blank. Houlton remained the proposed shire town.

Opposition in the form of a counter-petition to the Houlton petition appeared immediately, written by Penobscot County representatives opposing the establishment of the new county on the grounds that Penobscot would loose part of its northern area. The legislature finally acted, accepting Houlton's most recent petition as the basis for its actions. The Act of Establishment gave the county the name of Restook, which was later amended to Aroostook. The bill was passed and signed by Governor Fairfield on March 16, 1839. With the new county of Aroostook formed, the first Aroostook deed was recorded June 18th of that year. The boundaries between the county and Canada were finally determined in 1842, when Daniel Webster, then Secretary of State, and Lord Ashburton, acting for Great Britain, signed a treaty to settle the boundary problem.

Early Court Buildings

For ten years after the formation of the county, court sessions were held in the Black Hawk Tavern, erected in 1813 by builder Samuel Wormwood for pioneer settler Aaron Putnam. The tavern was constructed of wood cut and sawed on site, and was walled up with brick on the outside in an attempt to make it bulletproof. The court was held in a room of the second floor of the tavern. The corner occupied by the judge's bench was marked by four-foot tall wainscoting on the walls of the room. The first county jail was a dungeon in the basement, where rings in the

Early court sessions were held in the Black Hawk Tavern in Houlton, which had a jail in the basement.
Joe Inman, Houlton

walls were used to chain prisoners in their cells. There was no provision for ventilation for the prisoners in the basement.

Samuel Gooch became the first counselor at law at Houlton. He became a prominent figure early in the town's history. Other early attorneys in town included Henry C. Field who began practicing in the Court of Common Pleas in 1832. In 1834 he was joined by Isaac W. Tabor.

Sessions of the Aroostook County Courts and the Maine Supreme Judicial Court were moved from the Black Hawk Tavern when Trustees of the proposed Houlton Academy planned a school building which would have space for sessions of the courts. In 1848, the Maine Legislature authorized conveyance of one-half of Township 14 Range 3 (now Woodland) to the Academy Trustees, if they would agree to construct "a good and convenient academical building" and begin holding school sessions "before the final Monday in October 1849." The Trustees purchased a centrally-located lot of four acres in Houlton, facing the Military Road. The lot, located between Garrison Hill and the Creek on Military Street, was elevated land cleared of timber by Edmund Cone in 1818. The land was purchased from Collins Whitaker "for a fraction of its value." On this site, the Trustees built a two story frame building with schoolrooms on the lower floor. On the second floor a courtroom was built to be used for the sessions of the Supreme Judicial Court and county Courts of Common Pleas and General Sessions of the Peace. This room was occupied by the courts for eleven years, until a separate courthouse was built. [2]

The 1859 Aroostook County Courthouse in Houlton

In 1857 the county commissioners found a surplus in the county treasury that was sufficient to begin planning for a new courthouse. Commissioners Benjamin Hawes, Moses White and Bellony Violette determined to use these funds and the proceeds from a loan to construct a new building. Residents of Aroostook immediately took issue by writing their comments to the *Aroostook Times*, objecting to the anticipated new taxes. The county commissioners responded by citing the state legislation that makes it the duty of the county commissioners to provide for the erection of courthouses and other necessary buildings for the use of the county. The commissioners agreed that commission chair Hawes would contact a competent architect and begin the steps necessary to construct the courthouse. The chosen architect, Gridley J. F. Bryant, was known for design of other public buildings including the Androscoggin County Courthouse in Auburn. [3]

In an effort to closely monitor costs, the commissioners asked Bryant to develop two designs from which to choose. Bryant sent two sets of drawings for two designs of a building with identical exterior dimensions, but with different exterior decoration and interior arrangement of rooms, stairways and entrances. Bryant proposed to save funds by using square windows instead of arched ones and a roof balustrade instead of a cupola. But he was persuasive: "…the omission of these features will not injure the utility of the building although the exterior effect will be somewhat less imposing and attractive. A cupola however would seem to be an important adjunct …if only to contain a bell." The county commissioners chose the arched windows and cupola, and the French Mansard roof that Bryant recommended. [4]

The commissioners directed Benjamin Staples, clerk of courts, to retain Bryant to translate the chosen design into plans and specifications for the new building. Advertisements were placed in the *Aroostook Times* for a contract to begin construction in the spring, with completion by November, 1859. Harrison D. Clement of Lawrence, Massachusetts, won the initial contract with his low bid of $14,400.00.

The commissioners continued to work with Bryant to keep costs down. They listed their proposed alterations and potential cost savings:

> 1st Dispense with the cellar, but lay the foundation walls of sufficient depth for and as required for a good and permanent wall. $933.00
>
> 2nd Dispense with stone steps and iron railing and use good wood instead $350.00

The Aroostook County Courthouse in Houlton was opened for use in 1859.

Maine Historic Preservation Commission

3rd Dispense with cement and use good lime mortar for brickwork	$150.00
4th Dispense with the roof ventilating apparatus	$190.00
5th Dispense with double thick glass and use single thick of same quality instead	$ 75.00
6th Dispense with a portion of the gravel around the walls	$ 60.00
7th Dispense with copper gutters and use wood of suitable quality instead	$300.00
8th Dispense with windows in cupola and have balustrade instead	$ 25.00
TOTAL	$2,083.00

In addition the commissioners ordered the omission of a slate roof and substitution of a tin roof instead. The builder was directed to make the changes and deduct them from his bill. At the same time the commissioners arranged for the purchase and installation of two fireproof safes. [5]

On a site fronting on Military Road, construction of the courthouse began in April, 1858 and was completed in seven months as planned in November. The structure cost a total of $35,000. The clock was added at a later date, a gift to the town from generous individuals. Up the hill from the courthouse, the new county jail was finished at a cost of $27,000. The local media described the building: "This is a building for use and not ornament, still it is due to the Commissioners and Designer to admit that it is a fine looking structure and an addition to the looks of the place." [6]

A lynching in Maine

The community did not always rely on the courts to dispense punishment. A local tale about a lynching went as follows: [7]

Two brothers by the name of Hayden did the threshing for the farmers in that vicinity. They were rumored to be fine men, and first class story tellers. Their coming was always a great pleasure to which we looked forward and made a break in the long, long winter. Later one Hayden who had become Sheriff was sent to a camp 20 miles in the woods to arrest a man named Jim Cullen. He reached there at night. Cullen agreed to go out with him in the morning. Some time during the night he killed the sheriff with an ax, set the camp on fire and fled. When Sheriff Hayden failed to return, men went in search for him, found the camp still smoldering, and Hayden's partly burned body in the ruins. Several days later the murderer was captured and brought by sleigh to Presque Isle by a deputy sheriff. He was met outside the village by a mob. They dug a hole in the road where the sleigh runner would go and covered it with brush and snow. Men were lined up on each side of the road. When the sleigh runner went down, men took the horse by the head, others pulled the deputy sheriff from the sleigh and sat on him while some put a rope around the neck of the prisoner, dragged him to a tree and hanged him.

Expanding the Houlton Courthouse

Growth in local and county needs led to the expanded use of the courthouse. By 1882, even the town library was housed in a "small locker" or box for books kept at the courthouse. In 1889, plans for modification of the courthouse were prepared by Wilfred E. Mansur of Bangor, who also designed a new county jail. The project got underway in 1895. The new addition to the courthouse contained eight rooms, four on each floor. The addition extended the 1859 building and virtually replicated the earlier architecture. Its cost was $20,000.

A major fire in Houlton destroyed much of the downtown area in 1902, but the courthouse escaped undamaged. Remarkably, the Black Hawk Tavern, the original site of court terms, also escaped destruction in the fire. In 1928, another addition to the courthouse was made, with a long new wing on the north end of the courthouse. At the same time, gambrel roofed pediments were built over the 1895 portion of the building.

It was during this period that the writer of *The Meddybemps Letters* jokingly described the county as a place "where it was customary to promise everyone anything they wanted and then take it yourself if you could get hold of it. …" The author of the letters described the Republican Party of that time as "…a cross between a crowd of archangels and a gold mine." [8]

The Courthouse in Caribou

Sessions for the Aroostook County Superior Court in Caribou were authorized in 1885. The first sessions of the court were held in Clark's Hall, with Judge Robinson presiding. Clark's Hall was a three story wooden building at the corner of Main and Sweden Streets. On the first floor were two stores. On the second floor were law offices, first occupied by attorneys George I. Trickey, William P. Allen, and Louis C. Stearns. The third floor of the building was a hall where for many years gatherings of all kinds—plays such as "Uncle Tom's Cabin," public dances, dance schools, town meeting—were held. It was in this hall that the first court in Caribou convened.

The legislature transferred jurisdiction of the Superior Court to the Supreme Judicial Court in 1893, and provided that "the county of Aroostook should furnish proper and convenient rooms and accommodations in the Town of Caribou for the use of the Supreme Judicial Court." Terms for the Supreme Court were set for the fourth Tuesday of April and the third Tuesday of September at Houlton for civil and criminal business, and at Caribou the first Tuesday in December for civil business alone. For the next two years, the Supreme Judicial Court sat in Clark's Hall. [9]

A special law was passed in 1895 authorizing the construction of the Caribou Courthouse. The Legislature directed the county commissioners "to construct of brick and furnish a suitable courthouse in Caribou, in which to hold such terms of the Supreme Judicial, probate and insolvent courts as might, by law, be held in Caribou at a total expense of twenty thousand dollars. Provided, however, that there should be first tendered to the Commissioners a good and sufficient deed of land in Caribou village, running to the county, free of charge, upon which to build the Courthouse." [10]

The courthouse in Caribou was designed by Wilfred Mansur in 1895. The building has a facade with three arches and a large triangular pediment above the second story. This design may have been a precursor to the architect's plan for the Bangor/Penobscot County Courthouse, constructed eight years later.

There was considerable difficulty in finding a lot that suited everyone, but the deadlock was broken when Lyman Stevens offered to give the town the lot where the courthouse was built. Constructing the courthouse, the first brick building in town, cost $21,000 for the building and its furnishings. It was built during the summer of 1895 and occupied by the December term of court. The Caribou Courthouse was expanded by an addition in 1975, which provided for county offices, judge's chambers, and a large new law library.

[1] Putnam, Cora M., *The Story of Houlton*, Portland: House of Falmouth, Inc., 1958, p. 119

[2] Id, p. 249

[3] *Id.*, p. 253

[4] U.S. Department of the Interior, National Register of Historic Places, Registration Form, Aroostook County Courthouse and Jail, p. 2

[5] *Id.* p. 3

[6] Barnes, Francis, *The Story of Houlton, from the Public Records, and from the Experiences of its Founders, Their Descendants and Associates to the Present Time*. Houlton: Will H. Smith, 1889, n.p.

[7] "Aroostook Then and Now" *The Lewiston Journal*, reprint Nov. 16, 1929 in Aroostook county: A colection of Articles published 1928-1970 Vol 1. p. 13, n.d.

[8] Pattengall, William R., *The Meddybemps Letters*, Lewiston: Journal Company, 1924

[9] White, Stella King, *Early History of Caribou, Maine*, 1843-1895, published by the author, n.d., pp. 107-108

[10] *Id.*, p. 135

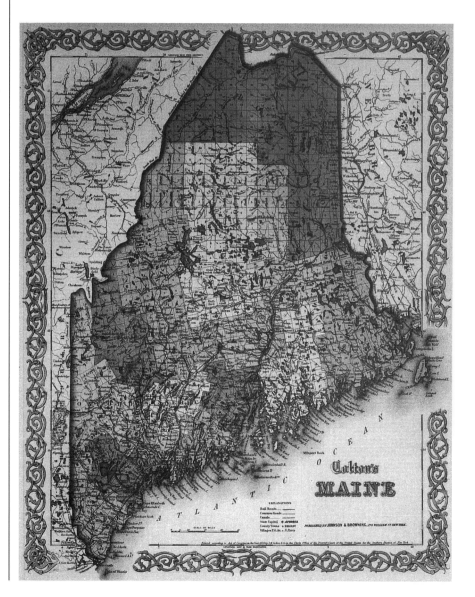

FIFTEEN

Androscoggin County
1854

At the rim of the cove ceiling in the newly restored courtroom in the Androscoggin County Courthouse in Auburn are the words: "Fidelity, Ethics, Morals, Truth, Justice, Mercy, Equity and Right." Embossed with gold leaf, the words, along with four State of Maine seals, comprise a pattern that merges with stenciled leaves above the windows and delicate tracery painted on the walls. The ceiling is highlighted by a skylight or "dome," planned when the original building was designed and built over 140 years ago. The principal courtroom, now gleaming and restored to its original state, has a high ceiling with fluted columns between large arched windows on each wall. The room is the highlight of a handsome brick building with a mansard roof.

Androscoggin County was one of the last counties set up in Maine, established as a consequence of the substantial growth of Lewiston and Auburn. In 1853 a proposal was developed in the state legislature to take land from Cumberland, Oxford, Kennebec and Lincoln counties to form a new county around the two towns. The sponsors of the act intended to have Lewiston designated as the county seat, but immediate opposition arose. When the final bill setting up Androscoggin County was passed by the legislature, a referendum was established for the residents of the new county to vote for the shire town. Three towns—Lewiston, Auburn and Danville—were candidates. After signing the bill on March 18, 1854, Governor William G. Crosby appointed temporary county officials to serve until an election could be held. Construction of the county building was postponed until the fall voting and selection of a shire town. In the meantime, Lewiston served as the site for county offices.

At the election on October 2, 1854, residents of the county chose

The New County and its Shire Town

Auburn as the shire town by a majority of 876 votes. Of the three towns vying for the privilege of being the county town, Danville cast most of its votes for its neighbor, Auburn. On November 15, Governor Crosby proclaimed Auburn as shire town of the county, adding that the voting throughout the county established the shire town "to all intents and purposes the same as if it had been designated by the act creating the county."

Immediately after the proclamation by the Governor, county offices were moved from Lewiston to Auburn into the "brick dwelling of Mrs. Davis," a building rented for administrative offices. Probate court was held in the Engine Hall on North Main Street. But the town moved slowly in finding a permanent site and home for the terms of the Court of Common Pleas and the Supreme Judicial Court. As a result, with no building constructed by the end of the year, Chief Justice Shepley of the Supreme Judicial Court adjourned the winter session of his court to Lewiston, where space was found in Jones Hall, which later became known as the lower railroad station. [1]

The county commissioners returned the court proceedings to Auburn in April, 1855. Space was rented for terms of court at Auburn Hall, a privately-operated meeting hall in the heart of town. Later that year, the county commissioners purchased a site for the new courthouse in the rapidly developing "Lewiston Falls" section of town, near the Lewiston-Auburn bridge. The property, at the corner of Main Street and the road to Turner, consisted of almost one acre of land in the farmstead of Thomas Little. The purchase price was $1,800. As the next step, the county administration commissioned plans for the new courthouse and other county buildings to be drawn up by Gridley J. F. Bryant of Boston, just beginning a career that would include designs for many other buildings in Maine. In November 1855, the commissioners voted to accept Bryant's plans, and began grading the site to prepare for construction.

Public bidding to construct the courthouse took place in early 1856, under the supervision of Isaac S. Small, Joseph Chase, and Samuel F. Waterman, county commissioners. The contract for the buildings was let to Albert Currier of Newburyport, Massachusetts for a total price of $69,753. The work of building the courthouse, county offices and jail was completed in only fifteen and one-half months, and the courthouse opened for business on January 1, 1857. Auburn commemorated the occasion by changing the street names in the center of town. Main Street became known as Court Street, and River Street was redesignated as Main Street.

At the site of the new courthouse, three major interconnected buildings housed the courts, the county administrative offices and the jail. The frontage of the complex was substantial: over one hundred feet long on the

Turner Street side, and over fifty feet on the Court Street side. The buildings were prudently designed to be fireproof, with vaults for county records, and fire doors between wings of the building. The most prominent part of the new construction housed the courtroom, county offices and the Register of Deeds. It fronted on Turner Street at the corner of Court Street. The first floor housed the county offices, the second the 55' x 50' courtroom and the rooms for jury deliberations. There was a partial third floor, initially used only for storage, behind the mansard roof. The roof was slate, rising in "hipped" fashion from each side of the building, to meet a flat portion at the top. In the center of the flat roof was a cupola or dome light which let natural light through the third floor into the courtroom.

At the northern end of the courthouse buildings were the jail keeper's

The Androscoggin County Courthouse in Auburn.
Maine Historic Preservation Commission

house and the two story jail. Between the court building and the jail was the section housing the Probate Court, which was described as two stories high, but the cellar raised the building significantly on the Turner Street side. Long stairways led to the front door of both the jail keeper's house and the courthouse from Turner Street.

The Knight Case [2]

The new courthouse was put to immediate use in a famous murder trial. In October, 1856, a woman was murdered in the town of Poland. Her husband, George Knight, was immediately suspected of the crime. Although Knight was "known as forehanded and a hard worker," he had made threats to his wife which she had reported to friends and neighbors. On the night of the murder Knight set out with a load of shingles for delivery in the town of Gray. According to the testimony at trial, he did not go far, but hitched his oxen to a tree in deep woods and stole back to his house. He found Mrs. Knight sleeping in his mother's room and cut her throat with a butcher knife. His mother ran shrieking from the room and her cries wakened a visiting niece and nephew who ran to the neighbors for help. No one including the mother saw the killer, but the niece saw the shadow of a man.

The neighbors caught up with Knight in Gray and told him what had happened. He "seemed unconcerned" and finished his delivery of the shingles. Although he denied a role in the murder, he was taken into custody and put in jail. County Attorney Goddard interviewed him, and noted Knight's composure. Goddard wondered how he had stayed so clean if he had been delivering shingles. In a dream that night, Goddard saw Knight in a blood-stained undershirt. He immediately went to see Knight and asked to see his undershirt. "At this the prisoner paled. He would have refused had he dared, but the men who guarded him were too grim. As he bared the long sleeve of his underwear, Goddard could see that it was soaked in blood "'clotted and caked to the cloth.'"

The trial in the winter of 1857 was a local sensation. It was conducted by Judge Walton. The prosecution was led by Maine Attorney General Nathan Appleton and Charles W. Goddard, the county attorney. The defense attorneys were Nathan Clifford and David Dunn. The trial began on February 16 and ended on March 10. The trial became so sensationalized that it caused comment in the *New York Times*:

"The Way They Manage Murder Trials in Maine — In one of the small towns of Maine, among an entirely rural population, they are enjoying the excitement of a Maine murder trial with as much gusto as any affair of the sort creates even in this wicked metropolis. A man named George Knight is on trial for the murder of his wife and to such a pitch is the excitement caused that a daily paper has been established expressly to chronicle the proceedings, while the place of trial is crowded with the fairer part of the population, who take their knitting and sewing with them, like German women at a concert, or the Boston women at a Lowell lecture. Murder trials have not yet become quite so prominent in New York."

Editors of the daily *Lewiston Journal*, transformed by the trial from a weekly, promptly retorted that murders in New York could never become sensational because they were such an everyday event. The *Journal* devoted most of the space in its daily edition to the trial, and the inauguration of the President in Washington, D.C. was "dismissed with a scant two stickfuls."

The trial raced onward with testimony from nephew and niece and observers. One witness testified to seeing Knight throw an object into the bushes which turned out to be a bloody butcher knife. Others testified to locked windows and doors which precluded an escape route for Mrs. Knight. Testimony was introduced about the expressed suspicions of Mrs. Knight that she was being gradually poisoned. Following final arguments, the jury deliberated for a total of 25 hours, returning a finding of guilty. Knight was sentenced in September of 1857. He spent the next 43 years in the state prison at Thomaston.

In 1867 two elderly women were murdered at their home in West Auburn. The two women—Susannah Kinsley and Polly Caswell—made their living by binding shoes at their home for a local shoe factory. Their murder was discovered by a friend, Issac Libbey, who frequently visited to see to their needs. On the cold day Libbey made his discovery, heavy snow covered the ground. Inside their home the two women were found, one with a fractured skull and the other with her throat cut. Because both bodies were frozen solid, it was not known immediately when the crime had occurred. The snow thoroughly obscured the footprints of the murderers.

Suspecting a connection to the shoe business, investigators located Clifton Harris who worked at the same shoe factory that employed the two women. Harris, a shoe worker, was found with blood on the edges of his boots. When questioned, he admitted having been at the scene, but accused another shoe worker, Luther Verrill, of the crimes. Harris stated that both men had been present, but that Verrill had committed the murders. Harris also stated that the two of them had gone there intending to rob the women, and had gained entrance through an unlocked window. Discovered by the women during the break-in, they panicked and Verrill hit them with chairs.

The Trial of Verrill and Harris[3]

Verrill testified to virtually the same story, but said he had not done the killing, but had watched as Harris murdered the two women. Both defendants testified, but Harris was more specific in describing the events. Although the jury found both Verrill and Harris guilty of the crime, Verrill was later released when Harris recanted part of his story. Harris was sentenced to one year in prison prior to hanging. He was just 20 years old. The execution took place in 1869.

The Mystery of the Headless Skeleton[4]

One of the most sensational events in the history of the Androscoggin County Courthouse was the trial heard by the Supreme Judicial Court at its annual term in Androscoggin County in 1875. The trial was based on the discovery of the headless skeleton of a woman, found some years after her death. The local media luridly described the scene: the body was "encased in a silk dress, in a secluded and desolate spot, yet within the precincts of a city, where it had lain above ground for years." The head was never found. The case turned entirely on identification of the woman's body by people who recognized her clothing and purse, and by witnesses to her relationship to her husband, James Lowell, the suspected murderer.

Lowell, age 31, was a railroad worker and farm helper who had served in the Civil War. Witnesses said he and his wife had an unpleasant marriage, with frequent loud arguments, and that Lowell had threatened his wife with a knife. On a carriage ride, when he had become enraged, she had jumped from the carriage and he pursued her, striking her with the horse whip. On another occasion, he threw water at her in a public place, saying she was "having a fit." After much abusive treatment, Mrs. Lowell began to live separately from her husband. Lowell persisted in contacting her. At her new residence, he appeared with a pistol and demanded she return to live with him, threatening to shoot her if she refused. A week later she was missing, and Lowell maintained she ran off with a man from a traveling circus from Australia.

Two years later, the bones was found and shortly after, the county coroner summoned a jury of inquest. Visiting the site early in the morning, the jury agreed on the indictment by 10:00 a.m. the same day. H.H. Richardson, the Lewiston City marshal, arrested Lowell in Lawrence and brought him to Lewiston on October 18, 1873. The grand jury brought the indictment on January 24, 1874. On the same day Attorney General H. M. Plaisted moved for arraignment of the prisoner. Judge Charles W. Walton presided. Counsel was assigned to Lowell: Eben Pillsbury of Augusta and M.T. Ludden of Lewiston.

The trial began on February 10, 1874 when the clerk called the list of the 50 traverse jurors summoned for the trial. An all-male jury was selected on the first morning of the trial. In the afternoon, opening statements began. Prosecutor Plaisted had assembled a great number of witnesses to testify against Lowell. The statements of the witnesses took five days. Witnesses testified that, after Mrs. Lowell disappeared, her husband sold her clothes, bartering them for a watch. Some time later, he bartered her fur cape in exchange for another watch. He bartered a pair of his own black-and-white checked pants in exchange for boots, then bought another pair of pants in exactly the same style and color. Blood was found on the pants he bartered away.

Letters to Lowell from his wife supposedly traveling with the circus – from New York, and from Lawrence and Lowell, Massachusetts—were presented. Additional letters, allegedly obscene in content, were found in Lowell's possession but were not presented by the State. The handwriting and spelling in the letters were compared with Lowell's handwriting. Experts agreed that the writing could be by the same hand. Witnesses saw Lowell and his wife go off together on the day she disappeared. All witnesses remembered the day, for it was the day when Central Hall in Lewiston burned. Some saw Lowell at the fire. Several saw the Lowells leave for a ride that day. One person overheard an argument between the Lowells about her talking or flirting with a man from the circus. Edward S. Wood, professor of chemistry in Harvard University medical department and Massachusetts General Hospital, a specialist in the analysis of animal tissues and blood, identified the blood on the bartered pants. At the last moment, the prosecution called as witness Thomas Littlefield who was allowed to testify that Lowell had pleaded guilty in 1873 to stealing seven tons of hay with a value of one hundred and twenty dollars. The fine had been $50.

The case for the defense began on the sixth day of the trial, Monday, February 16, 1874. Physician Benjamin F. Sturgis, was called and stated that there was no evidence that the head had been severed from the body by a knife, ax, or other instrument. Dr. A. Garcelon, a physician, testified that it was impossible for an unskilled hand, even with a sharp instrument, to sever head from body without leaving a trace on the bones of the neck. Dr. Harris, another medical specialist, testified that, when the soft parts of body have disintegrated, "the head will roll." Parents and friends testified to the time Lowell got home the day of his wife's disappearance. His mother said he went out to wash his wagon at a nearby brook. A friend talked of an injury to Lowell's face that spread blood on his "queer-looking" black-and-white checked pants. A crucial witness from the circus testified he saw Mrs. Lowell on the day after the alleged murder, and later saw her with the circus when it was in Rhode Island.

The prisoner testified as well. Lowell stated that he went for a ride on the fateful day, "…after 6:00 p.m., after my tea." He rode around Lewiston and Auburn, and passed the courthouse, returning to his father's house. Although he did not deny marital arguments, he denied the incident with the knife. He also denied writing the letters.

Judge Walton's charge to the jury pointed out aspects of the evidence that had not been fully explained, such as Lowell's possession of a chain and ring belonging to his wife. He then presented the options available to the jury: (1) not guilty; (2) guilty of manslaughter; (3) guilty of murder in the second degree; (4) guilty of murder in the first degree. At 6:35 p.m. the jury retired to the grand jury rooms – a suite of two rooms on the right of the main corridor on the first floor of the courthouse. The rooms were furnished "with comfortable oak seats and desks, … convenient for final discussion of the serious question which the jury had in hand." The judge turned to the sheriff, saying, "…court will be kept open. I shall go to tea. I wish you to preserve the propriety of the place in my absence, and send for me if the jury comes in either with a verdict or for instructions."

At 10:20 p.m. the jury returned with a verdict of guilty. It was the end of the tenth day of the trial. The sentence was death by hanging at the state prison. The execution of the sentence was scheduled for one year later, with Lowell to be retained in the state prison until that time. During that year it was said that Lowell confessed to Sheriff Littlefield that he did kill his wife on the night of June 12th, when they were riding up the Switzerland road. They got into a quarrel and he threw her out of the wagon, over the seat backwards, and broke her neck. But there was never any corroboration to Sheriff Littlefield's story that Lowell confessed to the crime.

Updating the Courthouse

The outward appearance of the Androscoggin County Courthouse has changed remarkably little over the years. Additions to the county buildings and interior renovations have not changed the exterior appearance of the original buildings significantly. In 1922 a three-story addition was added along Court Street. The addition was constructed under the supervision of the County Commissioners Fred L. Levitt, Albert B. Nealy, and Chester V. Chipman. The architect was Harry S. Coombs, and the contractor was George W. Lane and Co. The new building housed the Register of Probate and the Register of Deeds, along with new court-related rooms on the second floor. In 1970 and again in 1990 substantial additions were made to the county jail.

The old courtroom still serves its purposes admirably, and has been restored to its appearance when the building was constructed. A seated figure of Justice overlooks the room from a hemispherical mural painted by Harry Cochrane. The room retains unusual touches such as swivel chairs for the jury, and curtained doors at either side of the bench. The rooms of the Androscoggin County Historical society are located on the

Left: Auburn's Androscoggin County Courthouse today.

Below: The graceful court room on the second floor of the Androscoggin County Courthouse in Auburn.
Jacob Sloane

third floor of the courthouse, with a collection of American Indian implements and items of local historical interest, including files on historic trials in Androscoggin County. The building was placed on the National Register of Historic Places in 1983.

---

[1] Merrill, Georgia Drew, Ed., History of Androscoggin County, Maine, Boston: W.A. Ferguson and Co., 1891, p. 308

[2] Case material based on files and news clips compiled by the Androscoggin Historical Society, Auburn

[3] Case material based on files and news clips compiled by the Androscoggin Historical Society, Auburn

[4] *Trial of James M. Lowell, indicted for the Murder of His Wife, Mary Elizabeth Lowell*, Report of court stenographers, Portland: Dresser, McLennan & Co., 1875

SIXTEEN

Sagadahoc County
1854

The Sagadahoc County Courthouse was built on its hill in 1869 — some 15 years after the County of Sagadahoc was formed from a portion of Lincoln County. Just before the new building opened, nearly 130 years ago, the *Bath Sentinel and Times* editorialized: "It is now conceded by nearly the entire community that the best spot in the city was selected [for the courthouse]. It is on an elevation overlooking the city, the river, and surrounding country, and is the first building seen on approaching the city from any direction, by land or water."

Sagadahoc County was formed by a legislative act in 1854, and Bath was named the shire town or county seat. A courthouse was not immediately available to house terms of court or the county personnel. Until a courthouse could be built, the county commissioners accepted the city's invitation to house the court and its personnel in the existing Bath municipal building. A relatively large structure, the town house had been constructed in 1838 with funds the state had received as a windfall from the federal government. These funds came from an accumulation of revenue under the high tariff policies of the John Quincy Adams era. When President Andrew Jackson took office, the surplus in revenues had reached $40,000,000. After long deliberation, Congress decided to distribute the surplus to states in proportion to population. Maine in turn voted to pass the money on to its towns, *per capita*.

In 1837, Bath was notified it would receive $10,000 from this source. The townsfolk voted to spend $4,000 for a town hall, $2,000 as a loan to the ferry company, $3,000 for a new almshouse, and $1,000 to be saved until required for a new bridge at New Meadows. In April 1838 the town changed its mind, and some of the funds were distributed to residents *per*

The First Court Sessions in Bath

capita. However, the town collectively felt obligated under the earlier vote to move forward with the town hall. A resident questioned whether the town was obligated to build the town hall, and an opinion was sought from outside counsel. When consulted, three Portland lawyers—Prentiss Mellen, William Preble and Samuel Fessenden—concurred that the city was obligated, and the town borrowed money to construct the building.

The town hall was originally a mixed-use building, with retail stores on the first floor to bring in revenue. Stone steps spanned the front of the building, leading up to three doors. Two of the doors led to the space for retail establishments at the two front corners of the building. The middle door led to a small rear room used for a schoolroom and to a winding stairway to the second floor. Virtually all of the upper floor was occupied by the meeting hall, but there were two small offices for the town clerk and treasurer. The town voted to authorize selectmen to permit the use of the hall free of expenses for public meetings of citizens, military and other public purposes, excluding shows and theatrical performances. Persons using the hall were expected to be responsible for its "proper and safe use."

Parade celebration passes the Sagadahoc County Courthouse in Bath.
Maine Historical Society

Sagadahoc County courts were first held in the Bath City Hall.

By the time the court began to use the meeting room, the town hall had been slightly rebuilt. When Bath became a city in 1848, the building became the city hall. The retail stores on the first floor were removed, and their exterior doors were closed up. The retail space was divided into rooms for city council and principal officers. A vault was added under the stairs. When the court officials arrived in 1854, offices were provided from the remodeled space used by city officials.

Opening day of the court sessions in the great hall on the second floor was a matter of great pomp and ceremony. On the specified day court was to begin, a formal procession entered the room. First came the County Sheriff, then the Judge, followed by his deputies. Then came "all and every member of the Bar," carrying the traditional green bags with all their paraphernalia. By 1861, court was announced by a Paul Revere Bell, which had been purchased by the city from the 1803 North Church, and installed in a new belfry on the city hall.

The county commissioners began to plan for more permanent quarters for the court. In 1857 they voted to petition the legislature to borrow up to $10,000 for county buildings, and authorized the chairman to "attend to the Petition." The Legislature authorized a question on the county ballot to determine public sentiment about borrowing funds to build new buildings. The November 1859 election results, with all the towns in the county voting except Richmond, returned 2,088 votes, 961 voting for the loan and 1,127 voting against it. [1]

Voting for a New Courthouse

Despite this loss, the county commissioners continued in their quest for new buildings. The 1864 Legislature allowed the county to spend $8,500 toward a courthouse but did not approve the remaining $10,000 requested by the county. The commissioners pushed forward and bought a courthouse site for $1,500, meanwhile arranging to continue the use of the meeting hall in Bath's city hall at an annual rent of $200.

In 1867, the county commissioners asked the Legislature for permission to issue bonds in the amount of $10,000 to cover the expense of a courthouse. This time permission was granted, and the county hired architect Francis Henry Fassett to design the new building. Fassett had designed the old Bath High School, Bath Academy, and the medical school building (now Adams Hall) at Bowdoin College. He was Bath's resident architect until 1864, when he moved to Portland. For his courthouse work, Fassett received $300 in 1869 and $400 in 1870.

The commissioners, with plans in hand, divided the work into segments. They advertised for proposals in April, 1867 to construct the foundation of the courthouse. The two bids received from local contractors were for $9,400 and $7,985 for the special blasting needed to prepare the site for the new building and to construct the foundation and basement. To complete the building, the commissioners asked the voters of the county to authorize taking out a loan of $25,000. The election in September, 1867, although not entirely enthusiastic, resulted in 1,125 "Yes" votes in favor of the loan and 1,002 "no" votes. With this slim margin, the county commissioners were empowered to continue the new courthouse.

But the work of the commissioners was not finished. Another $30,000 would be required to fully finance the construction of the building. The approval of the legislature was sought for bonding this amount. Receiving approval in December of 1867, the commissioners issued the bonds in April, 1868, bringing the total cost for the new building to $65,000. Bids were solicited, and the award of the construction contracts went to Reed and Nichols for the "stone and mason work of the superstructure" and C.H. Hartwell and Co. for the "joiner work."

Progress on the new building was rapid. Within a year, the *Bath Sentinel and Times* reported:

"The county building, commenced about a year ago, is now nearly completed. … The offices are all well arranged and elegantly furnished, and the courtroom, which is 45 feet by 55, has no superior in point of arrangement and beauty of finish in New England. …Directly in front is the elegant monument erected in memory of fallen soldiers from Bath and vicinity. It is surrounded by an iron fence, enclosing what was once an unsightly vacant lot." [2]

In preparation for opening, the commissioners hired a new court messenger and the local paper remarked: "We are pleased to learn that the County Commissioners have employed Mr. William Willis, a gallant one-legged soldier of the 8th Maine Volunteers, as messenger at the new courthouse. Places like these, we believe, should never be filled by an able-bodied man when disabled soldiers can be found who will answer the purpose, and we are glad to know that our County Commissioners are of the same way of thinking." [3]

Before the building was occupied, it was struck by lightning. The newspaper reported the effects of lightning "fluid":

"The building is not yet supplied with lightning conductors, and the fluid, in consequence, shed about in a very miscellaneous way. It evidently first struck the top of the vane rod and followed the rod to its termination in a heavy timber in the upper part of the belfry. Enraged at finding its route cut off so suddenly, it knocked the belfry to smithereens in less than no time, shivering large timbers into fine fragments. The vane rod with its attachments was brought down and the northwest corner of the belfry was rent to pieces from top to bottom. …At the base of the belfry the fluid kindled a fire…[which] for a moment appeared to be serious, being in a position most difficult to get at; but the strenuous exertions of Mr. Commissioner Adams and Clerk of Courts Hayes soon made access to it and a few buckets of water did the business for it. … Mr. Willis was in the cellar of the courthouse and it knocked him down making him see 'stars'."

Repairs to the nearly-demolished belfry cost $200. [4]

The dedication ceremonies for the new courthouse occurred on August 18, 1869 with the Maine Supreme Judicial Court in attendance. Chief Justice Jonathan G. Dickenson delivered the dedicatory address. This eminent jurist had previously been principal of the Bath Academy and was at one time a contributor to the newspapers of Bath.

For the occasion, the *Bath Daily Sentinel and Times* described the new courthouse in some detail:

"The building now occupied for the first time by the Supreme Court is conceded to be one of the best courthouses in the State. In all its parts it is creditable to the skill and fidelity of those who have had control of the work. Mr. Fassett, the architect, Messrs. Couillard & Coombe, contractors for building the foundation and basement, Messrs. Reed & Nichols, contractors for the stone and mason work of the superstructure, and Messrs. C.H. Hartwell & Co., contractors for the joiner work, may all of them point to that structure as an evidence of what they can do in their respective branches of business. ... The building is 85 feet long and 53 feet six inches wide. The offices on the first floor are fourteen feet high in the clear. The first and second doors at the right hand open into the Probate Court room and the Register's office; the last door on the right admits to the Grand Jury room, and between this and probate office is a room for the accommodation of witnesses in attendance upon the Grand Jury. ... The first office at the left hand is that of the Clerk of Courts; next is the County Commissioners' room; and still beyond in the last room on the left, is the office of the Register of Deeds. ... A grand stairway, rising from either side of the hall, leads to the Court room and the adjoining offices. The Court room is 45 by 51 feet and 25 feet high. and in the finish and furnishing, it will not suffer by a comparison with any court room in the state. ... The fixtures in the court rooms are all made of black walnut and elaborately finished. The Judges' desk affords ample accommodations for five or six judges, should occasion require. The clerk's desk is admirably constructed both for convenience and for the safety of whatever he has in charge. 'The gentlemen of the bar' will no longer find themselves confined in the meager space they have hitherto been compelled to occupy. Lawyers, sheriff and sheriff's officers, jurors and witnesses are all furnished with an abundance of elbow room and ample accommodations. ... The private room for the Judge is situated adjacent to the Courtroom and may be entered either from the hall below or directly from the Court room. The room for the law library is opposite the Judge's room, and has the same facility of access. Both rooms are furnished so as to be admirably adapted to their appropriate uses. ... Fronting the Court room are the two jury rooms, one on either side of the entrance. Over each of the jury rooms and also over the Judge's room and law library, are lobbies which may be used for consultation with clients and witnesses and for the accommodation of parties having business in Court." [5]

Dedicating the Sagadahoc County Courthouse

The *Daily Sentinel and Times* continued with its coverage of the news of the opening of the building for court business:

"The occasion of the holding of the first session of the Court in the new Court building was deemed, by the members of the Sagadahoc Bar, as a proper one for the observance of exercises appropriate to the setting apart of the building to the purposes for which it was constructed. Accordingly at a meeting of the Bar last week the necessary arrangements were made, and public notice given that appropriate dedicatory exercises were to be held at the "coming in of the Court" yesterday morning. ... At 10 o'clock A.M., the Court Room being filled with ladies and gentlemen, the sheriff announced 'the Court,' and His Honor Judge Dickenson, accompanied by the Chaplain Rev. J.O. Fiske, D.D., came in and took their places at the desk. ... The exercises were opened with an exceedingly appropriate and fervent petition to the great Law Giver by Rev. Mr. Fiske, after which County Attorney Adams ...requested that the ordinary routine of business incident to the opening of the session be postponed, which request was granted. ... Hon. Henry Tallman—the oldest member of the Bar save one—then delivered the dedicatory address, which was attentively listened to and received with much favor."

It is worth noting that Mr. Tallman found it necessary to defend the jury system from its detractors in his dedicatory address:

"I believe that if there is any place in this world where we may go to find justice it is here: that is, in a courthouse. I have had some considerable experience with the verdicts of juries. I have heard verdicts which were thought to have been given under passion or inattention, but in referring back to a practice of more than thirty years, at the general character of the verdicts of juries, I am satisfied that such erroneous verdicts are an exception, and that the men who lift up their voices against this great bulwark—the trial by jury—know not what they do. It is the bulwark, the life and safety of all our institutions..."

His Honor Judge Dickenson, in reply, began in praise of national growth and the progress of civilization, and closed as follows:

"It is a little remarkable that while the hand of reform has dealt so unsparingly with every other department of civilization it has approached the common law with such deference and respect. And why is it so? Why is it that the elementary treatises of Coke and Littleton and Lord Mansfield and Erskin and Justice Marshall and Chancellor Kent are received at the bar and by the Court with the same authority as the decisions of living jurists? Why is it that conservatism has marked the character of the common law, with the exception of such changes as have been made in the law of evidence and the law touching the rights of married women? I look upon it as the highest compliment paid by the advancing civilization of the world to the common law, a system of jurisprudence that existed long before there was a railroad or telegraph or any very considerable and minute commercial relations between the different sections of the globe, and which was at the same time so flexible and comprehensive in its character that it is adapted to each of the ten thousand different questions that arise? Can it but be well denominated the perfection of human reason? ... And it is for the purpose of administering this law in all its purity, its fidelity and its power that this spacious edifice has been erected by the public spirit and enterprise of the good citizens of the County of Sagadahoc. Then let us one and all: Court and Bar and people, unite heartily together and dedicate this edifice to the cause of public order, to truth, to justice, to liberty and to law; and when, a century hence, posterity shall occupy the place we now occupy in the celebration of the anniversary of this day, God grant that it may be in a land of liberty protected by law." [6]

To close the ceremony, the County Attorney moved and the members of the bar concurred "that these proceedings be entered upon the Records of the Court, and the formal business of the Court suspended until tomorrow." Following the ceremonies, the members of the bar with a few invited guests dined together at the Sagadahoc House, with their President, Charles W. Larrabee, Esq., presiding. The *Bath Daily Sentinel and Times* could not help speculating about the meal: "As the affair was strictly private, we have not ventured to inquire as to what took place in the dining room though we doubt not that all present enjoyed themselves finely." [7]

At the time the Sagadahoc County Court was established in 1854, there were 22 practicing attorneys in the area. By the time of the dedication of the courthouse in 1869, the county bar comprised only eleven individuals. At the dedication of the building, Mr. Tallman noted this decline, and congratulated the county for its steadfastness and determination to proceed with construction of the building to show "the marks of justice and truth throughout the community." [8]

Improving the Sagadahoc Courthouse Facilities

Sagadahoc County grew steadily in economic importance after 1869. The courthouse was constantly improved. The old coal/wood burning stoves were replaced by steam heat in the 1880s. Hardwood floors were added to the courtroom and register's office and the floors in other areas were carpeted. In 1898, a large county flag was hung over the courthouse balcony, "falling within a few feet of the stone steps." A brick sidewalk was constructed in front of the building, with the city paying for the curb stone, and the county for the bricks. Steel shelves, filing cabinets and pigeon holes were installed for papers and records. Steel roller shelves were added to save wear and tear on most-used records. A metal roof to repel rain from the flat roof was installed after a portion of the frescoed

ceiling in the courtroom collapsed from accumulated moisture. The finish in the public rooms was frequently repainted, "…the furniture varnished and radiators, steam pipes and gas [lighting] fixtures …given new coats."[9]

The Commissioners cooperated with neighbors in annual rituals to maintain and improve the appearance of the courthouse. In 1905, they agreed to pay $25 to sprinkle water on High, Court and Center Streets to keep the dust down. To beautify the grounds, they brought in 150 loads of loam and sod, planted three flower beds, and built a road for a tidy approach to the coal chute. The belfry was repaired in 1919.

During the first World War, Bath Iron Works was booming, and the City of Bath was thriving economically. The courthouse bell rang out to celebrate the armistice in 1918. However, after the boom came the fall: BIW delivered its last ship to the Navy in 1925. With the termination of war contracts, a postwar shipping glut, and international agreements to limit size of navies, BIW seemed doomed. The company was unable to honor its obligation or devise a reorganization plan acceptable to its creditors. In October, 1925, BIW was auctioned off on the steps of the county courthouse. The winning bidder was a New York junk dealer, who scrapped out the yard, and left the buildings empty. In 1927 the company reorganized, and survived the depression with a 1931 contract for one Navy destroyer.

As WWII approached, BIW once more prospered, and the city hummed with activity. After WWII, improvements to the courthouse resumed. In the 1950s, the old heating system was replaced and in 1961,

paid off with rent from the probation and parole office, a County Extension office and the Superior Court. The state earmarked about $70,000 to aid the county in renovating the building to be accessible to the handicapped.

For the first time in nearly 35 years, the County of Sagadahoc voted to borrow money for capital improvements to a public building. Groundbreaking took place in a ceremony on May 21, 1986. The addition to the courthouse was completed and occupied in April, 1987. The renovation of the existing building continued, with the construction of fire stairs throughout. The old bell was relocated to the area that links the old and new portion of the building.

---

[1] Snow, Richard F., *Old Sagadahoc*, Topsham: R. Snow, 1987, p. 2

[2] *Id.*, p. 11

[3] *Id.*, p. 12

[4] *Id.*, pp. 12-13

[5] This account is from "The Court House–The Dedication," *Daily Sentinel and Times*, Bath, August 18, 1869; Snow, pp. 14 -15

[6] Snow, p. 20

[7] *Id.*, pp. 20-21

[8] *Id.*, p. 16

[9] *Id.*, p. 31, pp. 38-39

SEVENTEEN

Knox County

1860

Knox County, the newest of Maine's counties, is already over 100 years old. The history of the buildings used by the court has been well documented since the county's establishment in 1860. The present courthouse is unique in Maine for its diverse tenants: it rents interior space to a private engineering firm, and the courtroom has been used twice as a set for producing movies.

The area contained in the present Knox County was a part of Lincoln and Waldo counties until 1860. The rapidly increasing number of cases brought to court in Lincoln County required a seven week term by 1858, but most of the cases were from the eastern part of Lincoln County. Because of the overload, Rockland was made a half-shire town, and the next year a term of the Supreme Judicial Court was held in Rockland in Atlantic Hall, the upper portion of the Ulmer Block. The one term in 1858 was not sufficient to satisfy the east Lincoln towns and resulted in giving Rockland area boosters the justification for the need for a new county.

An 1859 plan was drawn up to form a new county from parts of Lincoln and Waldo counties, with Camden as shire town. The vote in the towns was overwhelmingly in favor but the Legislature did not agree to the plan.

In 1860, another proposal was made, but with Rockland as shire town. The Rockland City Council appropriated $500 to be used in furthering the idea. Local people cited the potential savings in expense and travel time. From some parts of the proposed county, the trip to Wiscasset for court was fifty miles each way. One case which lasted eleven days involved between 50 and 60 witnesses who were required to travel from St. George to Wiscasset. Fortunately, Republicans in Augusta determined to help the formation of the new county, with the goal of creating available positions

Creating a new county

The addition of Knox County in 1860 completed the roster of Maine counties.

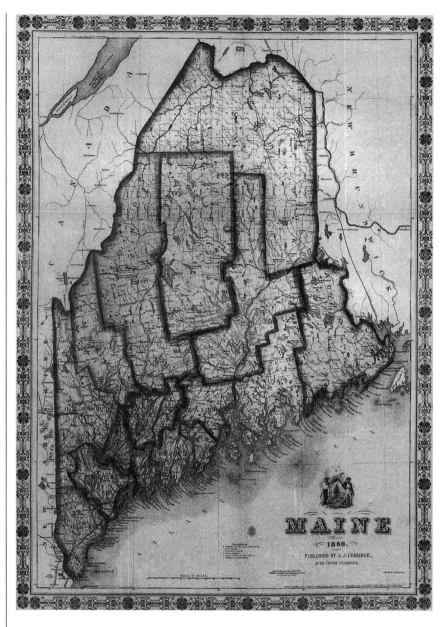

for loyal party members, since Lincoln County had a history of voting Democratic.

The 1860 plan proposed placing the question of forming a new county before the voters of the area. Initial reactions in legislative committee were negative, and Lincoln and Waldo county representatives led the opposition to the proposal. The legislature was preoccupied by the embezzlement of $94,073 by the state treasurer from state funds "which has converted the liquor traffic into a perfectly organized business carried on by licensed groggeries in every town to promote political ends."[1]

A second effort was made, omitting the proposal to take the plan to a local vote. This time the effort succeeded. A local paper fumed: "When a majority of the people were for the plan of '59, the Republicans defeated it. When they were against the plan of '60, the Republicans were for it." The legislative act secured the new county, and named it for Revolutionary War General Henry Knox, who had lived within the boundaries of the new county. A local newspaper speculated that the reason for denying the vote to the county residents was that the Republicans wanted to make the appointments of the county officers, and did not want to risk waiting until the fall election, when they might be turned out of office.[2]

The response in Rockland was instantly enthusiastic. Brass bands paraded through the town. There was a "vociferous ringing of bells, firing of cannons, a lavish use of fireworks, and burning of tar barrels." The need for a new building, as opposed to renting existing space, was initially viewed as being extravagant, "it being far cheaper to hire than to build." The newly appointed county commissioners were given power to establish county buildings, and the option to appoint a superintendent to build the building over two or three years. The county commissioners rented temporary space for the court in Atlantic Hall. County administrative offices were located upstairs in the Lime Rock Bank on Main Street. Soon after, the court and county offices were brought together in upper floors of the Pillsbury Block, and remained there until construction of the courthouse.[3]

In May, 1860, the Hon. Richard D. Rice of the Supreme Judicial Court came to the new county, and heard cases in Atlantic Hall. The grand jury came back with six indictments: one for murder, two for larceny, one for assault and battery and two against common sellers (violators of the prohibition law.) One man was convicted and sentenced to six months in the county jail for larceny from a vessel, but the other criminal cases were continued for hearing to the next term. The jail was located in Wiscasset and would not be replaced by a building in Rockland for several years.

On the morning of May 17th, 1873, in the Town of Warren, the news began to spread that "close on the heels of vice, murder dire had shown its fearful visage in this town for the first time since its settlement." The body of Dr. P.R. Baker, who had a large practice in the vicinity, was found lying on the floor of the bedroom used by Lucy Ann Mink in her brother's house. Baker had been shot in the heart. On the night of the murder Lucy Mink had gone to the house of a neighbor in her night clothes, acting "crazed or frightened," and stayed the night. No one entered the Mink house till morning, where the corpse of Dr. Baker was found. [4]

The Baker-Mink adultery was well known: gossip had it that Lucy had threatened to take Dr. Baker's life unless she were made mistress of his

The Supreme Judicial Court Comes to Rockland

house. Her guilt seemed clear. A coroner's inquest and a post mortem exam were held. After the arrival from New Hampshire of the "afflicted father and brother-in-law of the misguided man," the body was carried to Baker's home, and the funeral took place in the Baptist Church six days later. Many mourned for him as a physician and friend, and especially grieved for "his disreputable and untimely end."

Lucy Mink was arrested and, after a preliminary hearing, was arraigned and sent for safe keeping to Wiscasset Jail. Her trial took place at the October term of the Supreme Judicial Court at Rockland. Her testimony "condemned her of many crimes but not the shooting of Dr. Barker." The pistol used in the murder could not be found. After deliberation, the jury found her not guilty. Cyrus Eaton, author of "The Annals of Warren" disowns her: "She was not a native of Warren, and has since … taken the life in Lowell, Massachusetts of one Charles Ricker under similar circumstances. [5]

Planning the Knox County Courthouse

The need for a county courthouse became evident after the court and county offices had been in the Pillsbury Block for a few years. A committee was established by the county commissioners to investigate the possibilities for new court space. The committee was authorized:

1. To examine buildings now leased by the County for offices, determine their security and suitability, and what alterations, if any, were necessary for use for a term not exceeding 20 years from expiration of the present lease.
2. To report on terms for renewing lease of the present building.
3. To report on other buildings, presently or to be constructed in Rockland, which might be leased.
4. To procure plans and cost estimate for construction of a courthouse on the county lot at Union and Lime Rock Streets.
5. To prepare a notice to the municipal officers of the towns in the county of the intention of the County Commissioners to obtain a loan for such construction, with consent of the county communities, as required by law.[6]

The committee's completed report leaned toward construction of a new building. It included analyses of present leases, and registered disapproval that the vaults and safes were not fireproof, a critical matter for the records of the Registers of Deeds and Probate. It also reported: "The courtroom is in no respect suitable. For many years it has been a constant subject of complaint on the part of the judges, the Bar and those compelled to attend the courts. …the courtroom could not be heated adequately and in hot weather became almost unbearable. Open windows did little for court procedure, due to constant noise from Main Street traffic below, and this mode of ventilation was termed 'perilous to health.'" The cost of purchasing the Pillsbury Block was estimated to be $30,000 and with necessary improvements it would cost more than constructing a new building.[7]

In February, 1874, the Knox County Commissioners sent out a notice to all the towns of their intention to obtain a $50,000 loan to construct the courthouse. The estimate was based on the recently completed Somerset County Courthouse in Skowhegan, which had cost $48,000. Voting was favorable by a margin of 1434 to 606, with most of the opposition coming from Thomaston, Union and Warren. The architects chosen by the commissioners were Gridley J. F. Bryant and Louis P. Rogers. Bids for constructing the building were opened, and the contractors chosen were William H. Clover, Edward K. Clover, and Albert D. Lowry, with a low bid of $50,024.

The structure designed by Gridley Bryant was to be 85 feet in length, 55 feet wide, with exterior walls 46 1/2 feet tall, of solid brick stationed on a granite foundation. The roof would be hipped from all four corners and finished in slate. The first floor would contain the county offices and fireproof storage for records. The second floor would be taken up by the courtroom, occupying the full width and nearly the full length of the building. A gallery for visitors was projected for the rear of the courtroom.

Work began in June, 1874, under an agreement by the contractor to have all the work completed by March, 1875 or pay a penalty. All exterior work was completed before winter. Construction proceeded smoothly with one close call, when a block of granite weighing a ton and a half was being raised to the second floor level on a derrick. A stabilizing wire attached to the steeple of the Universalist Church nearby broke and the derrick fell into the partially constructed courthouse, taking down much of the interior wood staging before becoming wedged in a window opening. None of the workers was injured, but one worker fell from the derrick.

Plans for the building were changed somewhat during the construction period. The gallery in the courtroom was eliminated, with its space reallocated "for use by counsel." The walls of the building were made 5 inches thicker. Heating and ventilation cost an additional $3,000. The materials for the railings in the courtroom were changed from ash to black walnut. Iron fencing was added at $4,000, and $800 for furniture. All told, the extras would cost $33,146. [8]

The contractors rushed to meet the completion date in March, assigning eleven carpenters to finish the courtroom. A *Rockland Gazette* reporter viewed the courtroom, noting:

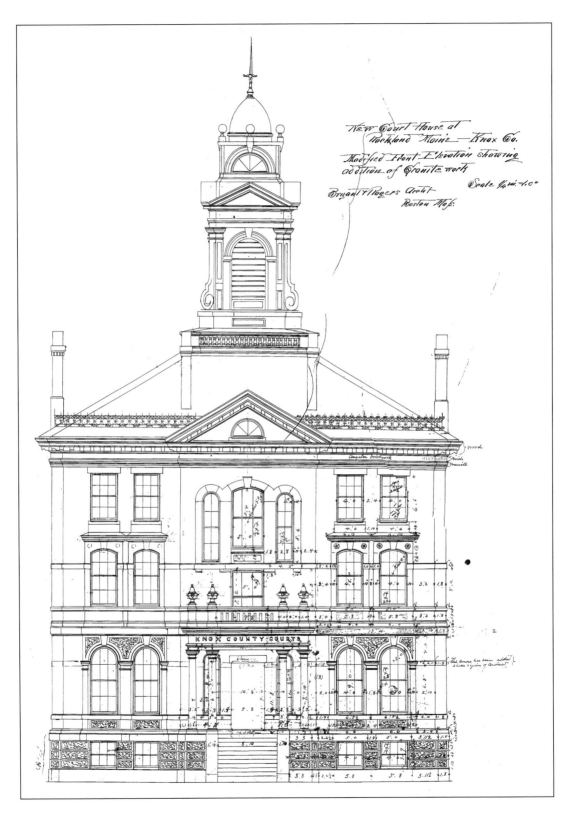

New Court House at
Rockland Maine — Knox Co.
Modified Front Elevation showing
addition of Granite work

Scale ¼ in.=1.0"

Bryant & Rogers Archt
Boston Mass:

KNOX COUNTY COURTS

"The finish is in ash, oiled, and is very handsome. …The courtroom is a noble hall 44 by 52 feet, and 24 feet in height. It has six ample windows, five feet wide and sixteen feet high, and in the evening will be lighted by four very handsome chandeliers of ten (gas) burners each, with porcelain shades. The judges' platform was raised three steps, and was furnished with a large black walnut desk of elegant style. The clerk's platform was raised a single step and displayed an elegant roll-top black walnut desk, and the bar enclosure was furnished with three handsome tables of corresponding style." [9]

Discussing the absence of the visitors' gallery, the *Gazette* reporter commented sourly, "The original plan was a recognition of this privilege of the public; the modification of the plan is a denial of it." [10]

The basement of the building was described as "rustic." It provided boiler rooms, and lockups for prisoners waiting trial, as well as the building's principal rest rooms. The first floor contained the probate offices with a fireproof vault room for storage of records. Across the hall were the offices of the county commissioners, the clerk of courts and the Register of Deeds, the latter of which was housed in a fireproof room. The fireproofing included extra thick walls, vaulted brick ceilings and floors, cast iron double doors, and windows with cast iron shutters. The interior first floor halls had black and white marble flooring in a checkerboard pattern.

The exterior of the building was impressive in its Italianate design. A half story base of granite supported the brick building and required a flight of stairs to the entrance, covered by an elegant portico supported by Doric columns. A Palladian window above the portico looked out onto a little balcony surrounded by a granite balustrade with four granite urns. A large triangular pediment above the Palladian window completed the facade, but the design continued upward with another balustrade around the flattened portion of the hipped roof, a cupola and a pointed weather vane. The sides of the building were graced by the two-story windows which provided light for the courtroom. Surrounding the roof line was a heavy cornice with an iron balustrade around it. Four chimneys on each side and two on the front facade completed the design.

The first term of the Supreme Judicial court in the new courthouse began on March 9, 1875. The first case was a civil action brought by Anson Bowler against the Town of Washington for injuries received from an alleged obstruction in the public highway. A second case became notorious in the history of capital punishment. An injunction was sought to prevent the Knox County sheriff from executing a death sentence on Louis H. F. Wagner, the Smutty Nose (Isles of Shoals) murderer, and

The Courthouse Opens for Business

John True Gordon, who had been convicted of the murder of his brother, sister-in-law and niece at Thorndike. Defense counsel presented numerous points of law, but the court denied the petitions for injunction. Wagner and Gordon were hanged at the State Prison in June, 1875, in a period when capital punishment was beginning to be viewed as barbarous. The public uproar over the hangings led the legislature to abolish capital punishment in Maine, although the death penalty was later restored briefly to allow three more persons to go to the gallows.

An indictment of Nathan Hart for murder became sensational when the Knox County Grand Jury's findings were released in the March Term of the Supreme Judicial Court for the year 1878. The murder took place in mid-December of 1877 at Tenant's Harbor. Sarah Meservey, wife of Capt. Luther Meservey, was found murdered on Jan. 29, 1878 in their own house. At the murder scene, on the floor of the kitchen, was a note written in pencil on brown paper: "I came as a Woman when She was out, and

The 1874 Knox County Courthouse in Rockland.

wait till She Come back not for money but i killed her." On February 1, 1878, an anonymous letter was received by Abby L. Hart, wife of Levi Hart. The letter, written in pencil, had been mailed at Philadelphia and went as follows:

> "To Mrs. Livi Hart—i thought i would drop you a line to tell you to tell your husband to be careful how he conducted things about Tenants Harbor cause if he dont he and a good many others of the men will get An ounce ball put threw them for tell them that it is no use trying to catch this chap for he will not be caught—so be careful who you take up in St George you shall hear from me again in three months. DM" [11]

The letter was thought to be a clue to the identity of the murderer. A relative, A.K. Meservey, married to a sister of Nathan F. Hart, suggested the name of Nathan to the authorities. A sample of Hart's handwriting was sought. Capt. Meservey produced an old log-book containing some of Hart's writing dating between 1856-1875. A handwriting analyst, asked to compare the sample of writing, concluded they were from same person. But shortly before the grand jury began its work, additional writings were found that did not match. The handwriting analyst did not refer to them in testimony before the grand jury.

There was testimony by Vina Wall that Nathan Hart revealed the precise method by which Mrs. Meservey was murdered, with her hands "tied together over her head with a cod-line tied in a square knot; that her cloud or scarf was wound three times around her neck and tied in a square knot." Pending trial, Nathan Hart was incarcerated. While Hart was in jail, a second letter of 3,000 words was received from Providence. Hart was released and immediately claimed that Meservey had murdered his own wife and filed libel suits worth $15,000. Ten handwriting experts—three from New York, five from Boston, and two from Maine—were scheduled to testify that the handwriting could not have been Hart's. But the experts from New York were not allowed to testify, because they were an hour late owing to a snow-storm blocking their route. The jury was unconvinced that Hart was truthful, and Hart lost his libel case against Meservey.

In 1879, a prisoner was awaiting trial for robbery in one of the holding cells in the courthouse basement. Samuel D. Haines, a 23-year-old, had been convicted of robbing the post office in Patten in 1872 and had spent four years in the jail at Bangor. Convicted of stealing two watches and other items from his uncle in Patten, he spent another year in jail in Bangor in 1877. Searching for new territory, he came to Rockland and

Murder in the Courthouse

drafting table, some new bookcases in front of the old, fluorescent lights, telephones, and new map files. In the two other rooms are a roll top desk, more map files, records of real property surveys, a patriotic painting in a gold frame, and another computer. The present occupants were pleased to have located the oldest known manuscript map of the State of Maine, drawn in 1795 and now housed in the Osher Map Library at the University of Southern Maine.

Film companies have twice come to the courthouse. The first film was the movie, *Peyton Place*, filmed in the courtroom and in Camden. The second, in 1995-96, was the movie, *Thinner*, based on a book by Stephen King. For this movie, the film company installed a temporary sound system disguised to blend with the architecture of the room, and temporary scaffolding outside the courtroom to control the exterior light source and

The vault of the Registry of Deeds in the Rockland Courthouse.

make it a constant sunny day. Appointments in the room were returned to the way they may have looked in the 1960s, including the replacement of plastic water flasks on the bench and bar tables with older glass versions.

In 1978 a substantial addition to the building was constructed to house the district court, the Registry of Deeds, a law library and offices for the superior court clerk. Offices were also provided for the use of superior court justices and district court judges, as well as supreme judicial court justices. The architects for the new addition were Woodard and Associates and the contractor A.P. Whitaker and Sons.

The Knox County Courthouse is listed on the National Register of Historic Places. Its nomination includes the following citation:

"This massive structure characterized the gravity and authority which is associated with government affairs. Municipal architecture which captures the spirit and translates it into a building form is rare. As an early and well designed example of this tradition, the Knox County Courthouse holds an important place in Maine architecture." [13]

[1] "A Bill for Knox County," *Rockland Democrat and Free Press*, Feb. 15, 1860

[2] "The Knox Papers I," *Rockland Democrat and Free Press*, Mar. 14, 1860, "The Knox Papers II," *Rockland Democrat and Free Press*, March 21, 1860; Rockland Bicentennial Commission, *Shore Village Story: An Informal History of Rockland, Maine*, Rockland: The Commission, 1976, p. 71

[3] "The Knox Papers IV," *Rockland Democrat and Free Press*, April 4, 1860; Eaton, Cyrus, *History of Thomaston, Rockland, and South Thomaston, Maine*, Hallowell: Masters, Smith & Co., 1865, p. 5

[4] Eaton, Cyrus, *The Annals of Warren*, Hallowell: Masters, Smith &Co., 1851, p. 464

[5] *Id.*

[6] "Second Century of Operation Nears for Court House," Part II, *Rockland Courier Gazette*, Sept. 28, 1974, p. 10

[7] "Second Century of Operation Nears for Court House," Part III, *Rockland Courier Gazette*, Oct. 1, 1974, p. 2

[8] Knox County Commissioners Minutes of Meetings in 1874, pp. 5, 34-35

[9] "Second Century of Operation Nears for Court House," Part IV, *Rockland Courier Gazette*, Oct. 3, 1974, p. 9

[10] *Id.*

[11] Case notes from Dunton, Alvin R., *The True Story of the Hart-Meservey Murder Trial*, Boston: published by the Author, 1882

[12] "Statement and Death of the Victim: Haines' Flight and Arrest," *Rockland Courier-Gazette*, 1879

[13] U.S. Department of the Interior, National Register of Historic Places, Registration Form, Knox County Courthouse, 1976, n.p.

The Merchants Exchange building in Portland became the Federal Courthouse in 1839.

EIGHTEEN

The United States Courthouses of Maine

United States courts have served Maine since 1789. For the first fifty years, federal courts had no separate courthouse in Maine. The first sessions of the United States District Court in Maine were held in Portland at the Cumberland County Courthouse, then located on Congress Street. For cases attracting substantial public interest, court was held in a larger room, such as the nearby meetinghouse.

District court sessions were initially scheduled for Pownalborough and Portland. In 1811 Congress agreed to transfer the Pownalborough sessions to Wiscasset, while maintaining sessions in Portland. A second term of the United States District Court was authorized by Congress to be held in Bangor, beginning in 1843. A term of the federal district court was authorized to be held in Bath in 1862. In the twentieth century, Congress established Northern and Southern Divisions of the United States District Court within the District of Maine, and courthouse buildings were constructed for the two divisions in Portland and Bangor.

The area called the United States District of Maine was formally defined when Congress assumed appellate jurisdiction of all maritime cases in 1778. To receive and administer these cases, Congress divided Massachusetts into three seaboard districts—Southern, Middle and Northern. The Northern District included the three eastern counties—York, Cumberland and Lincoln—and was known by the familiar name, "District of Maine." The judge of this district was Timothy Langdon, a lawyer from Wiscasset. Nathaniel Thwing of Woolwich was clerk.

The Judiciary Act of 1789 established the country's federal court system. Implementing the directives of the Constitution, Congress established a system of federal courts including the Supreme Court, the Circuit

Setting up the United States District of Maine

237

Courts and the District Courts. For the United States District Courts, Congress divided the United States into thirteen judicial districts, one for each of the eleven states that had ratified the Constitution, one for Kentucky (then a part of Virginia) and "one to consist of that part of the State of Massachusetts which lies easterly of the State of New Hampshire, and to be called the Maine District." The act provided for a:

> "District Court, in each of the districts, to consist of one judge who shall reside in the district, to which he is appointed, and shall be called a District Judge, and shall hold annually four sessions …in the following named places: to wit, in the District of Maine, at Portland and Pownalborough, alternately, beginning at the first [session]." [1]

After Wiscasset replaced Pownalborough as the shire town of Lincoln County, the District Court sat in Portland and Wiscasset.

The judges of the United States District Courts were limited in their jurisdiction to maritime cases and miscellaneous litigation depending on the citizenship of the contending parties. They also had jurisdiction over penalties and forfeitures under federal law, and a small number of criminal cases. District court judges would occasionally be called upon to join the Supreme Court justices to form a circuit court.

With the establishment of federal district courts, new judges were needed. The first district judge commissioned to serve in the District of Maine was Judge David Sewall, appointed by President George Washington.

The U.S. District Court Opens in Portland

Judge Sewall arrived in Portland for the first session of the U.S. District Court on the first Tuesday of December, 1789. On opening the session in the Cumberland County Courthouse, oaths were administered to the Judge, and to other new appointees in the district, including the Marshal, the U.S. Attorney, and the District Clerk. The business of the court began on preliminary matters, such as admitting attorneys to practice before the court. These matters continued through the second session of the court held in the Pownalborough Courthouse in March, 1790.

In the June, 1790 term in Portland, a grand jury was summoned for the first time. To provide for upcoming trials, two juries were summoned. The first jury trial was a civil case, *United States v. George Tyler*. Tyler, of Deer Isle, had allegedly smuggled "one barrel of West India rum and one bag of brown sugar, being articles of foreign growth and manufacture." During its deliberations, the jury found Tyler guilty of smuggling, and he was fined $400. [2]

The first capital trial and conviction in the United States courts occurred in Portland that summer in 1790, when Hans Hanson and

Thomas Bird were tried for piracy and murder. Hanson and Bird had allegedly taken over a ship where they were seamen and killed the vessel's captain, known for his cruelty to the crew. Bird confessed and admitted that he fired the gun which killed the captain, but he justified his action on grounds of the captain's cruelty to his crew.

The trial of Hanson and Bird took place a year or more after the events on which it was based. The delay resulted because the newly-established District Court of the United States had not yet organized the new maritime laws of the young country, and required time to set up a session in Maine. During that year, the defendants were confined to jail.

Public interest in the spectacular case grew daily as it became known that the case was finally coming to trial. As the Cumberland County Courthouse was too small to accommodate the crowds, the court decided to reconvene in the nearby meetinghouse to allow space for spectators. It was a noisy scene, as the crowd came and went. The pew seats were hinged boards which were raised to allow standing during prayers, and which clattered loudly when dropped to form a seat for the parishioners. One observer noted the irony that each of the meetinghouse pews resembled the prisoners' box in the courthouse.

The trial ended with a verdict of guilty for Bird and an acquittal for Hanson. Sentencing took place several days later in the courthouse. Bird's counsel immediately applied for a pardon for his client on the grounds that the case was the first capital conviction in a United States court. This petition for pardon was forwarded to President Washington who denied its application. Late in 1790 Bird was hanged on a gallows set up at the corner of Congress and Grove Streets in Portland.

Judge Sewall became involved in a maritime case in the middle of the War of 1812. The British had occupied Castine, and a British sloop destined there with a cargo of baled goods valued at $40,000, was captured by American forces and taken into Camden. The British Captain Mountjoy sailed rapidly from Castine to Camden, demanding the return or restoration of the cargo captured, threatening to burn both Camden and Lincolnville. Judge Sewall was consulted as to the need to return the sloop or the goods. He concluded that the goods did not need to be redelivered to the British. With that, Mountjoy seized two selectmen of Camden and carried them to Castine, declaring they would be detained until the goods were paid for or returned. The goods were never returned, and after several months, the selectmen returned to Camden.

The Federal District Court sat in Wiscasset to hear a series of disputes on property captured prior to the War of 1812. Silas Lee, appointed by President Jefferson as United States District Attorney for Maine, proceeded against the British brig *Boxer*, captured in a battle off Pemaquid on loses its principal architectural ornament, for the building was the finest in the State. It was the central object of the city, the point where our merchants and public men most did congregate; the general rendezvous of the citizens … The loss of any other single building would be scarcely felt in comparison with it." [4]

The fire also consumed the Natural History Society's collection, and Judge Ware's law library.

Within a year, a new federal building was built on the same site for use by federal agencies and the U.S. District Court. This 1855 building looked very different from the building it replaced. Designed in the fashionable Italianate architectural style, it was a new emblem of the city. The three-story building had thick walls constructed of brick and granite. All of the window and door openings were arched and recessed into the walls. High windows with arched sashes continued the theme. The front of the building on Middle Street was rounded, with an arcade on the first floor that was approachable from three sides of the building. Heavy stone courses defined each floor, and the third floor was topped with a dominant cornice, with six tall chimneys on each side of the building.

The 1855 Federal Building in Portland was constructed to be fireproof.

The 1855 federal building contained many improvements over the old Merchants Exchange Building. It was designed specifically for use by the

federal agencies and the U.S. District Court. The courtroom was designed to federal specifications. The entire building was believed to be fireproof.

Then came the Great Fire of 1866 in the Portland business district. The interior of the new building did not survive the fire, but the shell of the building was intact. Because of the immediate need to deal with the ruins, a first step was to determine whether the thick walls were reusable in a new structure. Treasury Department architects were sent from Washington to examine the building. The federal inspection team found that the building was unsafe and unsightly. They decreed that the building needed to be taken down and totally rebuilt.

The Treasury Department recommended that a fund of $150,000 be appropriated for the new structure. Congress acted, and architect W. R. Emerson was appointed to design the new building for use as a post office, courthouse and internal revenue office. A separate customs house was recommended for another location. In May, 1867, the shell of the burned building was demolished. The federal tenants were temporarily relocated to other buildings during the construction period. The cornerstone of the new building was laid on May 6, 1868.

The 1855 Federal Building after Portland's Great Fire of 1866.

The third federal building opened in 1871, with an exterior of Vermont marble, of a "remarkable fine, clear grain." Its cost was almost $500,000. One local commenter noted: "The pure white walls are in strong contrast to the warm-colored brick buildings around it and it looks a little cold in its elegance and chasteness." The *Portland Transcript* announced:

> "At length our splendid new post office is complete and we may well be proud of the provision government has made for our convenience. It is an elegant (Vermont) marble building of the pure Corinthian order." [5]

The ground floor of the 1871 building was occupied by the post office and the whole second floor was used by the U.S. District Court for courtroom and office space. The building was very classical in appearance, with high arches above windows and doors on the ground floor, and a four columns on a porch at the Middle Street side of the building. Flat columns surrounded the building on three sides, with windows in each bay formed by the columns. A heavy cornice and balustrade surrounded the top of the building, and a gable emphasized the Middle Street porch.

The 1911 United States Courthouse in Portland

Within 30 years, the 1871 building was insufficient to continue serving the personnel of both the court and the post office department. The federal court made plans for moving out of the old building.

In searching for a site, the court was assisted by several events. First, due to the City Hall fire in 1908, the Cumberland County Commissioners were planning a new building on a site facing Lincoln Park, not far from City Hall. Second, the City Beautiful movement sweeping the country was encouraging many cities to build civic centers or groupings of public buildings. Third, the site for the new grouping of buildings was close to the financial district, retaining the close linkages between the court and business and professional people.

As part of the civic center development and to make a more formal setting for the public buildings, the City of Portland enlarged Lincoln Park in 1908 by extending it into the city block bounded by Congress, Market, Federal and Pearl. The newly added park land at Lincoln Park, Mayor Leighton noted, "will not only increase the attractiveness of that 'beauty spot' in the heart of the city's business district, and get rid of a number of unsightly buildings, but will set off to the best advantage, the new city hall, the county courthouse and the federal courthouse." [6]

The site chosen for the new building faced the south side of the expanded Lincoln Park. To the east, its neighbor was the proposed Cumberland County Courthouse, housing the Cumberland County Superior Court and the Maine Supreme Judicial Court. Several prominent churches lined the north side of the park, adjacent to City Hall. With the plan linking new and old buildings and focused on an expanded park, Portland could with pride join the cities around the country that were building focal points of government buildings.

Construction of the present United States District Courthouse began in 1908 and was completed in 1911. The design of the building was prepared

The 1911 Edward Gignoux U.S. Federal Courthouse in Portland.

by James Knox Taylor, supervising architect of the U.S. Treasury. The building, in the Second Renaissance Revival style, was constructed of Maine granite with an interior trim of Vermont marble. The courthouse was two stories high, with a hip roof which enclosed a third story. The roof sloped back to reveal dormer windows with arched pediments. Windows on the first two stories were elaborately treated with balustrade segments below them. They were surmounted by raised triangular or arched pediments. At the roof line a continuous frieze and dentil cornice and balustrade of open balusters and solid panels ran around the entire building.

In 1932 Congress appropriated funds for the enlargement of the courthouse to provide postal offices and 44 offices for other government bureaus, including the Internal Revenue Service and the General Services Administration. James A. Wetmore, the Supervising Architect of the United States Treasury at the time, designed the expansion of the building to meet the needs of businesses and professional people for a downtown post office branch, supplementing the new main post office on Forest Avenue. Doubled in size, the building surrounded a new courtyard. On the exterior, the original classical architectural style was retained and extended to the new addition.

In 1973, the building was modernized. Heating and air conditioning ducts were installed and suspended ceilings were provided to contain new lighting fixtures. As the work of the court expanded and space in the existing building became constricted, government offices such as the Internal Revenue Service moved out. In 1974 the downtown branch of the post office moved out of the courthouse into another nearby building.

In 1988, the courthouse was named in honor of Judge Edward Gignoux, who had served as the U.S. District Court judge from 1957 to 1982. At the ceremonies honoring Judge Gignoux, comments were offered by U.S. Circuit Court Judge Frank Coffin, Senator William Cohen, Senator George Mitchell, Congressman Joseph Brennan and Congresswoman Olympia Snowe. Judge Coffin celebrated

"a perfect marriage of a building and a name. This building ...is not arrogant in its size, it is of human proportions but it has the durability and integrity of the granite out of which it is constructed. Its corridors, most of the time, radiate a serenity that is rare in these frenetic times, but most important, this splendid courtroom in which we sit, epitomizes the spaciousness of thought and the gracefulness of the justice that has been dispensed here for the last three decades by the man we permanently and lastingly honor today. ...Noble building. Noble name." [7]

Following passage of the Judicial Improvements Act of 1990, the building was reconstructed. The Act authorized three federal district court judges for Maine, and two of the judges were assigned to sit in the Portland United States Courthouse. A new courtroom was needed to accommodate the second judge, along with chambers and offices.

Designs for the renovated courthouse were prepared by Leers, Weinzapfel of Boston. The improvements included two full-sized district courtrooms (one with a 14 person jury box and the other with an 18 person jury box), a third courtroom suitable for civil jury trials, and a magistrate judge's hearing room.

A wholly new courtroom was constructed inside the old building. The new courtroom was designed with modern sound systems, computer capabilities, and closed-circuit television, allowing judges, for example, to banish an unruly defendant to a holding cell equipped with television receivers for monitoring the court proceedings. A wall painting, *The Virtues of Good Government*, is a frieze located just below the courtroom's skylight. The mural by Dorothea Rockburne is "a modern contemplation on the virtues of prudence, faith, common good, hope and magnanimity, using pure geometry and vibrant color as meditative devices." [8]

The original courtroom was also modernized and updated, but here the goal of the renovation was to restore the original appearance of the courtroom. The dropped ceiling was removed to uncover the massive vaulted ceiling and to replace the original ornate plaster work while hiding modern heating and air conditioning equipment. Copies of the original chandeliers and wall sconces were crafted and installed in the original locations. The addition of new lighting fixtures improves overall available light, and a new sound system alleviated the historically difficult acoustics of the room.

From the beginning of the work of the U.S. District Court in Maine in 1789, sessions were scheduled for both the north and south portions of the state. In the south, sessions were scheduled for Portland, and in the north, in Pownalborough at the Lincoln County Courthouse. The single District Court judge was required to travel to the two locations for each of the sessions.

As the court began its work at Pownalborough it was preoccupied with smuggling and non-payment of duties. Stephen Smith, collector for the District of Machias, had filed two cases. The first, *Smith vs. 115 gallons of molasses and other goods* was the first case filed in the District of Maine. The second was *Smith vs. 33 shawls and other goods*.

Judge Gignoux described the first murder case to come to the federal court sitting in Pownalborough in Lincoln County:

The Federal Courthouse in Bangor

"Judge Sewall, sitting in the Maine District court, was one of three judges (Mr. Justice William Cushing of the United States Supreme Court presiding) who tried a memorable murder case....as reported by the Revernd Jacob Bailey, an Episcopalian Minister, in a letter from Pownalborough: 'We have a man in jail for murder.... Since my residence here in 1760, five or six murders have been committed on the Kennebec River, and neither the murderers nor the persons killed ever frequented any divine worship.' Nobody who did not go to meeting had any chance for his life in a murder trial in Maine in those 'good old days.'" [9]

In 1811 the court began sitting in Wiscasset, first in the Wiscasset Hall courtroom, and later in the Lincoln County Courthouse built in 1824. These sessions were discontinued in 1843 when Congress authorized sittings of the court in Bangor to accommodate the growth of the northern sections of Maine.

Bangor was at the time a boom town, building a rapidly expanding timber-based economy and an industry that was rife with speculative land development schemes. Court activity was trying to keep pace with the boom. A new Penobscot County Courthouse had been built in 1833, just as the boom was getting underway. When the U.S. District Court sat in

The 1915 U.S. Courthouse in Bangor, now the Bangor City Hall. Theodore Lund

Bangor, with no courtroom of its own, it probably shared the space occupied by the Penobscot County Superior Court in their new courthouse.

From 1843 onwards, the U. S. District Court sat for two terms annually in Bangor, with a schedule of regular fall and spring trial sessions. Bangor shared the sittings with Bath for a period of time after the Civil War. In 1903 the new county courthouse was opened with a main courtroom that invited shared use. The Bangor fire in 1911 missed the county courthouse, but destroyed federal offices and much of Harlow Street, affording an opportunity for construction of a new building.

In August, 1911, Congress authorized the purchase of a new courthouse site in Bangor. Land in a portion of a public park at the foot of Park Street hill was cleared for the new building in early 1912, and construction got underway. The new building, housing the courthouse and post office building, was completed in 1915. It was the first courtroom in Bangor that the U.S. District Court could call its own.

At the inauguration of the courthouse, United States Attorney John Merrill noted that the people of Bangor and Maine were to be congratulated on a fine new courtroom for the United States Court:

"In this district, I cannot but feel that the dignity of the Court and the administration of justice will be better maintained when the sessions of the court are held in a courtroom such as this, especially designed and constructed for the purposes for which it is to be used. The building, of which this courtroom is a part, with its beauty, dignity and solidity, aids by means of the impression which, consciously or unconsciously, these characteristics make on the minds of men, in establishing the solidity and supremacy of law in this community. Those whose duty calls them there to administer and to aid in the administration of justice, will feel more than ever their responsibilities and their obligation to see to it that the laws are enforced with absolute impartiality, while the rights of all, even to those of the humblest citizen, are protected." [10]

In 1916, Congress divided the District of Maine into Northern and Southern Divisions. While deciding that the terms of the court would be held for the Northern Division at Bangor and Southern Division at Portland, Congress provided for the maintenance of permanent court facilities in both cities. James Mitchell, president of the Penobscot County Bar Association, remembered the federal court in the 1920s as:

"a court definitely remote from the everyday practice of the Bangor lawyer, full of austerity. ... substantially concerned with bankruptcy matters. Judge Peters presided over the court with great dignity.

...[w}]hen Judge Peters turned over the direction of this court ... the only admonition he could give to Judge Clifford was one ... given to him years before by the preceding Federal Judge, Judge Hale. This advice was that the new judge when presiding in court especially on a warm spring or early summer day keep his robe tightly tucked around him with his legs crossed so that if he fell asleep in the face of the dazzling display of counsel before him in the courtroom, he would sharply be thrust awake." [11]

At the end of the 1920s, criminal litigation centered on enforcement of federal laws prohibiting the sales of intoxicating liquor. Civil litigation became more active as part of the social and economic legislation of the 1930s and the war years of the 1940s.

After 50 years, the old post office and courthouse were worn and in need of replacement. A new building was authorized by Congress to be constructed to take its place. The new building was finished and occupied in 1968. The old post office and courthouse were formally transferred to the City of Bangor for use as a city hall.

On Tuesday, May 7, 1968, a ceremony of dedication took place in the new courtroom at the U.S. Post Office and Courthouse in Bangor. Presiding were Judge Edward T. Gignoux of the U.S. District Court, and

The Margaret Chase Smith U.S. Federal Building in Bangor opened in 1968.

Theodore Lund

Chief Justice Robert Williamson of the Supreme Judicial Court of Maine. Speakers reviewed the history of the U. S. District Court and the lives of the people who played important roles in its advancement. At the close of the ceremony, a motion was made for a change of venue to the Tarrantine Club for refreshment, "for the convenience of the parties and in the interests of justice." [12]

In 1978 Congress passed the Federal District Court Organization Act, providing for the appointment of a second judge for the District of Maine. George Mitchell was nominated, confirmed and appointed to the position, joining Chief Judge Edward T. Gignoux on the bench. Maine continued as one district, but the court could for the first time sit simultaneously at Portland and Bangor, benefiting its docket and caseload.

The U. S. Post Office and Courthouse building was formally dedicated to Margaret Chase Smith, the former Senator from Maine, on Aug. 31, 1984.

[1] Judiciary Act, Sept, 24, 1789

[2] United States District Court for the District of Maine, Bicentenial of the U. S. District Court, Bangor, Sept. 25, 1989, p. 23; Coe, Harrie B., ed., *Maine: Its Resources, Attractions, and its People*, New York: Lewis Publishing Co., Inc., 4 vols, 1928, p. 730

[3] Frankfurter, Felix, and James M. Landis, *The Business of the Supreme Court: A Study of the Federal Judicial System*, New York: Macmillan Co., 1928, p. 65

[4] Shettleworth, Earle G., Jr., and William Barry, *Mr Goodhue Remembers Portland: Scenes from the Mid-19h Century*, Augusta: Maine Historic Preservation Commission, 1981, n.p.

[5] Neal, John, *Portland Illustrated*, Portland: W.S. Jones, Publisher, 1874, p. 19; Portland and Vicinity, Portland: W.S. Jones, 1874, pp. 75-76

[6] "Inaugural Address of the Mayor," Dec., 1908 in *City of Portland 15th Auditors Report*, Portland: Master Printing House, 1909, pp. 35-36

[7] *Dedication of the Edward Thaxter Gignoux United States Courthouse*, Sept. 10, 1988, Portland, Me., p. 13

[8] *Reopening Ceremony, Edward Thaxter Gignoux United States Courthouse*, June 26, 1996, p. 1

[9] *Proceedings at the Dedication of Courthouse Facilities at New United States Post Office and Courthouse*, Bangor, Maine, May 7, 1968, p. 5

[10] *Id.*, p. 21

[11] *Id.*, p. 28

[12] *Id.*, p. 36

New district court houses, such as this one in West Bath, bring court services closer to residents.

252

NINETEEN

The Continuing Evolution of the Courts

The court system in Maine has changed significantly during the state's history from colony or province, to a district of Massachusetts, and through the early years of the newly formed state. Many notable changes in the courts have taken place within the last 50 years. New courts with specific responsibilities have been added. The district court system was established in 1962 to replace the tangled system of lower courts – municipal courts in cities and towns and individual trial justices in smaller communities. The Administrative Court was established in 1973 to take over review and administration of licenses from state agencies. The Family Court was established in 1998 to take over the burgeoning numbers of cases dealing with divorces, children's needs and parental responsibilities. As Maine Supreme Judicial Court Chief Justice Daniel Wathen described them:

> "Courts are a safety net for those who have fallen through all other safety nets. Courts exist to protect those who are damaged or injured, by rendering justice promptly in individual cases." [1]

Changes in the courts have been made to respond to new service directions and needs of the state's residents. The district court system now in place resulted from studies made in 1927, 1932, and 1957. In 1959 the Legislature authorized a more intensive examination of the system and resulted in an analysis of the potential caseloads, costs and monetary savings of instituting a system of district courts. The 1959 study concluded that district courts would provide an expert and uniform disposition of cases, a closer liaison between courts and social services agencies, and assistance to the state's social and law enforcement programs. One result of the district court change was that local or district courts were no longer to be called "inferior courts." Chief Justice Robert B. Williamson of the Maine Supreme Judicial Court stated the philosophy of forming the new courts:

> "We have adopted the principle that justice at the local level must be of the highest order, administered by judges charged with professional responsibility and obligations only to the court. [2]

One visible result of the district court program was the need for facilities to house the court. In many cases, these new facilities were located within the familiar county courthouses, but some were located in separate quarters either built for the purpose or adapted from pre-existing buildings to separately house the court functions. For example, new courthouses were provided for the district court in West Bath and Augusta, and recently, in central Biddeford. District courts were housed in county-owned buildings in Bangor, Belfast, Rockland, Wiscasset, South Paris, Dover-Foxcroft and Portland. In still other locations, such as Newport and Calais, experimentation is now underway on the use of private facilities adapted for district court use.

Because of the growing number of cases in all categories throughout the state, the need for judicial services has required the state to take on an increasing share of the fiscal responsibility for housing and administering the courts. During much of the history of Maine, courts and courthouses were funded by county commissioners, who provided support personnel including clerks of court, and courtrooms, chambers and even furniture. Since 1975, the state judiciary department has worked with the counties and the court system to create more courtrooms, chambers, office space and office supplies and equipment. A standard computer system has been developed for use in recording proceedings in all courthouses. Clerks of court, no longer elected individually in each county, are now appointed by the state judiciary department.

The role of the county is still central to the operation and improvement of the county courthouses. In recognition of the importance of courts and their symbolic buildings, communities have placed six of the historic courthouses on the National Register of Historic Places. Extensive renovations and additions to several courthouses now provide additional space, update and protect the old buildings from further deterioration, and help them comply with the Americans with Disabilities Act.

Despite renewed interest from both the counties and the state, not all of the county courthouses have reached a stable physical status, and funding for their improvement remains uncertain. Yet it is clear that physical improvements to courthouses are a graphic reminder to citizens of the importance of the courts. Courthouses are the setting for an essential service to society that must be carefully guarded and maintained at the highest possible level.

---

[1] Wathen, Hon. Daniel, "The State of the Judiciary—Steady Progress, But Is It Enough?" A Report to the Joint Convention of the 118th Legislature, December, 1997

[2] Henry, Hon. Harriett P., *The Maine District Court: A Quarter Century of Progress 1962-1987*, p. 4

Bibliography

Allen, Charles Edwin, *History of Dresden, Maine*, Lewiston: Twin City Printery, 1931, reprinted by Jennie G. Everson and Eleanor L. Everson, 1977.

Allen, Neal, *A Brief History of the United States District Court in the District of Maine*, Prepared at the request of the Court and of the Maine Commission to Commemorate the Bicentennial of the United States Constitution, Sept. 25, 1989, pamphlet

Allen, Neal, ed., Court Records of York County, Province of Massachusetts Bay, Portland: Maine Historical Society, 3 v., 1958-75

Allen, William, *The History of Norridgewock*, Norridgewock: Edward Peet, 1849

Andrews, Charles M., *The Colonial Period of American History*, New Haven: Yale University Press, 1975

Andrews, Charles M., *The Colonial Background of the American Revolution*, Rev. Ed., New Haven: Yale University Press, 1931

"Aroostook Then and Now" *The Lewiston Journal*, reprint Nov. 16, 1929 in *Aroostook county: a collection of Articles published 1928-1970* Vol 1. p. 13, n.d.

Auburn Heritage, Inc., "Goff's Corner District," *Auburn Landmarks*, Auburn: Vocational Technical Institute, 1976

Augusta Centennial Souvenir, issued by *Daily Kennebec Journal*, 1897

Bacon, George F., *Calais, Eastport and Vicinity*, Newark, N.J.: Glenwood Publishing Co., 1892

Bacon, George, *Rockland, Belfast and Vicinity: Its Representative Business Men and its Points of Interest*, Newark, N. J. Glenwood Publishing Co., 1892

Banks, Charles Edward, "Courthouse, Gaol and Punishments," in Banks, Ronald, *A History of Maine*, Dubuque, Iowa: Kendall Hunt Publishing Co., 1969

Banks, Charles Edward, *History of York, Maine; Successively known as Bristol (1632), Agamenticus (1641), Gorgeana (1642), and York (1652)* 3 vols, Cambridge, Mass.: Murray Printing Co., 1935; Reprinted by Old York Historical Society; Portsmouth, NH: Randall Publisher, 1990

Barnes, Francis, *The Story of Houlton, from the Public Records, and from the Experiences of its Founders, Their Descendants and Associates to the Present Time*. Houlton: Will H. Smith, 1889

Barrow, John S., *Fryeburg, Maine, An Historical Sketch*, Pequawket Press, Fryeburg, 1938

Bearse, Ray, ed., *Maine: A Guide to the Vacation State*, 2nd ed. rev., Boston: Houghton Mifflin Co., 1969

Beerits, Henry C., and Martha Vaughn, "The Pre-Revolutionary Pownalborough Courthouse," *Maine State Bar Bulletin* Vol. 17, No. 2, March 1983, pp 33 et seq.

Biddeford, Maine, Public Library, *An Introduction to Biddeford's History and a Chronological Outline of Events*, prepared by the McArthur Library, 1944, *Stories and Legends of Old Biddeford*: Part I - 1660-1747, prepared by the McArthur Library 1946, Part II - 1740-1800, prepared by the McArthur Library, 1944-46, reprinted and repaginated by the Biddeford Historical Society as *Dane York's History of Biddeford*, 1980

Bolte', Mary, "Courthouse on the Kennebec," *DownEast* (Vol. XXII, No. 10, July 1976) pp. 63-68

Bourne, Edward D., *History of Wells and Kennebunk*, Portland: B. Thurston & Co., 1875

Butler, Francis Goule, *History of Farmington, Franklin County, Maine, from the Earliest Explorations to the Present Time, 1776-1885*, Farmington: Knowlton, McLeary and Co., 1885, Reprinted in 1983

Caribou Centennial Committee, *Caribou Centennial, A Century of Development in Maine 1859-1959*, Caribou Publishing Co., 1959

Centennial Celebration of the Settlement of Bangor, Sept. 30, 1869, Bangor: B. A. Burr, 1870

"City of Bangor," *Gleason's Pictorial Drawing-Room Companion*, Vol. V, No. 22, No. 127, Boston, Dec. 3, 1853

Chase, Fannie, *Wiscasset in Pownalborough*, Second Ed., Wiscasset Public Library, Publisher, 1967

Coburn, Louise H., *Skowhegan on the Kennebec*, 1941, Skowhegan: Independent-Reporter Press, 1941

Coburn, Louise H., and Henrietta Wood, "Taverns and Stage Coaches of Skowhegan & Norridgewock," in Daughters of the American Revolution, Maine Chapter, *Trails and Taverns of Maine*, 1932

Coe, Harrie B., ed., *Maine: Its Resources, Attractions, and its People*, New York: Lewis Publishing Co., Inc., 4 vols, 1928

Coffin, N., *Statement & Account of Expenditure of N. Coffin, Esq., County Agent for Building a Courthouse*, Text of Report (Lincoln County), 1824

Cosmopolitan Club of Dover-Foxcroft, *Bicentennial U.S.A. 1776-1976*, Dover-Foxcroft, Maine, Rockland: Courier-Gazette, 1976

Davis, Albert H., *History of Ellsworth, Maine*, Lewiston: Lewiston Journal Printshop, 1927

Davis, William T., *History of the Judiciary of Massachusetts*, Boston: Boston Book Co., 1900

Dedication of the Edward Thaxter Gignoux United States Courthouse, Sept. 10, 1988, Portland

Dedicatory Exercises, York County Courthouse, Alfred, Maine, October 1, 1934, Alfred: n.p.

Dibner, Martin, *Portrait of Paris Hill*, Paris Hill Press, 1990

Doudiet, Ellenore W., *Majabigwaduce: Castin, Penobscot, Brooksville*, Castine: Castine Scientific Society, 1978

Drisko, George W., *Narrative of the Town of Machias: The Old and the New, the Early and the Late*, Machias: Press of the Republican, 1904

Dunton, Alvin R., *The True Story of the Hart-Meservey Murder Trial*, Boston: published by the Author, 1882

Eastman, Harland H., *Alfred, Maine: The Shakers and the Village*, Sanford: Wilson's Printers, second ed., 1992

Eaton, Cyrus, *Annals of the Town of Warren*, Hallowell: Masters, Smith & Co., 1851

Eaton, Cyrus, *History of Thomaston, Rockland, and South Thomaston, Maine*, Hallowell: Masters, Smith & Co., 1865

Elwell, Edward H., *Aroostook: with Some Account of the Excursions Thither of the Editors of Maine*, Portland: Transcript Printing Co., 1878

Elwell, Edward H., *Portland and Vicinity*, Reprint of 1881 ed. published by Loring, Short & Harmon, Portland, Portland: Greater Portland Landmarks, 1975

Fairfield, Roy P., *Sands, Spindles, and Steeples*, (A History of Saco, Maine), Portland: House of Falmouth, 1956

"The First Courthouse in Penobscot County, Now the City Hall in Bangor", *Maine Historical Magazine*, Vol VII, July, 1891-June 1892, pp. 33-35, Bangor: Glass & Co, 1892

"The First Lawyer in Washington County," *Bangor Historical Magazine*, Vol II, No. II. Bangor Aug. 1886

Frankfurter, Felix, and James M. Landis, *The Business of the Supreme Court: A Study of the Federal Judicial System*, New York: Macmillan Co., 1928

Fredericks, Katherine M.E., *Bar-Bits from Old Court Records in Lincoln County, Maine*, Wiscasset: County Commissioners of Lincoln Co., 1960

Fryeburg, Maine, Maine Street '90 Committee, *Old Pequawket Days*, Fryeburg, Maine, A Celebration of Maine Street '90, July 7-14, 1990, 25 p., Fryeburg: The Committee; Hurricane Press, 1990

Fryeburg Webster Centennial, Celebrating the Coming of Daniel Webster to Fryeburg 100 years ago, Fryeburg, A.F. Lewis, 1902

Furbush, C. O., *Memorial of the Centennial Anniversary of the Settlement of Machias, May 20, 1863*, Machias: C.O. Furbush, 1863

Gilpatric, George A., *Kennebunk History*, Kennebunk: Star Print, 1939

Godfrey, Edward S., "Structure of the Maine Court System, 1956-1991," 43 *Maine Law Review* 353, 1991

Godfrey, John Edwards, *Journals: Bangor , Maine, 1893-1869*, Rockland, Maine: Courier-Gazette, Inc., 1979

Goold, Nathan, *Falmouth Neck in the Revolution*. Portland: Press of Thurston Print, 1897

Goold, William, "History of the Cumberland County Buildings in Portland, Maine," *Collections and Proceedings of the Maine Historical Society*, 2nd Series, Vol. 9, pp. 292-308

Goold, William, *Portland in the Past, with Historical Notes of Old Falmouth*. Portland: B. Thurston and Company, 1886

Hamilton, Brooks W., "The Fort Became a County Seat in 1786," *Augusta, Maine Sesquicentennial Observance 1797 - 1947*

Hamlin, Charles, "The Supreme Court of Maine," *Green Bag*, Vol. VII, Boston: Boston Book Company, 1895

Hanson, J.W., *History of the Old Towns of Norridgewock and Canaan, comprising Norridgewock, Canaan, Starks, Skowhegan and Bloomfield from their early settlement to the year 1849*, Boston: published by the Author, 1849

Haskell, T.H., *The New Gloucester Centennial, Sept 7, 1874*, Portland: Hoyt, Fogg & Donham, 1875

Haskins, George L., *Law and Authority in Early Massachusetts: a study in Tradition and Design*, New York, Macmillan Co, 1960

Henry, Hon. Harriett P., *The Maine District Court: A Quarter Century of Progress 1962-1987*, Portland: Tower Publishing Co., 1987

History of Federal Courts, 40 Federal Rules Decisions 140-145, 214

History of Penobscot County, Maine, with Illustrations and Biographical Sketches, Cleveland: William, Chase & Co., 1882

Hubbard, Bill, "Courthouse Addition a Building of and for Portland," *Portland Press Herald*, Nov. 9, 1988

"Inaugural Address of the Mayor," Dec., 1908 in *City of Portland 15th Auditors Report*, Portland: Master Printing House, 1909

Isaacson, Dorris A., Ed., *Maine: A Guide 'Down East'*, Second Edition, Revision prepared by the Maine League of Historical Societies and Museums and sponsored by the 104th Maine Legislature and the State Sesquicentennial Commission, Rockland: Courier-Gazette, Inc., 1970

Jordan, William B., *Portland's Famous Weathercock 1788-1981*, Westbrook, Maine: Westbrook College, 1981

Kendall, J., and G.H. Gilman, *History of the Town of Houlton, Maine, from 1804-1883*, Haverhill, Ma: C.C. Morse & Son, 1884

Kershaw, Gordon E., *The Kennebeck Proprietors 1749-1775*, Somersworth, N.H.: New Hampshire Publishing Co., 1975

Kingsbury, Henry D., *History of Kennebec County, Maine*, New York: H.W. Blake & Co., 1892

Knights, Ernest G., *Waterboro, York County, Maine*, 1954

Lapham, William B., and Silas P. Maxim, *History of the Town of Paris, Maine*, Paris, Maine: Printed for the authors, 1884; reprinted by Somersworth, N.H.: New England History Press, 1983

Leamon, James S., *Revolution Down East: The War for American Independence in Maine*, Amherst, Mass.: The University of Massachusetts Press, 1993

Leane, John J., *History of Rumford, Maine, 1774-1972*, Rumford: Rumford Publishing Co., 1972

"Lincoln County Honored at Its Century Mark," *Kennebec Journal*, July 24, 1924

Loring, Amasa, *History of Piscataquis County, Maine*, Portland: Hoyt, Fogg & Donham, 1880

Lowell, Mary Chandler, *Old Foxcroft, Maine: Traditions and Memories*, Concord, NH: The Rumford Press, 1935

Lynch, John F., *The Advocate: An Autobiography and Series of Reminiscences*, Portland: George D. Loring, 1916

Maine Historic Preservation Commission, (Earle G. Shettleworth, Jr.), *A Biographical Dictionary of Architects in Maine: Gersham Flagg 1705-1771*, Vol. V., No. 9, Augusta: the Commission, 1988, pamphlet

Maine Historic Preservation Commission, (Roger Reed), *A Biographical Dictionary of Architects in Maine: George Burnham 1875-1931*, Vol. I, No. 1, Augusta: the Commission, 1984, pamphlet

Mallet, Richard P., *The Last 100 Years: a Glimpse of the Farmington We Have Known*, Wilton, Maine: Wilton Printed Products, 1991

Mallett, Richard, with Paul H. Mills, "Crime and Punishment "(1843-1922) in *The Early Years of Farmington, 1781-1860*, Wilton, Maine: Wilton Printed Products, 1994

Martin, Kathleen A., ed., *Voice on the Kennebec: A Description of the Development of Skowhegan During the Years 1941-81*, Skowhegan: Community Action Group, 1983

Martin, Kenneth R., and Snow, Ralph L., *Maine Odyssey: Good Times and Hard Times in Bath, 1936-1986*, Bath: Patten Free Library, 1988

"Materials for a History of Machias, Maine, from the Town Records," Excerpt from *Historical Magazine*, July and August, 1870

McGrath, Anna Fields, ed, *The County: Land of Promise*, Norfolk, Virginia: The Donning Company, 1989

McKenna, Martin, "Courthouse Work Will Go Before Zoning Board," *Times Record*, Brunswick, Jan. 17, 1986

McKusick, Hon. Vincent L., "Opening Ceremonies for the Session of the Law Court," Kennebec County Courthouse, *Maine Reporter* 522-536 A.2d cccxliii et seq., 1988

McKusick, Hon. Vincent L., "Opening Ceremonies for the Session of the Law Court," Penobscot County Courthouse, *Maine Reporter* 522-536 A.2d cccxlix et seq., 1988

McKusick, Hon. Vincent L., "Opening Ceremonies for the Session of the Law Court," Piscataquis County Courthouse, *Maine Reporter* 522-536 A.2d cccxliv et seq., 1988

McKusick, Hon. Vincent L., "Opening Ceremonies for the Session of the Law Court," Aroostook County Courthouse, *Maine Reporter* 522-536 A.2d cccxlviii et seq., 1988

McKusick, Hon. Vincent L., "Opening Ceremonies for the Session of the Law Court," York County Courthouse, *Maine Reporter* 522-536 A.2d cccxlxii et seq., 1988

McKusick, Hon. Vincent L., *Opening Remarks*, Law Court Session in Wiscasset, Week of May 29, 1990

McKusick, Hon. Vincent L., "The Upcoming Tercentenary of the Supreme Judicial Court, *Maine Bar Journal*, Jan., 1992

Melvin, Charlotte L., ed. *History of the Houlton Area: Bicentennial articles published in the Houlton Pioneer Times in 1975 and 1976*, Houlton: *Pioneer Times*, 1977

Merrill, George A., "Historical Sketch of Foxcroft, Maine," in *Sprague's Journal of Maine History, Proceedings of the Centennial Celebration, Oct. 1, 1912*, Dover, Me., J.F. Sprague: 1917

Merrill, Georgia Drew, Ed., *History of Androscoggin County, Maine*, Boston: W.A. Ferguson and Co., 1891

Miller, Samuel L., *History of the Town of Waldoboro, Maine*, Wiscasset: Emerson Printer, 1910

Mitchell, H.E., *The Town Register: Alfred, Lyman, Dayton, Hollis, and Waterboro, 1905*, Brunswick: H. E. Mitchell Co., 1905

Moody, Edward C., *Handbook History of the Town of York from Early Times to the Present*, August: York Publishing Co., 1914

Moody, Robert E. "The Lincoln County Courthouse," *Old-Time New England*, Vol. 56, pp. 61-62

Myers, Denys Peter, "The Historic Architecture of Maine," in *Maine Catalog Historic American Buildings Survey*, Augusta: Maine State Museum, 1974

Moulton, Augustus F., *Portland by the Sea, an Historical Treatise*, Augusta: Katahdin Publishing Co., 1926

Moulton, Augustus F., "The County of Lincoln," Excerpt from *Sprague's Journal of Maine History*, Vol. 13, No. 1

Nash, Charles Elventon, *The History of Augusta, Maine*, Augusta: Charles E. Nash & Son, 1904

Neal, John, *Portland Illustrated*, Portland: W.S. Jones, 1874

Nelson, Florence Hunt, *The New Gloucester Book: An account of the one hundred and fiftieth anniversary celebration of the Incorporation of the Town of New Gloucester Maine, together with a comprehensive review of the history of the Town, 1774-1924*, published by the Executive Committee of the Anniversary Celebration, Auburn, Maine: Merrill & Webber Co., 1925

North, James W., *History of Augusta from Earliest Settlement to the Present*, Facsimile of 1870 ed., Somersworth, N.H.: New England History Press, 1981

Owen, Henry Wilson, *The Edward Clarence Plummer History of Bath*, Bath: The Times Company of Bath, 1936

Palmer, Kenneth T., G. Thomas Taylor and Marcus A. Librizzi, *Maine Politics and Government*, Series of Politics and Government of the American States published by the University of Nebraska in association with the Center for the Study of Federalism, Lincoln, Nebraska: University of Nebraska Press, 1992

Paris Cape Historical Society, *Paris, Maine: The Second Hundred Years, 1893-1993*, Camden, Maine: Penobscot Press, 1994

Parker, Herbert, *Courts and Lawyers in New England*, New York: The American Historical Society, Inc., 1931

Parsons, Usher, *A Centennial History of Alfred, York County, Maine*, Philadelphia: Collins, Printer, 1872

Pattangall, William R., *The Meddybemps Letters*, Lewiston: *Lewiston Journal* Company, 1924

Patterson, Hon. William Davis, "Centennial of Lincoln County Courthouse, 1924," in *Sprague's Journal of Maine History*, Vol, 13, No. 1, pp. 17-28

Pierce, Ann, "A History of Maine's County Courthouses," *Maine Bar Journal,*, Vol. 1, No. 3 May, 1986

Piscataquis County Historical Society, *Historical Collections of Piscataquis County, Maine*, papers read at meetings of the Society, Dover: Observer Press, 1910

"Pownalborough and Lincoln County," *Bangor Historical Magazine*, Vol. III, No. VII, Jan., 1888

Proceedings at the Dedication of Courthouse Facilities at New United States Post Office and Courthouse, Bangor, Maine, May 7, 1968

Putnam, Cora M. *The Story of Houlton*, Portland: House of Falmouth, 1958

Raymond, Ellen G., *Maine State Court Organization Profile*, State Court Organization Profile Series, Williamsburg, Va.: National Center for State Courts, 1978

Reed, Parker McCobb, *History of Bath and Environs, Sagadahoc County, Maine, 1607-1894*, Portland: Lakeside Press, 1894

Reilly, Wayne, "The Harris Horror," *Down East*, Vol. XLIII No. 4, Nov. 1996, p. 64 et. seq.

Remich, Daniel, *History of Kennebunk from its Earliest Settlement to 1890*, Portland:

Lakeside Press, 1911

Reopening Ceremony Edward Thaxter Gignoux United States Courthouse, June 26, 1996, pamphlet

Rockland Bicentennial Commission, *Shore Village Story: An Informal History of Rockland, Maine,* Rockland: The Commission, 1976

Sewall, Rufus K., *Memorials of the Bar of Lincoln County, Maine, 1760-1900,* Wiscasset: Sheepscot Echo Publisher, 1900

Shettleworth, Earle G., Jr., and William Barry, *Mr Goodhue Remembers Portland: Scenes from the Mid-19h Century,* Augusta: Maine Historic   Preservation Commission, 1981

Skinner, Ralph, et. al, *Auburn 100 years a City, 1896-1969,* Auburn: Auburn Historical Committee, 1968

Silsby, Hon. Herbert T., II, "Clara H. Nash: Legal Pioneer," *Maine History News 7* (April 1972)

Silsby, Hon. Herbert T., II, "County's Judicial System Has Long, Colorful History," *Ellsworth American,* May 1, 1980

Silsby, Hon. Herbert T., II, "Ellsworth: A Brief History," in *Historical Record and Program: Bicentennial Celebration July 20-27, 1963,* Ellsworth, Me., Ellsworth Bicentennial Corporation, 1963

Silsby, Hon. Herbert T., II, "History of the Maine Superior Court," Maine *Bar Bulletin,* Vol. 14, No. 4, July, 1980, p. 109 et seq.

Silsby, Hon. Herbert T., II, "History of the Maine Superior Court,"*Maine Bar Bulletin,* Vol. 14, No. 5, September, 1980, p. 1 et seq.

Silsby, Hon. Herbert T., II, "Interesting History of Old County Courthouse Buildings," *Ellsworth American,* September 28, 1960, October 5, 1960, and October 19, 1960

Silsby, Hon. Herbert T., II, *A Speech Delivered...before a Special Session of the Supreme Judicial Court of the State of Maine ...Commemorating the 200th Anniversary of the Incorporation of Hancock County,* Unpublished Manuscript, Ellsworth, 1989

Smith, Edgar C., "The Early History of Dover and Foxcroft," in *The Piscataquis Observer,* Vol 65, Oct., 1902

Snow, Richard F., *Old Sagadahoc,* Topsham: R. Snow, 1987

Sprague, John Francis, *Piscataquis Biography and Fragments,* Bangor: Chas. H. Glass & Co., 1899

Stahl, Jasper J. *History of Old Broad Bay and Waldoboro,* Two Vols., Portland: Bond Wheelwright Co., 1956

Stevens, Louis, *Booming! Dover and Foxcroft from 1881-1892,* Newport, Maine: Newport Print Shop, 1996Stevens, Louis, *Dover-Foxcroft – A History,* Somersworth, N.H.: New Hampshire Printers, 1995

Sunrise Research Institute, *Sunrise County Architecture: Significant Buildings of Washington County,* Machiasport: Sunrise Research Institute, 1979

Surrency, Edwin C. "Federal District Court Judges and the History of Their Courts," 40 *F.R.D.* 150 (1966)

Thompson, Deborah, *Bangor, Maine 1768-1914: An Architectural History,* Orono, University of Maine Press, 1988

Thompson, Deborah, *Maine Forms of American Architecture,* Waterville, Maine: Colby Museum of Art, 1976

Trial of Ebenezer Ball Before the Hon. Samuel Sewall, George Thatcher, and Isaac Parker, Esquires, for the Murder of John Tileston Downes, at Robinstown, Jan. 28, 1811, Castine: Printed and Published by Samuel Hall, 1811

Trial of David Lynn, et al., for the murder of Paul Chadwick at Malta, in Maine on Sept 8, 1809, taken in short hand by John Merrick, Esq., Hallowell: Ezekiel Goodale, *1810*

Trial of Dr. Valorous P. Coolidge for the Murder of Edward Mathews at Waterville, Maine, *Boston Daily Times* reprint, 1848

Trial of James M. Lowell, indicted for the Murder of His Wife, Mary Elizabeth Lowell, Report of court stenographers, Portland: Dresser, McLennan & co., 1875

Trial of Moses Adams, High Sheriff of the County of Hancock, before the Supreme Judicial Court of the Commonwealth of Massachusetts, on an Indictment for the Murder of His Wife, Boston: Printed and Published by E.B. Tileston, 1815

Trial of Seth Elliot, Esq. for the Murder of His Son, John Wilson Elliot Before the Supreme Judicial Court at Castine, October Term, 1824, Belfast: Published by Fellows and Simpson, n.d.

United States District Court for the District of Maine, *Bicentennial of the U. S. District Court,* Bangor, Sept. 25, 1989

Usher, Parsons, *A Centennial History of Alfred, York County, Maine,* Philadelphia: Collins, 1872

Vaughn, Martha C.M., *John Adams at Pownalborough Courthouse,* A Bicentennial Project of Lincoln County Cultural and Historical Association, Wiscasset, 1976, pamphlet

Vickery, James B., ed, *An Illustrated History of the City of Bangor, Maine,* rev. ed. Bangor: Bangor Bicentennial Committee, 1976

Wasson, Samuel, *A Survey of Hancock County, Maine,* Augusta: Sprague, Owen & Nash, 1878

Wathen, Hon. Daniel, "The State of the Judiciary - Steady Progress, But Is It Enough?" A Report to the Joint Convention of the 118th Legislature, December, 1997

Wheeler, George Augustus, *History of Castine, Penobscot, and Brooksville, Maine, including the Ancient Settlement of Pentagoet,* Bangor: Burr & Robinson, 1875

Wheeler, George A. and Henry W. Wheeler, *History of Brunswick, Topsham and Harpswell, Maine,* Boston: Alfred Mudge Printers, 1878

White, Stella King, *Early History of Caribou, Maine, 1843-1895,* , 1945

Wiggin, Edward, *History of Aroostook,* Vol. 1, Presque Isle: Star-Herald press, 1922

Williamson, Grace Whitney, *A Survey of Maine Courthouses* by the Historical Activities Committee, National Society of Colonial Dames of America Resident in the State of Maine, June, 1965 (mimeo)

Williamson, Joseph, "Capital Trials in Maine," *Collections and Proceedings of the Maine Historical Society,* Second Series, Vol. I, 1890, pp. 159-172

Williamson, Joseph, "The Professional Tours of John Adams in Maine," *Collections and Proceedings of the Maine Historical Society,* Second Series, Vol. I, 1890, pp. 301-308

Williamson, Joseph, *History of the City of Belfast, in the State of Maine,* 2 Vols.,Vol. I, Portland: Loring, Short & Harmon, 1877; Vol. II, Boston: Houghton Mifflin Co., 1913

Williamson, William, *The History of the State of Maine*, Hallowell: Glazier, Masters & Co., two vols., 1832, reprint, Freeport, Maine: The Cumberland Press, 1966

Willis, William, *History of Portland*, Facsimile of 1865 ed., Somersworth, N.H.: New Hampshire Publishing Co., 1972

Willis, William, *History of the Law, the Courts and the Lawyers of Maine*, Portland: Joseph S. Bailey, 1863

Willis, William, *Journals of the Reverend Thomas Smith and the Reverend Samuel Deane, Pastors of the First Church in Portland, with Notes and Biographical Notices; and a Summary History of Portland.* Portland: Joseph S. Bailey, 1849

Wolfe, Jason, "Courthouse Face Lift Combines Function, Form," *Portland Press Herald*, Sept. 5, 1994, p. 1A

Wolfe, Jason, "Renovated Courthouse Finds Original Charm with Updates," *Portland Press Herald*, Sept. 5, 1994, p. 1B

Wood Henrietta D., *Early Days of Norridgewock*, Skowhegan: The Skowhegan Press, 1933, Reprinted, 1941

Writers' Program (Maine), *Portland City Guide*, American Guide Series, Work Projects Administration in the State of Maine, Portland: Forest City Printing Company, 1940

Wroth, Kinvin, "The Maine Connection: Massachusetts Justice Downeast, 1620-1820," in Osgood, Russell, Ed., *The History of the Law in Massachusetts: The Supreme Judicial Court 1692-1992*, Boston: Supreme Judicial Court Historical Society, 1992

Wroth, Kinvin, "Maine 175: The Bench and Bar of the District of Maine in 1820," *University of Maine School of Law Alumni Quarterly*, Fall, 1995, pp. 10-13

Yarborough, Nancy L., *Gridley J. F. Bryant and the Aroostook County Courthouse*, Unpublished paper, Cary Library, Houlton

Appendix A

Members of the Supreme Judicial Court
with Residences and Periods of Service

1.	Prentiss Mellen **C.J. 1**	Portland, Cumberland	C.J. 7/1/1820-10/11/1834 (resigned)
2.	William Pitt Preble	Portland, Cumberland	7/1/1820-6/18/1828 (resigned)
3.	Nathan Weston Jr. **C.J. 2**	Augusta, Kennebec	7/1/1820-10/22/1841 (retired) C.J. 10/22/1834-10/22/1841
4.	Albion K. Parris	Portland, Cumberland	6/25/1828-8/20/1836 (resigned)
5.	Nicholas Emery	Portland, Cumberland	10/22/1834-10/22/1841 (commission expired)
6.	Ether Shepley **C.J. 4**	Saco, York	9/23/1836-10/22/1855 (retired) C.J. 10/23/1848-10/22/1855
7.	John S. Tenney **C.J. 5**	Norridgewock, Somerset	10/23/1841-10/23/1862 (retired) C.J. 10/23/1855-10/23/1862
8.	Ezekiel Whitman **C.J. 3**	Portland, Cumberland	C.J. 12/10/1841-10/23/1848 (retired)
9.	Samuel Wells	Portland, Cumberland	9/28/1847-3/31/1854 (resigned)
10.	Joseph Howard	Portland, Cumberland	10/23/1848-10/22/1855 (commission expired)
11.	Richard D. Rice	Augusta, Kennebec	5/11/1852-12/1/1863 (resigned)
12.	John Appleton **C.J. 6**	Bangor, Penobscot	5/11/1852-9/20/1883 (retired) C.J. 10/24/1862-9/20/1883
13.	Joshua W. Hathaway	Bangor, Penobscot	5/11/1852-5/11/1859 (commission expired)
14.	Jonas Cutting	Bangor, Penobscot	4/20/1854-4/20/1875 (retired)
15.	Seth May	Winthrop, Kennebec	5/6/1855-5/6/1862 (retired)
16.	Woodbury Davis	Portland, Cumberland	10/10/1855 removed by address 4/11/1856 reappointed 2/25/1857 resigned 1865
17.	Daniel Goodenow	Alfred, York	10/10/1855-10/10/1862 (retired)
18.	Edward Kent	Bangor, Penobscot	5/11/1859-5/11/1873 (retired)
19.	Charles W. Walton	Auburn, Androscoggin	5/14/1862-5/14/1897 (retired)
20.	Jonathan G. Dickerson	Belfast, Waldo	10/24/1862-9/1/1878 (died)
21.	Edward Fox	Portland, Cumberland	10/24/1862-3/27/1863 (resigned)
22.	William G. Barrows	Brunswick, Cumberland	3/27/1863-3/24/1884 (retired)
23.	Charles Danforth	Gardiner, Kennebec	1/5/1864-3/30/1890 (died)
24.	Rufus P. Tapley	Saco, York	12/21/1865-12/21/1872 (retired)
25.	William Wirt Virgin	Portland, Cumberland	12/26/1872-1/23/1893 (died)
26.	John A. Peters **C.J. 7**	Bangor, Penobscot	5/15/1873-1/1/1900 (retired) C.J. 9/20/1883-1/1/1900
27.	Artemas Libbey	Augusta, Kennebec	4/23/1875-4/23/1882 1/11/1883-3/15/1894 (died)
28.	Joseph W. Symonds	Portland, Cumberland	10/16/1878-3/31/1884 (resigned)
29.	Lucilius A. Emery **C.J. 9**	Ellsworth, Hancock	10/5/1883-7/26/1911 (retired) C.J. 12/14/1906-7/26/1911
30.	Enoch Foster	Bethel, Oxford	3/24/1884-3/24/1898

			(commission expired)
31.	Thomas H. Haskell	Portland Cumberland	3/31/1884-9/24/1900 (died)
32.	Wm. Penn Whitehouse **C.J. 10**	Augusta, Kennebec	4/15/1890-4/8/1913 (retired) C.J. 7/26/1911-4/8/1913
33.	Andrew P. Wiswell **C.J. 8**	Ellsworth, Hancock	4/10/1893-12/4/1906 (died) C.J. 1/2/1900-12/4/1906
34.	Sewall C. Strout	Portland, Cumberland	4/12/1894-4/12/1908 (retired)
35.	Albert R. Savage **C.J. 11**	Auburn, Androscoggin	5/15/1897-6/14/1917 (died) C.J. 4/9/1913-6/14/1917
36.	William H. Fogler	Rockland, Knox	3/25/1898-2/18/1902 (died)
37.	Frederick A. Powers	Houlton, Aroostook	1/2/1900-3/31/1907 (resigned)
38.	Henry C. Peabody	Portland, Cumberland	11/29/1900-3/29/1911 (died)
39.	Albert M. Spear	Gardiner, Kennebec	3/1/1902-3/1/1916* 6/25/1917-7/7/1923 (retired) *was not reappointed 1916; was out 16 months
40.	Charles F. Woodard	Bangor, Penobscot	12/14/1906-6/17/1907 (died)
41.	Leslie C. Cornish **C.J. 12**	Augusta, Kennebec	3/31/1907-3/1/1925 (retired) C.J. 6/25/1917-3/1/1925
42.	Arno W. King	Ellsworth, Hancock	6/28/1907-7/21/1918 (died)
43.	George E. Bird	Portland, Cumberland	4/13/1908-8/28/1918 (retired)
44.	George F. Haley	Biddeford, York	4/12/1911-2/19/1918 (died)
45.	George M. Hanson	Calais, Washington	7/26/1911-4/4/1924 (died)
46.	Warren C. Philbrook	Waterville, Kennebec	4/9/1913-11/29/1928 (retired)
47.	John B. Madigan	Houlton, Aroostook	3/2/1916-1/19/1918 (died)
48.	Charles J. Dunn **C.J. 16**	Orono, Penobscot	1/28/1918-11/10/1939 (died) C.J. 7/18/1935-11/10/1939
49.	John A. Morrill	Auburn, Androscoggin	2/25/1918-5/31/1926 (retired)
50.	Scott Wilson **C.J. 13**	Portland, Cumberland	8/7/1918-10/7/1929 (retired) C.J. 3/1/1925-10/7/1929
51.	Luere B. Deasy **C.J. 14**	Bar Harbor, Hancock	9/25/1918-2/7/1930 (retired) C.J. 10/12/1929-2/7/1930
52.	Guy H. Sturgis **C.J. 18**	Portland, Cumberland	8/14/1923-3/1/1949 (retired) C.J. 8/8/1940-3/1/1949
53.	Charles P. Barnes **C.J. 17**	Houlton, Aroostook	4/17/1924-7/31/1940 (retired) C.J. 11/21/1939-7/31/1940
54.	Norman L. Bassett	Augusta, Kennebec	3/26/1925-9/15/1930 (retired)
55.	William R. Pattangall **C.J. 15**	Augusta, Kennebec	7/2/1926-7/16/1935 (retired) C.J. 2/7/1930-7/16/1935
56.	Frank G. Farrington	Augusta, Kennebec	11/16/1928-9/3/1933 (died)
57.	Sidney St. Felix Thaxter	Portland, Cumberland	9/16/1930-2/28/1954 (retired)
58.	James H. Hudson	Guilford, Piscataquis (Chambers: Augusta, Kennebec)	11/20/1933-8/21/1947 (died)
59.	Harry Manser	Auburn, Androscoggin	7/18/1935-3/20/1946 (retired)
60.	George H. Worster	Bangor, Penobscot	12/21/1939-7/31/1942 (retired)
61.	Harold H. Murchie **C.J. 19**	Calais, Washington	8/8/1940-3/7/1953 (died) C.J. 3/3/1949-3/7/1953
62.	Arthur Chapman	Portland, Cumberland	11/4/1942-8/5/1945 (retired)
63.	Nathaniel Tompkins	Houlton, Aroostook	8/23/1945-4/22/1949 (died)
64.	Raymond Fellows **C.J. 21**	Bangor, Penobscot	5/1/1946-9/15/1956 (retired) C.J. 4/7/1954-9/15/1956

65.	Edward P. Murray	Bangor, Penobscot	9/18/1947-4/6/1948 (retired)
66.	Edward F. Merrill **C.J. 20**	Skowhegan, Somerset	6/2/1948-4/7/1954 (retired) C.J. 3/18/1953-4/7/1954
67.	William B. Nulty	Portland, Cumberland	3/16/1949-9/11/1953 (died)
68.	Robert B. Williamson **C.J. 22**	Augusta, Kennebec	5/5/1949-8/21/1970 (retired) C.J. 10/4/1956-8/21/1970
69.	Frank A. Tirrell Jr.	Camden, Knox	3/18/1953-6/4/1955 (died)
70.	Donald W. Webber	Auburn, Androscoggin	10/8/1953-7/31/1973 (retired)
71.	Albert Beliveau	Rumford, Oxford	3/3/1954-3/25/1958 (retired)
72.	Walter M. Tapley Jr.	Portland, Cumberland	5/5/1954-6/30/1969 (retired)
73.	Percy T. Clarke	Ellsworth, Hancock	6/29/1955-6/7/1956 (retired)
74.	F. Harold Dubord	Waterville, Kennebec	10/4/1956-12/10/1962 (retired)
75.	Francis W. Sullivan	Portland, Cumberland	10/4/1956-7/10/1965 (retired)
76.	Cecil J. Siddall	Sanford, York	5/7/1958-2/27/1965 (retired)
77.	Harold C. Marden	Waterville, Kennebec	12/19/1962-11/15/1970 (retired)
78.	Abraham M. Rudman	Bangor, Penobscot	3/30/1965-12/14/1966 (retired)
79.	Armand A. Dufresne Jr. **C.J. 23**	Lewiston, Androscoggin	8/24/1965-9/3/1977 (retired) C.J. 9/30/1970-9/3/1977
80.	Randolph A. Weatherbee	Bangor, Penobscot	12/21/1966-5/20/1976 (died)
81.	Charles A. Pomeroy	Windham, Cumberland	7/2/1969-1/1/1980 (retired)
82.	Sidney W. Wernick	Portland, Cumberland	9/30/1970-8/24/1981 (retired)
83.	James P. Archibald	Houlton, Aroostook	1/27/1971-1/1/1980 (retired)
84.	Thomas E. Delahanty	Lewiston, Androscoggin	9/5/1973-8/31/1979 (retired)
85.	Edward S. Godfrey	Portland, Cumberland	8/18/1976-9/1/1983 (retired)
86.	David A. Nichols	Lincolnville, Waldo (Chambers: Rockland, Knox)	5/23/1977-5/31/1988 (retired)
87.	Vincent L. McKusick **C.J. 24**	Cape Elizabeth, Cumberland	C.J. 9/16/1977-2/28/1992 (retired)
88.	Harry P. Glassman	Portland, Cumberland	8/3/1979-5/15/1981 (died)
89.	David G. Roberts	Cumberland, Cumberland	1/11/1980 -9/2/1998 (retired)
90.	Gene Carter	Bangor, Penobscot	9/15/1980-7/5/1983 (resigned)
91.	Elmer H. Violette	Van Buren, Aroostook	8/31/1981-8/1/1986 (retired)
92.	Daniel E. Wathen **C.J. 25**	Augusta, Kennebec	8/3/1981 - C.J. 3/20/1992 -
93.	Caroline D. Glassman	Portland, Cumberland	8/30/1983 - 8/30/1997 (retired)
94.	Louis Scolnik	Lewiston, Androscoggin	9/7/1983-7/31/1988 (retired)
95.	Robert W. Clifford	Lewiston, Androscoggin	8/1/1986 -
96.	D. Brock Hornby	Cape Elizabeth, Cumberland	7/10/1988-5/7/1990 (resigned)
97.	Samuel W. Collins Jr.	Rockland, Knox	9/16/1988-4/40/1994 (retired)
98.	Morton A. Brody	Waterville, Kennebec	6/6/1990-8/9/1991 (resigned)
99.	Paul L. Rudman	Bangor, Penobscot	6/5/1992 -
100.	Howard H. Dana Jr.	Portland, Cumberland	3/4/1993 -
101.	Kermit V. Lipez	So. Portland, Cumberland	5/12/1994 -6/30/1998 (resigned)
102.	Leigh I. Saufley	Portland, Cumberland	10/20/1997 -
103.	Donald G. Alexander	Winthrop, Kennebec	9/2/1998-
104.	Susan W. Calkins	Portland, Cumberland	9/2/1998-

Appendix B

Members of the Statewide Superior Court
January 1, 1930 to Date
Residences and Periods of Service*

*Guide to symbols in right-hand column:
r. - retired; resíd. - resigned; d. - died; e. - elevated to Supreme Judicial Court
** Holdovers from County Superior Courts
T Date of qualification for start of term on County Superior Courts.

1.	Arthur Chapman**	Portland, Cumberland	(3/12/25) T -11/4/1942	e.
2.	William H. Fisher**	Augusta, Kennebec	(5/21/24) T -8/31/1940	r.
3.	Harry Manser**	Auburn, Androscoggin	(4/1/28) T -7/18/1935	e.
4.	George H. Worster**	Bangor, Penobscot	(11/24/24) T -12/21/39	e.
5.	George L. Emery	Biddeford, York	1/1/1930-10/2/1944	d.
6.	James H. Hudson	Guilford, Piscataquis	1/1/1930-11/20/1933	e.
7.	Sidney St. F. Thaxter	Portland, Cumberland	1/1/1930-9/16/1930	e.
8.	Herbert T. Powers	Fort Fairfield, Aroostook	10/1/1930-7/1/1941	r.
9.	Herbert E. Holmes	Lewiston, Androscoggin	11/20/1933-5/6/1935	d.
10.	Edward P. Murray	Bangor, Penobscot	7/18/1935-9/18/1947	e.
11.	Albert Beliveau	Rumford, Oxford	7/18/1935-3/3/1954	e.
12.	Raymond Fellows	Bangor, Penobscot	12/29/1939-5/1/1946	e.
13.	Robert A. Cony	Augusta, Kennebec	10/31/1940-1/1/1945	d.
14.	Nathaniel Tompkins	Houlton, Aroostook	10/1/1941-8/23/1945	e.
15.	Arthur Eugene Sewall	York, York	12/16/1942-3/1/1953	r.
16.	Earle L. Russell	Cape Elizabeth, Cumberland	12/20/1944-8/5/1947	d.
17.	Edward F. Merrill	Skowhegan, Somerset	1/23/1945-6/2/1948	e.
18.	Robert B. Williamson	Augusta, Kennebec	9/5/1945-5/5/1949	e.
19.	Frank A. Tirrell, Jr.	Rockland, Knox	5/15/1946-3/18/1953	e.
20.	William B. Nulty	Portland, Cumberland	9/18/1947-3/16/1949	e.
21.	Percy T. Clarke	Ellsworth, Hancock	10/1/1947-6/29/1955	e.
22.	Donald W. Webber	Auburn, Androscoggin	9/1/1948-10/8/1953	e.
23.	Francis W. Sullivan	Portland, Cumberland	4/1/1949-10/4/1956	e.
24.	Granville C. Gray	Presque Isle, Aroostook	5/18/1949-9/2/1956	d.
25.	Harold C. Marden	Waterville, Kennebec	3/1/1953-12/10/1962	e.
26.	Randolph A. Weatherbee	Hampden, Penobscot	3/25/1953-12/21/1966	e.
27.	Cecil J. Siddall	Sanford, York	8/19/1953-5/7/1958	e.
28.	Leonard F. Williams	Auburn, Androscoggin	11/4/1953-3/30/1964	d.
29.	Walter M. Tapley, Jr.	Portland, Cumberland	3/3/1954-5/5/1954	e.
30.	Abraham M. Rudman	Bangor, Penobscot	6/9/1954-3/31/1965	e.
31.	F. Harold Dubord	Waterville, Kennebec	6/29/1955-10/4/1956	e.
32.	James P. Archibald	Houlton, Aroostook	10/4/1956-1/27/1971	e.
33.	Armand A. Dufresne, Jr.	Lewiston, Androscoggin	10/4/1956-8/24/1965	e.
34.	Charles A. Pomeroy	Portland, Cumberland	10/4/1956-7/2/1969	e.

35.	John P. Carey	Bath, Sagadahoc	5/7/1958-12/10/1958	r.
36.	Thomas E. Delahanty	Lewiston, Androscoggin	12/31/1958-9/5/1973	e.
37.	William S. Silsby	Aurora, Hancock	12/20/1961-8/1/1972	r.
38.	James L. Reid	Augusta, Kennebec	12/28/1962-9/1/1975	r.
39.	Harold J. Rubin	Bath, Sagadahoc	5/20/1964-1/15/1979	r.
40.	Alton A. Lessard	Lewiston, Androscoggin	8/24/1965-8/1/1974	r.
41.	Lincoln Spencer	Kennebunkport, York	8/24/1965-9/1/1977	r.
42.	Albert Knudsen	Portland, Cumberland	5/4/1966-12/1/1973	r.
43.	David G. Roberts	Bangor, Penobscot	2/22/1967-1/11/1980	e.
44.	Sidney W. Wernick	Portland, Cumberland	7/2/1969-9/30/1970	e.
45.	William E. McCarthy	Rumford, Oxford	10/8/1969-4/8/1984	r.
46.	Lewis I. Naiman	Augusta, Kennebec	9/30/1970-12/31/1979	r.
47.	James A. Bishop	Presque Isle, Aroostook	1/27/1971-7/16/1977	d.
48.	Ian MacInnes	Bangor, Penobscot	12/22/1971-10/10/1983	r.
49.	Harry P. Glassman	Portland, Cumberland	12/22/1971-8/31/1979	e.
50.	Edward Stern	Bangor, Penobscot	12/20/1972-12/20/1979	r.
51.	Elmer H. Violette	Van Buren, Aroostook	9/5/1973-8/31/1981	e.
52.	Sumner J. Goffin	Portland, Cumberland	10/10/1973-12/22/1984	r.
53.	Robert L. Browne	Bangor, Penobscot	3/20/1974-11/26/1984	r.
54.	Louis Scolnik	Lewiston, Androscoggin	12/10/1974-9/7/1983	e.
55.	David A. Nichols	Lincolnville, Waldo	10/1/1975-5/18/1977	e.
56.	Stephen L. Perkins	S. Portland, Cumberland	9/16/1977-4/30/1993	r.
57.	Daniel E. Wathen	Augusta, Kennebec	9/16/1977-8/31/1981	e.
58.	Herbert T. Silsby, II	Ellsworth, Hancock	9/16/1977-2/28/1992	r.
59.	Robert W. Clifford	Lewiston, Androscoggin	6/8/1979-8/1/1986	e.
60.	William E. McKinley	Portland, Cumberland	1/11/1979-1/31/1990	r.
61.	Donald G. Alexander	Winthrop, Kennebec	2/15/1980-9/2/1998	e.
62.	Jessie Briggs Gunther	Dover-Foxcroft, Piscataquis	4/11/1980-2/1/1986	resíd
63.	Morton A. Brody	Waterville, Kennebec	7/18/1980-6/7/1990	e.
64.	Carl O. Bradford	Yarmouth, Cumberland	10/23/1981-8/31/1998	r.
65.	William D. Brodrick	Kennebunkport, York	12/9/1981-2/28/1995	r.
66.	Thomas E. Delahanty, II	Lewiston, Androscoggin	11/4/1983-	
67.	Paul T. Pierson	Stockholm, Aroostook	1/17/1984-	
68.	G. Arthur Brennan	York, York	4/12/1984-	
69.	Bruce W. Chandler	Unity, Kennebec	9/21/1984-9/30/1994	r.
70.	Eugene W. Beaulieu	Bangor, Penobscot	1/25/1985-1/17/1992	resíd
71.	Kermit V. Lipez	S. Portland, Cumberland	6/14/1985-5/12/1994	e.
72.	Jack O. Smith	Bangor, Penobscot	3/27/1986-9/30/1992	r.
73.	Paul A. Fritzsche	Kennebunk, York	7/31/1986-	
74.	Roland A. Cole	Wells, York	9/25/1986-	
75.	Margaret J. Kravchuk	Bangor, Penobscot	3/27/1990-	
76.	Andrew M. Mead	Bangor, Penobscot	5/28/1992-	
77.	Nancy Diesel Mills	Cornville, Somerset	2/18/1993-	
78.	Francis C. Marsano	Belfast, Waldo	4/9/1993-	
79.	Leigh I. Saufley	Portland, Cumberland	4/9/1993-10/20/1997	e.

80.	Robert E. Crowley	Kennebunk, York	6/14/1993-
81.	John R. Atwood	Damariscotta, Lincoln	5/17/1994-
82.	Donald H. Marden	Waterville, Kennebec	12/8/1994-
83.	Susan W. Calkins	Portland, Cumberland	5/21/1995-
84.	S. Kirk Studstrup	Hallowell, Cumberland	10/20/1997-
85.	Jeffrey Hjelm	Dixmont, Penobscot	9/2/1998-
86.	Thomas E. Humphrey	Springvale, York	9/2/1998-
87.	Thomas D. Warren	Brunswick, Cumberland	9/2/1998-

e.

Appendix C

Distribution of Supreme Judicial Court Justices and Superior Court Justices by County of Residence

County	Supreme Judicial Court	Superior Court
Cumberland	35	19
Kennebec	18	12
Penobscot	14	14
Androscoggin	9	10
Aroostook	6	7
Hancock	5	3
York	5	10
Knox	3	1
Oxford	2	2
Somerset	2	2
Waldo	2	2
Washington	2	0
Piscataquis	1	2
Sagadahoc	0	2
Lincoln	0	1
Franklin	0	0
	104	87

Appendix D

United States District Judges
for the
District of Maine

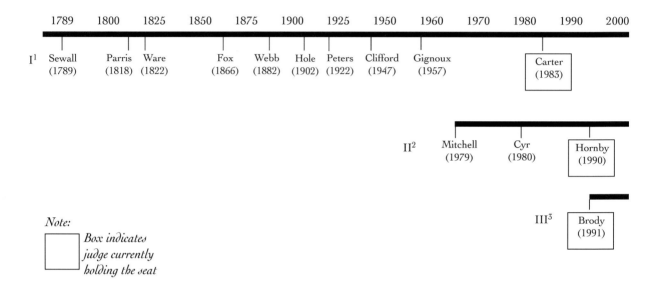

Note:

Box indicates
judge currently
holding the seat

Legislation Creating Seats
1. Judiciary Act of 1789
2. Omnibus Judgeship Act of 1978
3. Civil Justice Reform Act of 1990